THE ANGLER'S BOOK OF DAILY INSPIRATION

THE
ANGLER'S BOOK OF
DAILY INSPIRATION

A Year of Motivation, Revelation, and Instruction

KEVIN NELSON

CB
CONTEMPORARY BOOKS

Library of Congress Cataloging-in-Publication Data

Nelson, Kevin, 1953–
    The angler's book of daily inspiration : a year of motivation,
revelation, and instruction / Kevin Nelson.
        p.   cm.
    ISBN 0-8092-3069-0
    1. Fishing—Miscellanea.   2. Fishing—Quotations, maxims, etc.
3. Fishing—Philosophy.   I. Title.
SH441.N44   1997
799.1'2—dc21   96-40271
                                                                       CIP

Interior design by Kim Bartko

Preface

"I love any discourse of rivers, and fish and fishing."
—Izaak Walton

This is a book for fishermen. Its sole purpose is to encourage and inspire people—men and women, boys and girls—to fish.

It is written for beginning fishermen as well as longtime veterans of the craft. It covers lake fishing and ocean fishing and river fishing, with an admitted author's bias toward the latter. But it is sincerely hoped that every type of fisherman— bait, spinning, fly—wherever he fishes, salt water or fresh water, will find something useful in these pages.

This book is less about the *how* of fishing and more about the *tao*. Within its inspiration-a-day format, it is a meditation on fish and fishing, the wonders of the natural world, the virtues of solitude, and the ways that fishing brings families and friends together. It's about how to become a more patient fisherman, how to make more time for fishing in your life, the importance of a sense of humor in the face of fishing's inevitable disappointments and frustration, and many other subjects related to the ancient custom of dipping line into water.

Fish, and everything will be all right. That's the simple message of this book. You will learn what you need to know. You will grow as a fisherman. You will have grand adventures and lifetime experiences. You will come to know the amazing world of water and fish. You will find out things about yourself that you never knew.

But first, you must get there. You must fish. Engage your whole being and all your skills and all your life experiences into this most fascinating and rewarding of pursuits, and you will receive far more in return.

The literature of angling is a vast pool that dates back centuries. This book casts a light line, with perhaps a Royal Coachman attached, into the quiet edges of this pool. If after being inspired by something you've read in these pages, you pull a beautiful golden or rainbow out of a brook, this author's job will be happily complete.

—Kevin Nelson
Benicia, California

January 1

"There is nothing that attracts human nature more powerfully than the sport of tempting the unknown with a fishing line."
—Henry Van Dyke

Make this the best year of your fishing life.

Whether you've been fishing for sixty years, or you started yesterday, make this the best year of your fishing life.

That means fishing more—more than you ever have in a single year. That means getting away on the weekends whenever you can, even cutting out midweek if you can swing it. That means possibly going to a fishing lodge for a week this summer, or taking off and going someplace like the Bahamas or Alaska or Idaho, somewhere you've never been.

Having the best year of your fishing life means that you're going to do what you've always wanted to do, really tempt the unknown, really chase your fishing dreams big time.

Those dreams don't have to be grandiose. You don't have to go out and snag Moby Dick on a 5X tippet. They can be whatever you want to make them. Perhaps simply spending more time with your kid on a free-running High Sierra stream.

Forget that you've made this resolution before (if you have). This is a different sort of New Year's resolution, one that is going to last the entire year.

Starting today, the best year of your fishing life.

Resolved: I make this year the best year of my fishing life.

January 2

"My philosophy is: Enjoy yourself. You cannot survive unless you enjoy yourself."

—John Hersey

John Hersey, who fished the fighting blues off the Atlantic Coast and witnessed the horrors of the Hiroshima bomb, got it right. Enjoyment is everything. It's not merely a luxury, it's a matter of survival. This is especially true in fishing.

You're not going to catch fish unless you enjoy yourself. If you don't enjoy yourself, you're not going to be out there in the first place, and no matter what anyone tells you, it is impossible to catch fish without fishing.

So it all begins with enjoyment. That's the source of all good things in fishing. Everything proceeds from that.

You're a better fisherman when you're enjoying yourself. You learn more and you learn faster. You're more receptive to the natural world unfolding around you. You're more willing to try different things, seek out new places to fish. And when you're having a good time, all you want to do is fish. So enjoyment leads directly to more fishing and more fishing leads to better fishing and the better your fishing, the more you are apt to enjoy it. May the circle be unbroken.

So that's today's message. A simple one, but easily overlooked. The next time you go fishing, whether it's today or in six months, let this be your thought: let the good times roll.

Resolved: When it comes to fishing, I let the good times roll.

January 3

"Let the blessing of St. Peter's Master be upon all that are lovers of virtue; and dare trust in His Providence; and be quiet; and go a-angling."

—Izaak Walton

There are hard days fishing and there are easy days fishing.

When it's hard, it's hell. The wind blows off the river like an invisible knife, the water is polar bear cold, and the fish are sensibly vacationing in the Bahamas (taking it easy).

When it's easy, it's a far different story. The trout leap out of the river and greet you at the trailhead.

"May we park your car?" they ask.

"Sure," you reply, and you let one of them walk you down to a heretofore unknown trout pool where a bunch of goldens is fighting over which one gets to be caught first. It's such a fight, they have to take numbers.

The worst thing you can do as a fisherman (well, there are a lot of bad things, but this is one of them) is to make an easy day hard. Hard days will happen. They will come as surely as the morning sun. You don't have to go out and look for them.

So when an easy day comes, step back and let it happen. Go with the flow (a favorite river term). It's an attitude of trust as much as anything. Trust that good things, including a trout rising to the fly, will come to you if you let them.

Resolved: I let the fish come to me.

January 4

There are hundreds, if not thousands, of books on fishing. There are more words entombed in books about fishing than there are wild trout. Well, maybe not, but it's close. And as wild trout get scarcer and scarcer, more books get written about fishing.

Funny how that works.

With all this help around, it's quite easy to become an excellent book fisherman. Book fishermen are almost as plentiful as fishing books. There are many advantages to becoming a book fisherman.

You never get wet. You never fall in and get washed downstream. Flying things never bite you. You never get so bone-tired that you can hardly see straight. You never drag in after dark with your head throbbing from the sun pounding on it all day. You never get dirty and muddy. You never straggle into camp with a hole as big as a crater in your stomach from not eating. And you never feel miserable and desperate from being beaten up all day by a bunch of swimming creatures you never even caught sight of.

Then again, a book fisherman will never know what it feels like to pull out a steelhead glistening silver under a blue moon.

Guess you might say it's a trade-off.

Resolved: I put down this book and go fishing.

January 5

"Psssst. Did ya hear? . . ."

Getting tips on where to fish is like getting directions when you're driving. Sometimes you can trust them, sometimes you can't.

A tip can come out of the blue and leave you blue. Sometimes a tip from a guy you love and trust and respect will lead you twelve miles down a dirt road to a dried up cow pond.

Other times you will be sitting drinking coffee at the Pillar Point Cafe and a man with a grizzled beard who looks like he roomed with Ahab will collapse onto the stool next to you.

"Deep Reef," he will say between sputtering coughs of phlegm into a blackened kerchief. "Salmon."

What the heck, you've got nothing else going, so you wander down to Deep Reef and catch salmon. By the truckload.

It's anybody's guess when it comes to fishing tips. But one thing is clear: you must *hear* the tip first before deciding whether to check it out. You must listen. You must engage your eyes and ears and be aware of the opportunities that can arise, quite unexpectedly, in the world of fishing.

"Psssst. Did ya hear? . . ."

Resolved: I keep my eyes and ears open. A good tip may come my way.

January 6

"You need to become the fish. You visualize what the fish wants, not what you want. You let the intuitive side override the thinking part of your brain."

—John Tavenner, fishing guide

Right-brained and left-brained fishing? Many fishermen would just call that harebrained.

Well, it is and it isn't.

If a strong mental approach meant everything, then the Amazing Kreskin would be down at the trout stream hauling in fish, rather than bending spoons with his mind the way he supposedly does.

There are two basic questions that every fisherman wants answered: (A) Are there fish? and (B) What are you using? Everything else is fluff.

Still, fishing guides like Tavenner and lifelong fishermen— guys who really know their stuff—do not discount the merits of visualization and intuition—the mental side of the sport. It's not just a matter of rod and tackle and what you're throwing at them. You must be aware.

As John Tavenner says, "You must be intuitive to anticipate what they [fish] want. Thinking is a slowing-down process." Every fisherman knows the benefit of slowing down and firmly concentrating on the task at hand. These are only two of the ways in which the mental side of fishing can contribute to success.

There are many, many more. Today, and over the course of the next year, make a pact with yourself to explore the mental side of fishing.

Resolved: I open myself up to the mental side of fishing.

January 7

"The satisfaction of taking fish by proven techniques cannot compare with the thrill of catching fish whose capture seems a miracle."

—Harold F. Blaisdell

There is a right way and a wrong way to teach a kid how to fish.

The right way is the way that gives a kid joy and makes him want to go out again. The wrong way is one that makes him throw down his rod in frustration because he's not doing it *right*—that is, the way his father told him.

A kid can fish by the book, but if he's not having a good time, it's a bad book. Harold Blaisdell writes, "I think it is a mistake to try to cram a technical knowledge of fishing down a youngster's throat. Not only may it sour him on the whole deal, but it will deny him the fun of learning through trial and error. No boy enjoys doing as he's told, but when left to his own devices there is no limit to the effort he will expend in satisfying his own curiosity."

Let your child be. Give him space in a trout stream as you would anyone else. Let him figure it out himself.

Your child will thank you for it, if not this year, then in the years to come when he's reached manhood and the two of you are still fishing, still roaming the trout streams of Idaho together, father and son.

Resolved: I give my son space.

January 8

"I sat there ruefully wondering what a Hewitt or LaBranche or Bergman would do. They'd probably rig up and go fishin' at length I sensibly told myself."

—Robert Traver

It's Friday afternoon, quitting time. What are you gonna do this weekend?

Rig up and go fishing.

Your wife just left you. The kids can't stand you. The mortgage company is foreclosing on your house. What's a fella like you supposed to do?

Rig up and go fishing. (Well, it can't hurt.)

You just got fired from your job. Now that you've got all that free time on your hands, rig up and go fishing.

Whatever your situation, either good or ill, it will only get better if you rig up and go fishing. That is the most appropriate response: rig up and go fishing.

Don't think about it too long; all you will do is come up with reasons why you shouldn't do what you most definitely want to do, and that's no good. So keep the thinking to a minimum, and rig up and go fishing.

And when you have done it, when you have managed to slip away from all the ties that bind, park your car by the side of your favorite out-of-the-way trout stream and go down and check out what's happening. Is it mayflies or midges or what? You sit and ponder and maybe you're sure what to use and maybe you're not.

What should I do? you ask yourself.

But you already know the answer to that.

Resolved: I rig up and go fishing.

January 9

"The simplicities work. The basic skills that we learn first are the ones that carry us through a lifetime."

—John Randolph

You know a lot.

You know a lot and can do a lot. The next time you go out, focus on what you know and what you can do, instead of the negatives that invariably swarm around every fisherman's head like mosquitoes.

Okay, so you don't know everything. Who does? So you're not Lee Wulff. Who is? Wulff's dead anyway, so what does he know?

Extend this attitude to all areas of your fishing life. Your gear, for one. You may not be wielding a super-light, super-strong, tournament-ready rod with all the assorted gimcracks, but the one you have has worked in the past and you trust it like an old friend and you know it won't let you down when you need it. That's pretty good, when you think about it.

Focus on what you have, rather than what you lack. The same goes for the amount of time you spend fishing. Maybe the only time you have to go fishing is when you're on vacation. Maybe it's only one weekend a month, or one weekend a year. At least it's something. Use the time you have to the fullest, rather than thinking about all the time you could be fishing and are not. That's just a way to make yourself miserable, and fishing is plenty miserable enough without adding more misery to it.

What you know is enough. What you have is enough. Exploit them to their fullest in the time that you have.

Resolved: I focus on what I know.

January 10

"The pessimist thinks 'always' and 'never.' The optimist thinks 'sometimes' and 'lately.'

—Dr. Martin Seligman

The power of positive thinking can only take you so far in fishing.

Still, it can't hurt and it might even do some good. It might even put you in a better frame of mind and cut out all those what-in-God's-name-am-I-doing-out-here? thoughts that everybody has from time to time.

Just imagine it. See yourself on the McCloud or the Deschutes. It's sunny, it's beautiful. You're all alone. You've found a spot to yourself. It's a nice quiet pool and lurking under the surface is something very large, of German stock. It moves ominously through the water like a U-2. Your cast is perfect and the brown moves up to it and takes it and then it's just you and him, for the rest of the day, up and down the river, until finally he gives in and gives up, one champion bowing to another's greater spirit.

Now that's a pretty picture.

Resolved: I imagine positive images before I fish.

January 11

Not to sound too Pollyannaish, but you know why it hurts so much? Because you love it, that's why.

Right, right. What's love got to do with fishing? Nothing, you say. Or maybe on second thought there *is* something: they both smell. That's it. Both love and fish smell.

Funny, hah hah. But think about the rest of your life—your job, for instance. Sure you care about it because you need the dough. But forgetting that for a moment, how much do you really care?

And how much do you care about it compared to fishing?

It's probably not even close. And that's the case with a lot of the other areas of your life when you stand them up next to fishing, a thing you truly love. They pale. There's nothing there. They crumble like a brick building in an earthquake.

And you know why you love fishing? Because you are living large, that's why. You're out there. Nobody's telling you what to do. You make your own hours, you come and go as you please. There's no one to answer to except you and the fish, and unlike your boss, at least you respect the fish.

So that's why you get disappointed. That's why the lows can seem so low, like you've hit the curb and you're never going to get up. That's the price of love.

Make a pact with yourself: never let the lows bring you down too low. Always remember, a high is close behind.

Resolved: I never let the lows of fishing get me down too low.

January 12

"That is where I want to be; that is how I am renewed."

—Joan Salvato Wulff, on fishing

Find ways to bring fishing into your life. Not just on the odd weekend that you can get away, or over the summer. But every day.

Fishing is a year-round pastime. That is one of its enduring charms. Make fishing your year-round pastime.

Be inventive. Find a way to bring fishing into your life when the closest water for a hundred miles is the spray from a broken fire hydrant down at the corner. It's possible. Anything's possible if you've got the desire (and the yearning to hunt the piscine).

Read about it (in this book, for example) before you turn out the lights for bed. Subscribe to the magazines. Some of the best fishing found anywhere is on the printed page.

Go out in the yard and practice casts. Learn to tie flies. Learn to tie them better if you already know how. Hell, become a fly-tying master.

It's not as if you need to turn fishing into some kind of daily regime, like taking vitamin C or doing aerobics. But a little bit on a semiregular basis can lead to a lot more on a more regular basis. And that's what you want, right? More time spent fishing.

Resolved: I find ways to bring fishing into my life.

January 13

"One of the reasons I love to fish is the relaxing rhythm of the sport—the total removal, in place and purpose, from the stress and competition of work."

—Judy Muller

Whatever you're doing, take a fishing break.

How important is it really? Take a break from it. Go fishing.

You definitely need a break if the project is a large and demanding one. You cannot go full blast on a large and demanding project and expect to make it all the way through with any assurance of quality. So take a break. Go fishing.

And when you return to it—rejuvenated by the sight and sound and feel and taste of a river or lake—your project will be much the better for it. You can turn up the throttle and finish it. Then after you're done—before starting something else—take another break. You deserve it.

Apply the same principle for the small projects in your life. Small projects are, by definition, *small*. Why sweat it? It'll get done. Take a break and go fishing.

The idea is to turn your thinking around. You probably see fishing as a break from your ordinary life. You use it to get away from job, family, responsibilities, etc.

Instead of seeing fishing as a break, see your life as a break from fishing. Life is what you have to endure between fishing trips. Where you want to be is fishing. Everything else just gets in the way.

Give yourself a day or just an afternoon. That may be all the break you need.

Resolved: Whatever I'm doing, I take a break from it and go fishing.

January 14

"To the dull mind nature is leaden. To the illumined mind the whole world burns and sparkles with light."

—Ralph Waldo Emerson

What to do about boredom?

Every angler experiences it from time to time. It's like a vital connection has gone bad or gotten fuzzy for some reason.

The French have a great way to say it: *"je m'ennui,"* which roughly translated means, "I bore myself." In other words, if you're bored, you don't have to look too far to find the reason.

Boredom is a standard complaint of nonfishermen about fishing. Kids use it on a Saturday morning when they've been dragged out to the municipal wharf by their dads. Saying they're bored and moping around is an excellent way to get back to their familiar habit of sitting in front of a TV, which we all know is a most exciting form of recreation.

It may be time for a break if you find yourself getting bored. Maybe you're just plain tired. Find a nice shade tree, tip your hat over your eyes, and take a snooze.

Sometimes, too, you can get into a habit of mind which goes something like this: "I'm fishing. I've been waiting a month for this chance. I'm gonna have fun, damn it." But it doesn't seem like much fun because you've put so much pressure on it and weighed it down with so many expectations.

Fishing gives back. Let it happen. Open yourself up to it. Do this and you'll find plenty to keep you busy—plenty.

Resolved: I take a break from fishing if I find boredom setting in.

January 15

You can tell.

Like no one else, you can tell. Are there fish, or not? You can tell.

Ask yourself. Your self knows. A book won't help you. Only you can help you. What do you say?

You've read water before. It's not hieroglyphics. There are tricks to it, things to know. You know some of them; you know lots of them, in fact. Trust what you see. Trust your experience to tell you what you see.

Listen to others, of course. Check out the one-eyed tackle shop owner who's seen it all (or at least half of it). Search out the locals, maybe enlist a guide. They know the river like no one else. They live with it year-round and you're just a visitor. Soak up as much information as you can from them.

Still, it ultimately boils down to you. Your vision, your wisdom, your experience, your inner voice.

People will think you're crazy if you follow that voice. Sometimes you'll have to go out on your own, to a place where no one has ever gone, or at least where no one has been in a long time, because that is where your voice is telling you to go. But if you listen to that voice and trust it, more times than not, you will catch fish.

Resolved: I trust my fishing instincts.

January 16

"I've never regretted the things I've done in my life. It's the things I didn't do that I've always regretted."

—Michael Caine

Go around the bend.

How many chances are you going to have to fish this river? So fish it, if you're going to fish it. Go around the bend.

We've all been there before. Tired, full of doubts. Should I pack it in and call it a day, or should I fish a little more? Maybe go down around the bend and see what it looks like from there.

Listen to this voice, the voice that tells you to go around the bend.

You'll have plenty of time to rest. Camp will still be there when you get back. If daylight slips away, so be it. Fishing is like baseball now at Wrigley Field. You can play it both day and night.

Think of the stories you will have to tell, the stories that may be lurking around the bend. But don't do it just to have something to brag about to your buddies back at camp. Do it for yourself. Do it because it's there. Go around the bend.

You may never pass this way again. Seize the opportunity. You're not chasing fool's gold. You've lived long enough to know that what's around the bend will probably pretty much resemble the stretch of river you're already standing knee-deep in.

That's not the point. The point is don't live a life of regret, missed chances, and unfulfilled hopes. Do the things you see yourself doing in your mind's eye. Go around the bend.

Resolved: I go around the bend.

January 17

"Fish fine and far off is the principle rule for trout angling."

—Charles Cotton

No finer rule than this: fish fine and far off. Told in dialog form, here is more basic advice from the great Mr. Cotton, the seventeenth-century champion of fly-fishing and Izaak Walton's old streamside pal:

"Viator: 'Did you see that, sir?'"

"Piscator: 'Yes, I saw the fish; and he saw you too, which made him turn short. You must fish further off, if you intend to have any sport here.'"

And more:

"Piscator: 'Why now, let me tell you you lost that fish by your own fault, and through your own eagerness and haste; for you are never to offer to strike a good fish, if he do not strike himself, till you first see him turn his head after he has taken your fly, and then you can never strain your tackle in the striking, if you strike with any manner of moderation.'"

Fish fine and far off. Don't be too eager. Never offer to strike a fish if he does not strike himself. These are excellent precepts, and you probably have a few of your own that you live by.

That's today's message: stick with the basics. They'll never fail you. Whether the lessons come from Charles Cotton or Mel Krieger or your own hard-won experience (the best teacher), if they work for you, use them, no matter how old or outdated they may seem to others.

Resolved: I go back to the basics in a pinch.

January 18

"If a man fishes hard, what is he going to do easy?"

—Roy Blount Jr.

Think easy, not hard. Think simple, not complicated.

Angling instructors have a trick when they're teaching a more complicated knot, say a blood knot, to beginning fishermen. Instead of emphasizing how difficult it is, they introduce it by saying how easy a knot it is to tie, how simple.

The reasoning is obvious: talk up-front about how difficult a thing is and inevitably people, especially beginning knot-tiers, panic. They go into brain lock.

When they believe a blood knot (or whatever) is a simple task that's easy to learn, the attitude of beginners is much different. They jump into the project. They're enthusiastic, ready to learn. Granted, they may encounter difficulties as they go along, but at least they've gotten over the initial mental barriers to learning something new, barriers which can seem so formidable as to stop the beginner dead in his tracks.

This approach can pay dividends even if you can tie a blood knot in your sleep, even if you've tied it a thousand times. Whatever your skill level in fishing, there are always new challenges, new things to learn. Focus not on the difficulty of those challenges, but on how doable they are, how attainable. Say you simply want to spend more time fishing, but all you can think of are the obstacles that prevent you from doing it. The more you think about those obstacles, the more power you give them. Eliminate or lessen the obstacles in your mind, and they will have less force in reality.

Resolved: I think easy, not hard.

January 19

"There comes a time in life when, because you are on an adventure, even an uncomfortable one, you enjoy yourself. It is not the old routine, whatever it may be, and there is no knowing how many chances life will bring you to do something madcap."

—William Humphrey

That time in life has come. Go on an adventure. Get out of the old routine. Do something madcap.

Fish for blues in the blistering winds off Nantucket. Hook a tarpon in the waters of the Gulf Stream, Ernest Hemingway's old stomping ground. Go to Alaska or Montana. Go to Newfoundland in search of salmon. Better still, try Outer Mongolia. I hear they're really big over there.

Go not in pursuit of fish so much as a rarer and more precious thing: the person you were, are, and still could be. There is nothing necessarily wrong with the old routine. The old routine works; that's why it's become routine. It has its place.

But you have to be sure that you define your routine, rather than letting your routine define you. Be eternally vigilant that you control your habits, rather than letting your habits control you.

The best way to figure out a new and better routine is to get out of your old one for a while. Try on a new way of doing things. Test yourself, go on an adventure. How many chances do you expect to have? Do you seriously think you can put it off indefinitely? What are you waiting for?

Resolved: I get out of my old routine. I go on a fishing adventure.

January 20

The popular perception of fishing is stuck in the nineteenth century. When people think about fishing—well, some people anyhow—they picture something out of a Mark Twain novel as painted by Norman Rockwell.

A boy is lying on the bank of a slowly meandering river. He's asleep, a straw hat blocking his eyes from the sun. Trees line the river. It's a beautiful, peaceful landscape. There's no one around except the boy, who's barefoot. A string is tied to his big toe and it leads off into the water. Not far away a trout is jumping high out of the water, almost winking at the boy, who of course, is fast asleep and doesn't see it.

Now a lot of dyed-in-the wool fishermen resent this image. They know that fishing is far more vigorous than that, and they certainly know that if they did happen to fall asleep by the stream, as soon as that big trout hit the water they'd be up in a flash recasting their string in its direction.

Nobody likes to be called lazy, especially when he's not. But if you can't be lazy when you're fishing, when can you be?

We are privileged, as fisherman, to be able to say good-bye to all that, at least for a while. Let the rest of the world rush by pell-mell as it will. We get to say stop, and slow the whole business down. We get a shot at contentment and peace of mind. If some want to call that laziness, so be it.

Metaphorically speaking, never forget to tie a string to your big toe when you go fishing.

Resolved: I take it easy the next time I go fishing.

January 21

"When I have made a difficult cast and landed it the way I wanted, or fished over a difficult fish and finally caught it, I feel true reward."

—Jennifer Smith, fly-fisher

Fishing is in the casting. Get into a good casting rhythm, send the line where you want it to go, easily, smoothly, effortlessly, and everything will fall into place, fish included.

The first, essential step to good fly casting is this: see the cast before you make it. See what you want to do before you do it.

Technique supports vision. See first what you need to do, and your technique will follow in line. Without this clear-sightedness, technique will only carry you so far and no farther.

Technique is the arm (and by extension, the fly rod); vision is the mind. Use the arm to serve the mind.

Casting against the wind? Have a difficult, obstructed side cast? Want to cast to a pool far upstream? Whatever you're doing, whatever situation you're in, see it first. See the line coiling and recoiling, making beautiful arcs in the air. See the fly landing in the spot where you want it.

Before taking a swing, Jack Nicklaus plays a movie in his mind of the way he wants his golf shot to go. All great athletes do much the same thing: they see the results they want prior to the act.

It works for fishermen, too. See it, then do it. The seeing of it will help you do it.

Resolved: I see a cast before I make it.

January 22

"If you spend any time at all framed by the terrain, a sense of your own small stature is inevitable."

—Elizabeth Storer

What are the lessons you need to learn as a human being? You can learn them in fishing.

Not lessons on how to fish, but lessons on how to live. Lessons about yourself, your family, other people, the natural world. You may not know what the lessons are, but they're there, if you have a mind to learn.

You may not think you need lessons. Lessons are for school, for kids. You don't need any more lessons.

Or you may think you can guide your education. You strive to learn a specific thing because that's where you feel a certain lack and where you want to get better. But then you receive a lesson of a wholly different sort, one that you weren't expecting, not by a long shot.

Fishing is like that. It keeps you off balance, surprises you.

It takes humility to learn, to accept that you may need a lesson or two even in your advanced stage of enlightenment. The lessons you learn when you're on a stream or in the middle of a lake on a boat have a way of spilling over into the rest of your life when you're far, far away from streams and boats.

Keep a sense of perspective about yourself. Approach the natural world and fishing with humility and respect, and you will learn important lessons, the ones you need to learn.

Resolved: I maintain my perspective.

January 23

"Learn to labour, and to wait."

—Henry Wadsworth Longfellow

Ten minutes a week. That's all you need. Practice your casting for ten minutes a week, and you'll be as good as Mel Krieger or anybody.

Okay, maybe not Mel Krieger. But you'll be pretty good. Good enough to spin beautiful pictures in the air. Good enough to put your fly line where you want, when you want.

How much is ten minutes? Ten minutes is nothing. A shower takes ten minutes. That's how much time you need to spend—one shower's worth.

It takes longer to microwave a three-pound ham than it does to get in a week's worth of practice with a fly rod. Put the ham in, go out and practice your casts, then come back and have dinner.

Think about how much time you waste on freeways getting to and from work. That's an eternity compared to the little time it takes to make your casting just that much better. Postcommute is, in fact, the perfect time for it. Everybody needs to wind down after playing road warrior on the drive home. Spend your wind-down time in silent conversation with your fly rod. Afterward you'll be ready to wage the homefront battles—kids, dinner, spouse, etc.

Some fishermen hate the idea of practice. They only want to make their casts when they can hook a fish with one. That's understandable. But a little bit of easy labor every week can make a world of difference when you finally get on a stream or lake to fish for real.

Resolved: I practice casting for ten minutes a week.

January 24

"They play poker, bowl and fish together. They fish together every spring and early summer before family vacations, Little League baseball and visiting relatives can intrude."

—Raymond Carver

Give yourself the gift of time. That's the best thing you can do for yourself as a fisherman.

Time to fish. Time to get away. Time to really get into it, to hang out with your buds, to go on an extended fishing trip, to take that fishing adventure you've always dreamed about.

Whatever you want to do in fishing, whatever your desire or dream, it will require time. Give yourself that gift.

People tend to think of gifts only in terms of things. But that expensive new rod your wife gave you for Christmas will just gather dust in the garage unless you use it. And to use it you need time, that most precious of commodities.

But nobody is going to give it to you; you're going to have to take it for yourself. With all the pressures of making a living, family, modern life in general, it's easy for fishing—something you really care about, but which others might consider a luxury—to take a backseat, even get nudged out of the car altogether.

Don't let it happen. Don't let others intrude. Make a commitment to yourself. Find a way to carve a space in the schedule and then fight for it with all your might. It will be worth it.

Resolved: I give myself the time to fish.

January 25

"When a spot looks hot, cast as long as 20 minutes to it. When this doesn't work, do everything the opposite way. After the tried and true method you can use your wildest kind of imagination."
— Robert Zwirz and Morty Marshall, fishing authors

A popular visualization technique used by athletes is to envision a thing as having already happened prior to doing it. You start at the end and work back in your mind to the beginning.

Say an athlete is running the 100-meter dash. He sees himself busting the finish line first, ahead of the other runners in the race. He replays the race in his mind, working back to when he put his feet in the starting blocks. The idea is to develop a sense of the thing being accomplished—the race being run—before taking a single step. This technique helps him get control of the process.

He feels more relaxed, more confident, for he has already seen the ending. It's not a scary unknown like it was before. The drama has already been played out in a sense. What he does is act out an event that has already taken place in his mind.

Think about applying this technique to fishing. It's simple stuff, not mystical hocus-pocus. Start with the fish and work backward in your mind. You release the fish. Somebody snaps a picture. You net it. You bring it in. It makes a long, gallant fight and you stay with it all the way. You hook it, make the strike. The trout rises. You make a lovely cast into a pool behind a boulder. You make false casts. You see the trout. You pick your spot. You resolve to hunt trout.

Resolved: I visualize my fishing from finish to start.

January 26

"I have probably caught a half-million trout in my lifetime."

—A. J. McClane

A half-million trout? That's a lot of trout. Better get busy. You've got a lot of catching up to do.

Let's say you live until you're seventy. A seventy-year-old man must catch 7,143 fish a year in order to reach or surpass what the legendary McClane did in his lifetime. That's 137 fish a week, or nearly twenty fish a day. That is, however, somewhat less than one fish per hour, so if you haven't caught a fish in the last thirty minutes, you're still safe.

Well, you're safe for a while, or until you finish reading this section. But after you're done, no more tarrying. Or you'll never make it.

A half-million trout in a lifetime is almost a fantasy figure. Apart from the issues surrounding resources, do you know anyone who could actually do it? Who could actually spend days and nights tromping around pathless woods, up and down raging rivers, in pursuit of fish? Many of us wouldn't mind living that life, at least for a year or two, but only a few lucky souls pull it off.

A half-million in a lifetime may not be feasible, but fortunately there are still wild trout out there for you. Better get busy. You've got a lot of catching up to do.

Resolved: I get busy. I make plans to go fishing.

January 27

"I have no desire to latch onto a monster symbol of fate and prove my manhood in titanic piscine war. But sometimes I do like a couple of cooperative fish of frying size."

—John Steinbeck

A couple of fish of frying size. Now that's a worthy goal for every fisherman.

But you might think something is wrong with this—and you—if you read the weekly fishing reports published in the newspaper. It almost doesn't matter which paper you read; they're all the same.

"Jack Weathers and Pete McVie broke the 100-pound barrier for sturgeons on separate outings to Mare Island. . . . A 65-pound sturgeon was photographed at Rod and Reel. . . . Lenny Monroe weighed a 47-pounder near the Pittsburgh PG&E plant. . . . Capt. Rock Jackson of the Happy Trawler said his passengers released 80 to 100 rockfish. . . . Capt. Pappy O'Brien caught 83 halibut in two days on a weekend trip to Seal Rock. . . . Forty-five passengers on the New Tom Sawyer collected 51 salmon to 33 pounds, 32 halibut to 25 pounds, eight bass to 9 pounds and two ling cod. . . ."

And so it goes. It's not a fishing report, it's a shopping list. All quantities and poundage.

It's easy to get caught up in the numbers game when you're fishing. But all things considered, it probably won't offer as many long-term benefits as a more modest approach of a couple of fish of frying size.

Resolved: I catch a couple of fish of frying size.

January 28

"They have a mystery about them. The first time you catch a steelhead, it's like a bolt of lightning striking the tip of your rod."

—Jim Edmondson

The steelhead needs you. For years you've hunted them—felt that surge of lightning in your rod. Now they're in trouble and they need you.

A steelhead is a migratory fish. Its native range is from southern California up to the Gulf of Alaska and east into the northern Rockies. Zane Grey fished for steelhead on the Rogue River in Oregon. Normally they weigh six to ten pounds, but it's been reported fishermen have caught steelhead weighing thirty-five pounds or more, and the reports are true.

Oncorhynchus mykiss (that's Latin for "one helluva fish") spawn in fresh water but take to sea like merchant seamen and live their lives in salt water. Then that mysterious, inexplicable call comes and they return to their spawning grounds to breed and die.

That's where the trouble comes in. More than twenty steelhead stocks have been lost and another forty or more are headed for extinction unless we do something to stop the madness.

What to do? Join a conservation organization that is working to save the steelhead and other threatened fish. California Trout and Trout Unlimited are two. There are many others. Get involved. The steelhead—and your grandchildren, who may want to feel that lightning strike—will thank you.

Resolved: I join a conservation organization.

January 29

"If you wish to be happy forever, learn to fish."

—Chinese proverb

New to fishing? Want to learn? Why not take a class?

A class will give you some hands-on experience with a fly-fishing rod without having to worry about flies or fish. You'll learn to pick up and lay down. You'll learn that old standby, the roll cast. You'll learn to make false casts. You'll learn how to hold your hands on the (never call it a pole) rod.

Smart instructors teach their beginning students without hooks. You will thank them for that after you whip yourself in the face with the line.

You will cast until your arm hurts. You will learn the correct motion of the elbow and arm. You will be able to make a fool of yourself in a comfortable, no-pressure environment in which other people are making similar fools of themselves.

After casting for a couple of hours into a casting pool, you will move onto dry land and simulate the act of landing a fish. Another student will hold the end of the line and walk this way and that, back and forth, mimicking the motions of a fish in water. You will haul this human fish in and learn to use a net.

You will learn to tie basic knots, such as the surgeon's knot or the blood knot. You may become totally confused, or more likely, forget everything you learned the next day. The key to knot-tying—and casting, for that matter—is repetition.

Then, after taking a class, you will be ready for higher education on free-running streams and rivers.

Resolved: I take a fly-fishing class.

January 30

"It is something of an art and it comes with time. It is the art of reading water."

—Robert Zwirz and Morty Marshall

First Picasso sees, then he paints. His painting is an expression of what he sees.

First Updike sees, then he writes. His novels and essays are expressions of that unique vision.

It is no different with a fisherman. First he sees, then he fishes. What he uses to catch the fish, where he goes to catch them, how he goes about it—this is largely the result of what he sees. He reads the water.

It is impossible to learn to read water by reading a book. It is impossible to learn it from listening to others. To read water you have to study it, spend time with it, get to know it.

There are tricks you can pick up, little signposts that you recognize as you become more intimate with water. But there are no quick fixes, just as there are no quick fixes in learning to paint or write well. It takes time. It takes a lot of hard looking—and thinking.

Thinking is part of seeing. Reading water is not merely an act of the eyeball. You have to actively engage the cerebrum as well. It is not a passive act, like watching television or a movie. Water is a different world with different rules than the ones that govern us on land. To know this world you must enter into it fully and be willing to do more than simply drop a line and hope for the best.

First comes seeing.

Resolved: I really study the water. I really look at it hard.

January 31

Here's something to do: spend a week at a fishing lodge.

It doesn't matter if you're a big dog in the sport or just a pup. A week at a fishing lodge will do you just fine.

They're all over the place. They advertise in the fishing magazines, so you won't have any problem finding one that suits your type of fishing, your tastes, your choice of scenery.

It's all fishing, that's what's great about going to a fishing lodge. You fish in the morning, you fish in the afternoon, you fish in the evening. What could be better than that?

A fishing lodge will provide guide services, instruction, tours. The best thing about all of it is where it happens. You're not learning on some water-filled concrete ditch. You don't have to drive three hours to get there. You're already there. You wake up in the woods, and you go to bed in the woods. The sound of trout rising and falling in the water sings you softly to sleep.

After a day of sparring with wild trout, traipsing around the stream in your shorty vest like Brad Pitt, you come back hungry enough to eat a bear. Most fishing lodge menus do not include bear, but they feed you pretty good anyway.

Chances are you've wanted to check in at a lodge for quite some time. All you needed was a spur, a kick in the pants. Let today's message be that spur. Lay aside your other business. Make plans and go.

Resolved: I book a week at a fishing lodge.

February 1

"I always give myself three days to catch a fish: One for weather, one to get to know the water, and one for luck."
—Kay Kolt, fly-fisher

The key to catching fish? Well, there are lots of keys, but here is one of them: maximize your fishing time.

The only way to catch fish is to spend time doing it. Too obvious? Possibly, but no one yet has reported catching a fish while driving back to town to pick up their forgotten waders or rain parka. Or for that matter, while sitting on the bank untying tangles.

Some fishermen spend more time and energy getting out to the lake than they do on it. And it can drive you nuts to go on a trip with one of them. They do not seem to realize that going on the fishing trip they've been promising themselves for so long is only half the battle. There is this little matter of fishing, which must be attended to.

Make time your ally, rather than a thing you are constantly fighting. Plan ahead, prepare. Eliminate or minimize distractions. Give yourself fully over to what you're doing. Our lives are normally so fractured, with demands and commitments pulling us in many different directions at once, that it is sometimes hard to concentrate.

One way to sharpen your power of concentration is to give yourself plenty of time in which to fish. A feeling of too little time makes you rush, puts pressure on you, and prevents you from obtaining the results you seek.

Resolved: I make an effort to maximize my fishing time.

February 2

"The fact is that the fly fisherman is likely to raise his biggest and most difficult trout when he is on the stream alone, concentrating and undisturbed."

—R. Palmer Baker Jr.

For such a solitary sport, fishing can get awfully damned crowded.

Sometimes there are so many fishermen around, they seem like ants at a picnic. Crawling everywhere, getting into everything.

Turn left, and there's one at your elbow. Turn right, and there's another on your shoulder. Wade into the river, and you step on somebody's toe.

How do to get away from the crowds? Go upstream or down.

Fishermen fish rivers and lakes the way people drive on the freeway—all bunched together. Likely as not, they're bunched at a spot closest to the road, thereby decreasing the distance they have to walk.

Go upstream or downstream and you will leave them behind. Go a little farther and you can get away from just about everyone.

It's not a fail-safe method. You may never entirely escape the presence of human beings on popular fishing streams. But you have a much better chance of doing so if you take a nice, solitary stroll upstream or down.

Resolved: I beat the crowds. I hike upstream or downstream.

February 3

"Here's a guy standing in cold water up to his liver throwing the world's most expensive clothesline at trees."

—P. J. O'Rourke, on fly-fishing

Fishing and frustration go hand in hand. Nobody is more frustrated than a frustrated fisherman.

When faced with the inevitable frustrations of fishing, the angler may:

(A) Go stark-raving mad. Break his rod in half. Break it into tiny pieces and use it for kindling. Wrap that expensive clothesline around his neck, tie the end to a nearby tree, and swing. Another possibility is to wrap it around his buddy's neck. Failing that, he may fill his tackle box with stones and sink it to the bottom of the lake, so it never tortures human beings again. Afterward he can burn all his flies, his hat, vest, and waders and dance around the fire in a crazed expression of piscine catharsis.

(B) Accept the frustrations of fishing as part of the sport, and move on.

While many longtime fishermen follow option A, it is probably wiser to choose B.

Resolved: I accept the minor frustrations of fishing as part of the sport, and move on.

February 4

"Fishing is an act of subtlety. We walk away defeated in the pursuit, but pleased at having pursued."

—Charles H. Traub

The f-word in fishing is *failure*. It doesn't belong.

What is failure in fishing? Not catching fish? That's crazy. You can have the time of your life and not see a fish all day.

Okay, maybe that's stretching it. But almost everyone who's tied a worm to a hook would agree there's more to fishing than fish. You've got your head screwed on wrong if all you're thinking is capture, capture, and more capture.

That's where the failure syndrome comes in. It lodges in your head like a termite and relentlessly eats away at you until your brains turn to sawdust. Of course you're going to feel rotten if you're obsessed with catching fish and draw nary a nibble or a look-see all day.

You're hardly a failure, though. What you need is to redefine success for yourself.

It's not just semantics. It's a way of looking at fishing that values process over result, that draws lessons from every experience, no matter how seemingly fruitless or unfulfilling, and which ultimately cuts you, the fisherman, some slack.

Don't be so tough on yourself. Everyone wants to catch fish. But you take all the fun out of it if that's all that matters to you. It's doubtful you'll be all that agreeable a person to fish with, either.

Resolved: I eliminate failure from my fishing vocabulary.

February 5

"And God created great whales, and every living creature that moveth, which the waters brought forth abundantly after their kind, and every winged fowl after his kind; and God saw that it was good."

—Genesis 1:21

Fishermen may get the best glimpses of whales. They are out on the ocean in boats, and they see the whales swim by during migrations. To see a whale in its native habitat, to see its beautiful, massive form breach the surface of the water, must be one of the most extraordinary sights in all of nature.

In Melville's time they referred to whales as *monsters*. Perhaps many people today still see them that way. A blue whale can be one hundred feet long and weigh 150 tons. They're so big, so otherworldly. They're like dinosaurs of the sea, representatives of a lost, and seemingly scarier, time.

But in fact, whales are mammals like us. They breathe air the same as we do. They're warm-blooded, and whale moms produce milk for their babies like human moms do.

Some whale pods can be a thousand members strong. A thousand whales, swimming in the open sea—what a thought. Sperm whales can dive as deep as a mile under the sea. When they rise to the surface to breathe, they blow air out their blowholes. Their spouting can be seen for miles.

If you live by the coast, take a day to go look for whales during their seasonal migrations. Go by boat or station yourself at a whale-watching spot on land. It's a wondrous reminder, if one is needed, of the wonders of our world and the awesome power and majesty and mystery of the sea.

Resolved: I go whale-watching.

February 6

"Only the shallow know themselves."

—Oscar Wilde

You've fished every stream on the map, and some that aren't. Make a commitment to keep learning.

You've caught fish on a fly that you made up on the spot. Make a commitment to keep learning.

Your dad taught you fishing when you were five years old and you've been at it ever since. Make a commitment to keep learning.

You can tell a rainbow trout from a steelhead and a Dolly Varden from Dolly Parton. Make a commitment to keep learning.

You disdain planted trout and seek wild. Make a commitment to keep learning.

You've studied the hatching habits of the mayfly and stonefly and talked about it at a dinner party. Make a commitment to keep learning.

You are on a first-name basis with Mel Krieger. Make a commitment to keep learning.

You've caught big fish on lighter test line. Make a commitment to keep learning.

You've caught a 1,300-pound Atlantic blue marlin in Bermuda and coho in Alaska. Make a commitment to keep learning.

Whatever you've done in fishing, do more. Go farther. Stay longer. Expand your limits. Make a commitment to keep learning and in so doing, find out more about yourself.

Resolved: I make a commitment to keep learning.

February 7

"If there is no struggle, there is no progress."

—Frederick Douglass

Fishing is like anything else. You reach plateaus. It doesn't matter how good you are or how long you've been at it. At some point the learning curve is going to flatten out and you're going to wonder if you're making any progress at all.

It's like floating down a river. You're in the current, clipping along pretty well, making time. Then the river slows and your boat drifts. And drifts. After a while it feels like you're not going anywhere at all.

But, in fact, you are. When a boat is drifting it's still going somewhere, though maybe not be quite as fast as before. Look around you. There's still plenty of opportunity to learn, to have fun, assuming you relax and readjust your bearings to the slower pace.

Then again, you may not want to. You may want to get back in the current and book. Well then, take out the oars and *paddle*.

When you find yourself adrift, in life as well as fishing, engage yourself further. That is your only hope. Never withdraw. Disappointed at where you stand? Want to progress to a higher plane, or at a faster rate? The answer is clear: take out the oars and paddle.

Resolved: I engage myself further.

February 8

"A gentleman trying to get a fly out of the milk or a piece of cork out of his glass of wine often imagines himself to be irritated. Let him think for a moment of the patience of anglers sitting by dark pools, and let his soul be immediately irradiated with gratification and repose."

—G. K. Chesterton

There is a great poem by William Butler Yeats called "The Lake Isle of Innisfree." "I will arise and go now," he writes, "and go to Innisfree, and a small cabin build there, of clay and wattles made." Not exactly deluxe accommodations, but at least the twentieth century's greatest poet could get some quiet time there. "And I shall have some peace there, for peace comes dropping slow, dropping from the veils of morning to where the cricket sings."

The lake water of Innisfree—"lapping with low sounds by the shore"—occupied a special place in Yeats's heart. It traveled with him wherever he went: "While I stand on the roadway, or on the pavement grey, I hear it in the deep heart's core."

You may carry a similar spot in your heart's core. Not Innisfree, but a fishing spot that is special to you. It may not be a place the guidebooks rave about; you may like it only for your own personal reasons. Those are the best places, really.

The next time modern life threatens to overwhelm you, when you get really irritated or ticked off, you might take a moment and recall that spot in your mind. See yourself fishing at your personal Innisfree, and the irritation—whatever it may be—may gently ease away.

Resolved: I picture myself fishing and let the irritations of the moment slip away.

February 9

"Sweet is pleasure after pain."

—John Dryden

If fishing seems all pain and no pleasure, pack it in early and go seek pleasure.

Let your rod lay. Become Euell Gibbons for a day. Go in search of wild mushrooms or miner's lettuce. Check out the Indian grinding stone and the old logging bridge.

Downstream is an abandoned mining cave that's dark and wet and spooky. Take a flashlight and explore.

Climb a tree, see what you can see. Hike up a side canyon. Go up the pools of the creek, strip off your clothes, and go swimming. Bare your buns to the sky.

Watch for golden eagles. They say they're around there. Bask in the purple and blue lupine flowers spread across the hillsides like streamers of colored ribbon.

Go into town. Investigate the local sights and history (if there are any). After you're done with that—shouldn't take long—stop in at the Buffalo Head Saloon. Order yourself a pitcher, put two quarters in the slots, and rack up a game of pool. Maybe you'll meet a girl who saw *A River Runs Through It* and just loves fishermen.

In brief, there's no sense beating a dead horse. Go have some fun if the fishing is bad, or you're just not into it the way you want to be. The fish will still be there when you get back.

Resolved: I pack it in early and explore.

February 10

"Of all the cants that which are canted in this canting world, the cant of criticism is the most tormenting."

—Laurence Sterne

Every fisherman is a teacher. Fishermen teach their sons and daughters, but they teach other people, too: brothers and sisters, wives, other people's kids, friends.

It is no easy thing being a teacher. It's a weighty responsibility. You are a kind of gatekeeper. You hold the keys to this amazing world, and newcomers must pass through you to enter.

You can welcome them in, or you can block the door. It's up to you.

One thing is certain: more people have been turned off fishing by other people trying to get them "started right" than by any other way. Criticism has its place in the learning process. So do mockery and sarcasm. Just not at the beginning.

Teach others as you would present a fly on a rippling stream—lightly, delicately. Being overly disapproving of a beginner will make him pull back and quit trying. Is that what you want? And if you simply cannot resist—if you can't teach your wife to fish without getting angry at her or mocking her—get out of the role of teacher. Let someone else do it.

Fishing is a big-tent sport. Lots of people can do it and get something out of it. Be a supportive teacher. Be generous with your pupils. Ease off on the can'ts and don'ts, especially in the beginning.

Resolved: I ease off on the can'ts and don'ts with someone who's learning.

February 11

"To reach the river we had a hard climb, downwards of fully half a mile; then a plunge and zip! the first trout."

—William Freed

Make the hard climb. It'll be worth it.

Most fishermen are not going to make the hard climb. So you're already ahead of the game before your line even meets the water.

Go down into the canyon, follow the river. Get away from the road and all those other fished-out places. Make the hard climb.

You may have wanted to go to a certain spot, but its difficult location always stopped you. Make the hard climb and end the speculation.

It's a simple fact that you're not going to know what it's like until you go. Make the hard climb and find out.

Go off the trail. Bushwhack through the manzanita. Get your bearings on the granite outcropping across the canyon. Track along the hillside and follow the surging pools downward. Make the hard climb.

Make the hard climb and get into better shape. Then the harder climbs will seem easier and you can make even harder climbs.

The best views are at the top of the mountain. You can only see them if you get there. It's the same with fishing. A payoff will come after a hard climb. Never doubt that. You will reach the river, make the plunge into the cold waters, and zip! There will be trout.

Resolved: I make the hard climb.

February 12

"We catched fish and talked, and we took a swim now and then to keep off sleepiness. . . . We had mighty good weather as a general thing, and nothing ever happened to us at all."

—Mark Twain

On your next trip, let nothing happen at all.

The best fish stories are adventure stories. They tell of trips to strange, exotic places where you meet unique but charming characters and where amazing, fascinating, even bizarre things occur.

Those sorts of fishing trips are necessary and good. Everybody needs to take fishing trips like that from time to time.

But the other kind of fishing trip is useful and necessary, too. The kind where nothing at all happens.

Where you catch some fish and cook them over the wood fire in camp. Where you take slugs from a bottle of Jack Daniels and pass it around. Where you stand around and talk. Where you stagger off to your bag and fall asleep under a shining canopy of stars.

In the morning you get up and do pretty much what you did the previous day, and if you're lucky, what you'll do tomorrow. You fish. Around noon you eat sandwiches and talk on the bank while taking a break from the fishing. Maybe then you fall asleep.

Nothing much happens weatherwise. It's sunny the whole damn time.

Yep, those are great trips, maybe the best. Those trips where nothing happens, nothing at all.

Resolved: I take a fishing trip where nothing at all happens.

February 13

"Happy the man, and happy he alone,
He who can call today his own."

—John Dryden

Some things in this book you can do in a day. You can say, "Those are good ideas," and institute them immediately. Other things take more time.

This is one of the latter. You won't be able to do it today, or even next month or in six months. It may take years. You may never be able to pull it off.

Here it is: think about making a change in your life that will give you more time to fish.

Fishing is what you like. Fishing is what you want to do. But in the current arrangement of things it is nearly impossible to do it as much as you like.

So why not change your life?

Retirement is the traditional answer. That's when people finally get the time to pursue the pleasures they've had to deny themselves while working for a living.

But you may not want to wait until you're sixty-five or seventy. Are there other ways to create more time and space for fishing? Not just on weekends or vacations, but regularly, on a permanent basis. Can you simplify your life to allow more fishing, to make your days truly your own?

Think about it. It may not be as crazy or as far-fetched an idea as it seems at first glance.

Resolved: I consider a change of life that gives me more time to fish.

February 14

"Whenever you're casting, the idea is to fall into a hypnotic rhythm, so that you and the rod become one—so that thinking becomes impossible."

—Bill Barich

The way to get good with a fly rod is to practice. A good place to practice is a casting pool.

Go early in the morning, when it's just you and the ducks and maybe an occasional jogger. It's quiet then. Casting becomes a form of meditation as you work the line back and forth across the water.

A casting pool has built-in advantages over a stream or lake. There's no pressure to catch fish. You can work solely on technique without worrying about results.

Conditions are controlled. You don't have to fret about wind or rain or freezing cold feet or what's hatching. All you have to worry about is not hitting somebody with your back cast.

Probably while you're casting some kids will come up and ask what you're doing. Since you're only practicing and the pressure's off, you'll have the time to show them. Maybe you'll even let them take a few tries.

Practice fishing is the next best thing to real fishing and that's a heckuva lot better than most things. Going to a casting pool gets you away from the house and that's good in itself. Don't overlook an obvious resource such as a casting pool if it helps. Anything that helps your fishing is, by definition, good.

Resolved: I brush up on my technique at a casting pool.

February 15

"Just one steelhead a day on the North Umpqua makes a fisherman feel like a king."

—Ray Bergman

Feel like a king today. Just catch one fish.

Do not set your sights too high, nor too low. Just catch one fish. That is setting your sights exactly right.

Let it be on the North Umpqua or the Green or the Selway or the Tuolumne. Whatever your stream or river or body of water, wherever you are. Just catch one fish.

It can be a steelhead or a golden trout or a striper or a brookie. Just catch one of them.

A popular motivational technique for athletes in training is to do one of whatever it is they are doing. One repetition, one lap around the track, one exercise. After they do that first one, it is easier to do another and so on.

It is the same with fishing. After you catch (and release) one, you can catch (and release) a second. Then a third, and so on. But it starts with one.

On some days and on some streams, however, even catching one fish is a high and lofty goal, an achievement to be proud of. You've set out to do something and you've done it. Nothing is more satisfying, in life or in fishing, than that. Set your goal at one fish today (or the next time you go out), and do it.

Resolved: I feel like a king. I catch one good fish today.

February 16

"Look to your health; and if you have it praise God, and value it next to a good conscience; for health is the second blessing that we mortals are capable of; a blessing that money cannot buy."

—Izaak Walton

Like so many other things, old Izaak was dead-on on this one. What do you have if you don't have your health? We take it for granted until something bad happens. Then we realize how precious it is.

Many nonfishermen think of fishing as a sedentary pastime. But in fact it is an outdoor discipline that requires a level of fitness and toughness.

Before you go on your next trip, why not do something for yourself that promotes health, hardiness, endurance? You don't have to suddenly become Arnold Schwarzenegger. Do simple things. Incorporate fitness into your daily life. Instead of riding the elevator, take the stairs. Walk instead of driving. Do some easy stretching exercises in the mornings before work. Take your vitamin C. Eat an occasional carrot. Lay off the booze.

You'll figure out what works for you. Even little things can add up to a lot. The idea is: look to your health. Take care of yourself, so you're not huffing and puffing all over the place and slowing everybody down on your next trip. That's no good for you or anybody else. The more fit you are, the better you're going to feel about everything, including your fishing.

Resolved: I walk more.

February 17

"My advice is—go often and visit many localities."

—Charles Bradford, angler

Fish often—and at many different places. That's good advice. Charles Bradford, writing in 1900, offers some more pointed tips:

- Fish whenever you can. The best time of year to fish is the time you can get away.
- The best time of day to fish is after breakfast. "Never go before, for trout are not early risers," says Bradford.
- Though after breakfast is best, fish at various times during the day. Who can outguess trout? Not any man. "Trout will bite just when they feel like it, and the best way to ascertain their biting time is to give them frequent opportunity," Bradford says.
- Trout will bite when it is windy and when it is calm. They will bite on a cloudy day, but also on a sunny day. Additionally, trout will bite when it rains and when it is clear. Any questions?

Bradford shows similar logic on the eternal question of what fly is best. He says the best fly is "the fly the trout seem to fancy most on the day you are out."

"As conditions are innumerable," concludes Bradford, "it is difficult to make rules today which will not fail tomorrow." This may be his best rule. Be open to what comes, and be ready to adapt to conditions as you find them.

Resolved: I stay open to what comes.

February 18

"The weather turned to sweet milk; we watched the wind drive the ice down the lake. I met and lost the trout of my dreams; and there were flaming meteors in the night."

—E. Annie Proulx

You need to watch the wind drive the ice down the lake. You need to meet the trout of your dreams and see flaming meteors in the night. You need to take a fishing vacation.

A fishing vacation is a vacation where you just fish. What a concept. Morning, noon, and night, or whenever you like. All the fishing you can handle, and then some. You stay at one place. When you get tired of that place, you move down the road to another. When you get tired there, you move again—maybe into the next *state*.

A fishing vacation is more safari than vacation. Go in search of the perfect fishing hole. If there are people in your life who would not like this—kids, spouses, girlfriends, etc.—there is a simple solution: do not bring them.

Go to a faraway, exotic locale. Costa Rica. Alaska. New Zealand. The Bahamas. Any of these places would provide an excellent backdrop for a fishing vacation.

Try a type of fishing that you've never tried before. Never fly-fished? Explore the trout streams of Idaho. Never shore-fished for fighting blues? Why not Nantucket? Go big-game fishing. Fish for strange underwater creatures whose pictures you've only seen in books. Use your vacation to get out of your fishing rut and do things you've always dreamed of doing.

Think about it. Envision it. Plan for it. Then do it—a dream fishing vacation. You can worry about paying for it later.

Resolved: I plan my dream fishing vacation.

February 19

"Thinking and fishing go well together somehow."

—John Atherton

Think of the problems you encounter in fishing not as problems, but as challenges.

A problem implies difficulty, uncertainty, doubt. It needs to be solved. Sometimes it is, sometimes it isn't.

A challenge, on the other hand, is "a call or summons to engage in any contest," according to the dictionary. A test of skill or strength, a battle of wit and will. There is something inherently stimulating about a challenge, as opposed to a problem. A person *rises* to meet a challenge. He calls upon all the powers at his command, his skill and nerve and pluck, the best he has to offer, to do the thing that needs to be done and to do it well.

A problem can be intractable. You sometimes give up on a problem, deeming it too hard to solve. Most people view a challenge in a different light. They see it as something they can overcome, a hurdle rather than a wall, and they keep after it until they get over it.

This is a way in which thinking can help your fishing. When you have to wade a stream, see it as a challenge. When you must cast against the wind, see it as a challenge. When nothing you are throwing at them is working, see it as a challenge to find the thing that finally does.

Seeing fishing as a series of problems will only discourage you. View these same situations as challenges and you will be inspired and eager to take them on.

Resolved: I see the problems in fishing not as problems, but as challenges.

February 20

"Fishing can be whatever you wish to make of it. Angling is most rewarding to the boy or girl who puts the most into it."

—Tom McNally

It's easy to let things slide. Don't let them slide. Do what you need to do to make yourself a better fisherman.

You may be content where you stand now. Good for you. But if you want to get better, do the things that will help you get better.

Fish more. That's the surest way. Get out on the stream or lake and work it. Put your time in. Experience is not a fool-proof guide to capturing fish, but it helps.

Learn to read water. Reading rivers is like learning about the stars; it's impossible to exhaust the subject. While you're at it, study your friends the fish. The more you know about them, the more you will respect them and their habitat.

Fish in different conditions and at different times of the year. You will naturally gravitate to new places the longer you fish. Try different types of fishing. Fish in salt water if you are accustomed to fresh. You will learn wherever you go, however you do it.

Study your fellow anglers—the good ones. Watch what they do and how they do it. Copy them. Experiment. Abandon old, trusted methods if these methods no longer work.

"Whatever it takes" is a good rule of thumb. Do whatever it takes to make yourself a better fisherman. Fishing is like any other activity. Put a lot into it and you will get a lot out of it.

Resolved: I do what I need to do to make myself a better fisherman.

February 21

Once upon a time wealthy fishermen had custom rods made in six or more sections. These were called "Sunday rods." They could hide them under the blankets in their horse-and-buggies or even in their clothes. Then after church they'd politely excuse themselves and go off and fish.

Today's equivalent might be the eight-piece rods that fit snugly into small carrying cases. Businessmen-anglers can politely excuse themselves at the end of the day and go off and fish. More popular are the four- and five-piece rods.

In any event, the principle is clear: take your rod with you wherever you go.

Okay, that might be pushing it. Take it wherever it is practicable. But only go places where you can get away and fish at the drop of a popper.

You may not have any weekday time during a business trip, but before you come home, schedule a Saturday to explore the local waterways and fish.

Definitely take your rod on weekend getaways or family vacations, even if they are technically "nonfishing" excursions. You never know when you'll be driving on the highway alongside some lovely, inviting trout stream, and want to stop and check it out. With your multipiece buried under the blankets in the back of the car, you can do it.

Resolved: I take my rod wherever I go.

February 22

"The answer is to do what works best for you, based on experience."

—Silvio Calabi

That's the answer all right. Do what works best for you, based on experience.

Books and videos can only tell you so much. Other fishermen can only tell you so much. Do what works best for you, based on your experience.

That's scary advice, in a sense. It means you have to rely on yourself. It means that ultimate responsibility rests with you. You're the one who's accountable. You're the one who takes the rap if something screws up.

Scary, yes. But empowering, too. Self-empowerment is a trendy concept, but it applies to the ancient art of angling. When you do what works best for you, you demonstrate—to others, and more important, to yourself—that you have the capacity and power to meet the challenges you face. You stand on your own two feet.

Whatever the situation in fishing, whatever the question, ask yourself first and last. Trust yourself above all others. You know your abilities and interests better than anyone.

The worst thing is to take the advice of someone else and then have it not work. You feel cheated because it was someone else's idea, but you're the person who bears responsibility for it. Seek your own counsel—and rely on it. Do what works for you, based on your own experience and judgment.

Resolved: I do what works best for me, based on my own experience.

February 23

"In my view, the people who fish do so because it seems like magic to them, and it is hard to find things in life that seem magical."

—Howell Raines

Are you getting what you want from fishing?

Are you having fun? That's the question for the day. Are you enjoying yourself, or is it beginning to feel a little like . . . work?

Maybe you're fishing too much. It's possible, you know. Maybe it's just not as much fun as it used to be. The old magic isn't there.

Or the reverse. You get really psyched up to catch fish and then when you don't—or at least not as many as you want—disappointment sets in. And frustration.

Maybe you just don't get it anymore. You're sick of the challenge. Sick of trying to outthink creatures who don't think.

There are any number of reasons for fishing burnout. Maybe you have one or two of your own to add to the list.

The thing is, it's not the end of the world. You can be having the greatest sex in the world with the world's most beautiful and stimulating partner. But sooner or later you're going to want to stand up, get out of bed, and take a shower.

You may need a break from fishing. A break from not only doing it, but from thinking about doing it. Consider this a kind of mental shower. Let the shower last as long as you want—days, weeks, whatever. Then when you're feeling like your old vigorous self again, call up that beautiful partner of yours and get busy.

Resolved: I take a break from fishing if I need it.

February 24

"For most people, success in fly fishing is a matter of definition and attitude. I usually fish well enough to leave the water more satisfied than frustrated, and that is good enough for me."

—Susan Williams

Leave the water more satisfied than frustrated. That's a good rule, one of the best.

There are as many ways to get frustrated in fishing as there are fish. Don't let those petty frustrations and irritations get the better of you. Walk away with a feeling of satisfaction.

Satisfaction on a trout stream lies in how you define it. Your approach and attitude. You can catch (and release) a dozen in a day and still be frustrated as hell. You could have been looking for a big fish, or a fish that really challenged you, and not found it.

Find satisfaction in what you are doing. It's there for you, even amid the minor annoyances. Make satisfaction, not frustration, the defining element of your experience.

It's like the old saw about having an argument with your spouse and not going to sleep until it's settled. Treat a trout stream like your lover. Never walk away mad.

It's human nature to focus on the little things we do wrong, rather than all the things we do right. Think about the things you did right on the stream, your successes, rather than your failures. Feeling frustrated all the time is a form of self-criticism, or nagging. It's self-defeating. Quit nagging at yourself. Be satisfied when you walk away from a trout stream.

Resolved: I leave the water with a feeling of satisfaction.

February 25

"That virgin, vital, fine day; today."

—Stephane Mallarmé, poet

It's tempting to look beyond today. There are so many potential variables, so many things that could happen tomorrow or in the future.

Resist the temptation. Plumb today for all it's worth. After all, what could be better than right now?

You're on a river. Sun's out, mountains all around. The water's cold but nothing you can't handle. Your rod is like a magic wand with a Royal Coachman attached to the end. It drops ever so gently on the water, and bingo! A large, handsome brook trout slurps it up like it's chocolate.

There is a tendency when you're not fishing to look ahead to when you will be. But there's also a tendency to take yourself out of the moment when you finally *are* fishing.

When you go on a fishing trip, treat each day as a gift. Stay in the moment as much as possible. Leave yesterday behind, forget tomorrow. This may happen naturally, of course, but sometimes thoughts of the life you left behind just won't go away, like the proverbial 800-pound gorilla in your living room.

When that happens, take a step back and look around you. See where you are, what you are doing, and how lucky you are. A moment like this can snap you back to your senses almost as rapidly as a biting trout.

Resolved: When I go on a fishing trip, I treat each day as a gift.

February 26

*"Some people just don't seem to realize, when they're moaning
about not getting prayers answered, that no is the answer."*

—Nelia Gardner White

Go figure.

You can go out trolling on San Pablo Bay on a Wednesday
evening and hit the jackpot. Salmon do chorus-line kicks
jumping out of the water into your boat. It's like you're a river-
boat gambler and your lucky day has come.

So you go out again Thursday, thinking you'll play this hot
streak for all it's worth. Same conditions, same everything.
And you can't draw scratch. You get on your hands and knees
and beg, you tear your hair out, you beseech the heavens.
Nothing. You're busted. Your lucky streak has run out
overnight.

Every fisherman has felt lucky and come back with nothing. Or gone out with little hope and hit the jackpot. There
doesn't seem to be any rational explanation for why you are
blessed one day and passed over the next.

Well, there isn't. Except fate perhaps. Doesn't matter what
you use. Doesn't matter where you go. If the fishing gods aren't
smiling on you, there isn't a damn thing you can do about it.

Now you can rail against a bad day (and plenty do), or you
can just wipe the slate clean and start over again tomorrow.
Probably better for the blood pressure to take the latter
approach.

Resolved: I wipe a bad day off the slate and start over
tomorrow.

February 27

"There is a pleasure in the pathless woods."

—Lord Byron

Seek out the pathless woods. Jump in your car and go find them.

Leave behind the crowds. Say good-bye to all that. People who complain that the forests and mountains are overcrowded have never strayed from the trail and gone cross-country.

Go cross-country. Seek out the pathless woods and find a secret stream that's all your own.

This will take more work and more daring than blindly following the trampled-down routes of others. You'll need to bring a map and some wilderness sense. Precautions are in order. You want to be careful about private land and all that. But there are still wild, unknown places if you have an urge to find them.

All those great fishing spots they talk about in the guide books, the places everyone knows about? Once upon a time they were unknown. Somebody had to discover them.

The best places to fish are secret. The best places are the ones nobody talks about, the ones that aren't in the guidebooks. The people who know about them want to keep them all to themselves. That's not selfish; that's smart. Those places—the secret places—lie amidst the pathless woods.

Find your secret stream. Find a stream that you want to keep all to yourself. Seek out the pathless woods, and you will.

Resolved: I seek out the pathless woods and discover a secret stream.

February 28

"We do not obtain the most precious gifts by going in search of them but by waiting for them."

—Simone Weil

Take the long view when it comes to fishing.

The long view helps prevent frustration and curb disappointment. The long view makes a person think more in terms of the fishing experience, rather than evaluating it solely on results.

You may not get out to the lake as much as you want. And it frustrates you when you think about it. So you can do one of two things: (A) not think about it, or (B) take the long view. You know you're going to get out there one of these days and when you do, those bass are gonna be thumpin' the sides of the boat. That's the long view. It takes patience, but so does fishing.

Some people say, "Think like a fish." Take the long view on fish and you'll be better off.

Some days you're going to be on top of the world. Other days the world is going to flatten you like a pancake. By taking the long view, you'll know you're going to have good days and bad days, and there's no reason to get too worked up about either.

The short view triumphs only in the short run. Take the long view and like the turtle in his race against the hare, you'll come out ahead. For the turtle knew two skills vital to fishermen: how to wait and how to use time to advantage. Be a turtle when it comes to fishing.

Resolved: I take the long view in fishing.

February 29

February 29 comes around only once every four years, so enjoy it. And what better means of enjoyment than the noble art of angling?

Take your rod and reel and fish. That is a most productive use of leisure time.

Be serious about your fishing, but not too serious. Being too serious can lead to problems. You can take yourself so seriously that you lose your sense of humor. That is truly a disaster.

On the other hand, you do not want to regard fishing too lightly, either. It is not a superficial thing. You do not want to be seen as a dilettante or part-timer. To fully experience the joys and pleasures of fishing, you must fully commit yourself.

(Nonfishing types would probably agree that anybody who fishes should indeed be committed, but that's another story.)

Treat this day like a free day. It's a gift of sorts. The next February 29 you see will be in four years. Use this day in a most constructive and productive manner.

Fish.

Resolved: Happy Leap Year! I'm going fishing.

March 1

It's not like it's the wilderness or anything. You knew that to begin with. It's just the state park, not far from the freeway. You pay two bucks to park, and pull up under some trees. It's late afternoon and hot and nobody's around.

The stripers are running. You hear it's good. You've done this plenty of times before—fished here maybe fifty times—but still, you're excited. No matter how long you've been doing it, it's impossible to quell—that surge of feeling, every time you rig up.

You grab your rods—keeping your options open, you bring two—and you head off down a dirt trail that hugs the shoreline and reaches into a wetlands area where you've seen snowy egrets and blue herons and mallards. A quail bolts from the bushes, squealing like a baby, when you approach.

Then you come to the place where you want to fish and you see it. It's plastic and cardboard. A discarded package of surf leaders, twenty-five-pound test. Hand tied in China for distribution here. Well, it's been distributed all right.

There's no illusion. Of course, other fishermen have been there and fished there. And maybe someone dropped it by mistake. Still, you wish it wasn't there. You want to fish, you don't want to deal with somebody else's trash. You pick it up and stuff it in your back pocket, muttering a silent curse.

Resolved: I check over a spot for trash before I leave.

March 2

"Too much of a good thing can be wonderful."

—Mae West

Catch and release a trout. Have a piece of berry pie.

Catch and release two trout. Have pie and ice cream.

Never see a trout all day, let alone release one. Treat yourself to a New York steak, baked potato slathered with butter and sour cream, Scotch over, and *then* pie and ice cream. You deserve it, suffering through a hard day like that.

When you catch fish, treat yourself. When you don't catch fish, treat yourself. Whatever you want to do, however you like to do it, just treat yourself. Steak dinner, a big drunk, dancing and howling at the Kit-Kat Ranch, or all of the above.

Sometimes fishing can be pure agony, an act of self-torture. Treat yourself to something good when that happens.

Sometimes fishing can be pure bliss, heaven on earth. All the more reason to live it up afterward and treat yourself.

Then there are those middle-of-the-road days, a little good, a little not so good. Treat yourself on those days, too.

A fishing trip should be an occasion for all sorts of pleasures, not just those of the fishing kind. Don't be stingy. Pile pleasure on top of pleasure. Enjoy yourself, have fun, let go. You'll have plenty of time to rest up when you go back to work.

Resolved: I catch a trout and eat a piece of pie.

March 3

"The ark was built by amateurs, and the Titanic by the experts. Don't wait for the experts."

—Murray Cohen

Not sure what to do? What to use? How to use it? Here's a suggestion: make the simple choice.

The simple choice is always the best choice until proved otherwise. But it almost never is.

The simple choice is the one staring you right in your face, although you don't realize it. When you finally realize it, you see how simple the answer was all the time.

The simple choice is sometimes the most obvious, although not always. The simple choice is never the stupid choice. On the contrary, it is the most sublime, the most elegant, the wisest.

You can always go on to more complicated choices if the simple solution doesn't work. That's another of its virtues. It acts as a good starting point.

An expert will hardly ever make the simple choice first. The expert will say, "That's too simple," and choose a more complicated option. He will almost invariably be wrong. After going down all the other more complicated paths, even the expert may come to realize that the right path was the simplest one. And he knew the answer from the very beginning.

It takes great wisdom to reject the trappings of wisdom and make the simple choice. It takes great experience to do the same. The wisest, most experienced fishermen will value simplicity above all and make simple choices when they're on a boat or in the stream.

Resolved: I make the simple choice on a stream or boat.

March 4

"Almost nothing makes me happier than to leave on a fishing trip."

—Bill Barich

Make yourself happy. Leave on a fishing trip.

Imagine it. You're all packed. Your rods and reels are in the back of the car with the rest of your tackle.

You've packed the tapes, made your music choices for the drive up. Blues Traveler, Grateful Dead, Stevie Ray Vaughan, old Allman Brothers. Because where you're going, the radio blitzes out and you can't get anything. So you need some tunes to keep you company.

You pull out of the driveway, wave good-bye to responsibility, and hit the road.

One of the best things about a fishing trip is driving there. On the way back you're tired and burned out and maybe not all that happy about leaving. But on the way up you're charged about the thought of fishing, and you burn off some of that energy behind the wheel.

You slip Vaughan's "Love Struck Baby" into the tape deck and fly. Day has turned to night, and a full moon looms above the flat, hot farmland. The moon is like the music; it keeps you company when you climb into the mountains and finally reach the exit that takes you down to the dirt road that goes to the river. It's about two in the morning when you pull in, but you're wired from the drive and just happy to be there. You celebrate with shots of Cuervo all around, then fall into your bag, dreaming dreams of what the morning will bring.

Resolved: I make myself happy. I go on a fishing trip.

March 5

"However, sir," said the Captain, "that's no reason not to have a drink."

—Max Shulman

You've just fought a titanic life-or-death struggle with a marlin that turns out to be a wad of kelp. However, that's no reason not to have a drink.

A large swell washes you out of your fishing boat and it's an hour of bobbing in the open sea like a cork before anyone else in the party notices you're gone. However, that's no reason not to have a drink.

You take your wife fishing. She catches a 175-pound sturgeon on thirty-pound test, breaking a record, while you come up empty. However, that's no reason not to have a drink.

You have to cut your fishing trip short because you hook your nose while making a cast, and it requires five stitches to sew up. However, that's no reason not to have a drink.

You slip while fording a river and get swept downstream. Another fisherman who is unaware of your troubles hooks you and reels you in after a terrific battle. Furious that you are a human being and not the biggest fish of his life, he throws you back in the river. However, that's no reason not to have a drink.

You find the greatest fishing spot of your life. It's paradise. Trout in abundance, and you're all alone. You make your first cast. Then the bus pulls up and forty-five conventioneers from Fresno spill out. However, that's no reason not to have a drink.

Resolved: I have a drink.

March 6

"I hooked myself instead of fish; tangled my line in every tree; lost my bait; broke my rod; until I gave up the attempt in despair; and passed the day under the trees, reading old Izaak."

—Washington Irving

Some days will be like that.

You will hook yourself instead of fish. You will tangle your line in every shrub and tree. You will lose your bait and break your rod, perhaps voluntarily, over your own knee. And finally, you may even give up the attempt, acknowledging the truth of the axiom that every fishing rod has a line on one end and a fool on the other.

Did you remember to pack a book? A book can be a saviour at times like that, as valuable a piece of fishing gear as a Royal Coachman or waders. A book cannot help you untangle your line, but it can provide solace and philosophy when you do. It can turn a lost day into a memorable and sweetly pleasurable one. You say to yourself, "Well, that's enough of *that*," and you retire to a shady spot under the aspen and cottonwood trees, where the river passes gently by, and you lose yourself in Thomas McGuane or Le Anne Schreiber or Nick Lyons or whoever you like. Then after a while maybe you close your eyes and nap.

A book and a nap, either taken singly or in combination, will make you feel like a new man. You may even feel like trying your luck once more, saying farewell to despair, and casting your fly like a message of hope onto the ripples of the stream.

Resolved: I take a book with me.

March 7

"It was a chance to enjoy a beautiful river and all that lives in and with it. To be part of the current during the day and to sleep in its song by night."

—Sally Stoner

One of the great things about going fishing is that it gives you a chance to sleep by a river.

Is there such a thing as an ugly river? There have been rivers made ugly by man. But all rivers in their native, uncorrupted state are beautiful.

So many people live in apartments or houses where all they hear at night are the sounds of traffic and street life.

What a nice change it is to camp by a river. To be part of the current during the day and to sleep in its song by night.

River music is the best kind of background music. It's always there. It's like the bass line in a jazz combo, laying down a low, steady groove as you boil water for coffee in the morning, take a nap in the afternoon, or collect wood for the fire at night.

But step up to its banks, and it surges instantly forward. You hear a different side of it. The river as scat singer. Tripping up and down the scale, free and full of energy and power and musicality. It knocks your shoes off, this river song, and all you want to do is sit down and listen.

It's great to sleep by a river. You've spent the day on it or around it and now it eases you into the night. The endlessly flowing river seems to provide a rhythm that your day lacks in the city. You let the fire burn down and crawl into your bag. You're in an open spot with a clear view of the stars. Your eyelids close, and the river beats on.

Resolved: I go fishing and sleep by a beautiful river.

March 8

Take the right and wrong out of fishing. Think in terms of more optimum and less optimum.

Beginning fishermen especially are prone to thinking that they're doing something wrong. They get down on themselves and think they'll never get it right.

Banish right and wrong concepts from your fishing lexicon. Then substitute more optimum and less optimum.

More optimum means that you've found a better way to do it. Less optimum is maybe not as good, but that still does not make it wrong.

The only wrong in fishing is to give up and quit because you've become discouraged and frustrated and buried yourself in criticism.

Right-wrong thinking can rob fishing of much of its joy. More optimum–less optimum is a more forgiving, less punitive approach. It suggests there is more than one road to happiness. Do you enjoy fishing? Are you getting the results you seek? Those are the essential questions. If you find a way that works for you, and if you're happy with what you're getting from it, stick with it.

Resolved: I think in terms of more optimum and less optimum.

March 9

"The old man used to say that the best part of hunting and fishing was the thinking about going and the talking about it after you got back."

—Robert Ruark

When you need a haircut, you go to a barber. When your car breaks down, you go to a mechanic. When your dog needs a shot, you go to the vet.

And when you need fishing gear, go to a fishing store.

There's nothing wrong with going to a sporting goods store to get your gear. Lots of people wade in past the tennis rackets, basketballs, running shoes, skis, barbells, mitts, footballs, and basketball hoops to find what they're looking for. But it's not the same as going to a place that specializes in fishing and only fishing.

You can loiter in a tackle shop or fishing shop. Nobody is going to kick you out or look at you funny. Chances are they will engage you in a conversation about blue ribbon trout or some such thing.

There may be four or five guys loitering in the shop with you, all trading stories about fishing, some of which may even be true. They will tell jokes. They will gossip about who caught what and where, and what's happening. They'll talk about where they've been and where they're going next. Some of it may even be useful.

That's the best thing about a fishing or tackle shop. What they really have to offer is information and solidarity, and it's free.

Resolved: I stop by my local tackle shop and check out what's going on.

March 10

*"These men have had nine months of winter to catch up on
their sleep. The steelhead will start running soon, maybe
tonight, and there is no question about where they should be."*

—Pam Houston

There is no question where you should be, either. You've had
plenty of time to rest, all winter. The steelhead are running.
Go out and catch them.

It's easy to become complacent and lazy as a fisherman. It's
easy to think, "I've done that," and pass on opportunities that
come your way. But you're a fool if you do that consistently.

Get off the fence. Quit waffling. When you have a chance
to go fishing, take it. No matter how inconvenient it seems.

You may think, "Oh, there'll be another time." Oh really?
Can you say that for sure? To borrow from an old song, we—
and more exactly, the steelhead—may never pass this way
again.

Suppose you are right. Suppose you do get a second chance.
But you risk missing this run, this moment, which will be
unique and impossible to duplicate. And who knows? Maybe
the best ever.

Remember that old Latin phrase, *carpe diem*. Break that
phrase down. The first four letters spell "carp," which is a fish.
So another way of interpreting that phrase is: seize the carp.

Or as in this case, seize the steelhead. Seize the trout.
Seize the marlin. Seize the striped bass. Seize the sturgeon.
Seize the pike. Seize the catfish. There is no better day than
today, no better moment than now, no better opportunity
than this to catch fish.

Resolved: When I have a chance to go fishing, I take it.

March 11

"Every man has a fish in his life that haunts him."

—Negley Farson

It's one of the axioms of fishing: the one that got away. Every fisherman likes to tell the story of a big fish—it's always a big fish—that just wriggled out of his grasp.

Here's a novel thought: let it go.

Why hang onto a thought that tortures or haunts you, if indeed it does? Why let it attach itself to you like some kind of deer tick? Why let it bore into your skin and cause problems?

Grab its little black body and pluck it out. It serves no useful purpose. Let it go.

Sometimes it's fun to talk about the one that got away. It's like meeting a celebrity or a famous statesman. You can entertain others with how close you came to greatness.

But if it was a bad experience, one that truly still bothers you, forget it. It's a form of reliving your failures, and what's the point of that? You've already gone over the event again and again in your mind. You've learned everything you can from it and now you've gone way beyond education into self-recrimination, which will never help you catch fish.

It doesn't even have to be a big fish. If you lose *any* fish when you're out on the stream, forget about it. Move ahead.

Let go of your failures, if you insist on calling them that. Look ahead to what's coming, rather than back at what has passed. Clear your mind of the one that got away and focus on the big ones to come.

Resolved: I let go of the one that got away.

March 12

"The angler who is determined to catch the biggest fish or the most of them, by his own determination becomes a competitor and is self-poisoned."

—John Atherton

To borrow from the golfer Tommy Bolt, fishing is a sport where guts, stick-to-itiveness, and blind devotion will get you nothing but an ulcer. This is particularly true if you see fishing as a competition to catch the biggest fish or the most fish or whatever.

You wouldn't be human if it didn't hurt a little bit when your buddy brings in a bigger fish than you, or if he nets them left and right while you can't draw scratch.

Everybody wants to haul in a record-size catch or stand on the bank and lure fish like some kind of fish magnet. It's natural to feel that way.

But people get into trouble when everything becomes merely a matter of size and quantity. That's pure ego talking. There's no worse fate than to be stuck in a boat with a fisherman like that. You want to drop him over the side and leave him.

Fishing is simply not a competitive sport. That's not to say you can't compete in a bass or fly-fishing tournament and have a helluva time. But there has to be something else to it or you're probably not going to stay interested for long.

Try this: the next time your buddy hauls in a bigger fish than you, suck it up and give him a pat on the back for a job well done. On second thought, that might be pushing it a bit too far.

Resolved: I throw all ego-mad fishermen over the side of the boat.

March 13

"Weather is so changeable that even television weathermen are seldom right. I've seen too many fishing trips ruined by completely unreliable weather reports."

—David Richey

Here's one weather tip that will never prove wrong: expect changing conditions.

If it is calm, expect wind. If it is windy, know that it will be calm again in the morning, or the day after.

If the river is low, expect it to rise. If the river is rising, always know that it will come down again. When it comes down, be certain it will rise. Never be surprised by such changes.

Whatever the conditions, expect them to change. Nothing is static about a trout stream, or life. Conditions are always changing. Never expect otherwise.

The fisherman who is surprised by changing conditions is an unprepared fisherman. Be prepared for flux. Change is the one constant in nature. Never be surprised by it.

If the sky is clear, expect clouds by late afternoon. If clouds appear, consider the possibility of rain. If the skies have opened up like in the time of Noah, know that at some point the rain will stop. The one given with weather is there are no givens, except change.

Listen to the weathercasters if you dare. Read the weather report in the paper if you must. But you already know what conditions are going to be like when you get there: changing. Expect this, and you'll be ready when the inevitable occurs.

Resolved: I expect changing conditions when I fish.

March 14

"If fishing interferes with your business, give up your business."

—Saying

Suppose you took the morning off today and went fishing. What about it?

What's it like outside? Sunny, with a light breeze. Not a cloud in the sky. Perfect.

It's probably not possible to simply take the morning off and go fishing. Or is it? It's amazing what a person can accomplish when he has a mind for it.

Think of it this way: it's only one morning out of the week. You'll be able to catch up. You'll have four other mornings this week to do your work—six, if you count the weekend. That's plenty.

That's not even counting the afternoons. You've got the entire afternoon today to catch up on what you miss this morning, if anything. And you can work late if you can't get it all done in the afternoon.

Think of what you'll miss if you don't go fishing. That's what you should focus on. Work schmork. That pile of papers on your desk will still be there when you get back.

Preparation isn't everything in fishing, no matter what they say. Sometimes it's nice to throw preparation to the wind. Damn the consequences and act on the spur of the moment, like running off to Vegas to get married. Today, stick a ladder out your window, climb down, hop into your convertible, and elope with your fishing rod.

Resolved: I take the morning off and go fishing.

March 15

"Knowing a river intimately is a very large part of the joy of fly fishing."

—Roderick Haig-Brown

Get to know a river intimately. Get on speaking terms with it.

Because rivers are usually on a smaller scale than the sea or even a lake, it's possible to get to know them with a high degree of intimacy, as you would a friend or a lover. You can know them in all their moods: "their changes through the seasons," as Haig-Brown writes, "the shifts and quirks of current, the sharp runs, the slow glides, the eddies and bars and crossing places, the very rocks of the bottom."

Haig-Brown was one of the greatest of all fishing writers. The river he came to know best was the Campbell in British Columbia. He knew that in January the steelhead ran. In February, the cutthroats spawned, and in the two following months, so did the winter steelhead. By May he found the steelhead in Island Pools. In August he went to Canyon Pool in search of the big cutthroats. Then in October came the cohos. By December the cycle started over again with the steelhead. Ever the fisherman, Haig-Brown could find mayfly and stone-fly nymphs and knew which rocks the midges preferred.

Lord knows, you don't need to have the knowledge of a Haig-Brown to catch fish. But as he would tell you, an intimate knowledge of a river does enhance the all-around pleasure of fishing.

Resolved: I get on speaking terms with a river.

March 16

"As far as equipment goes, we are living in the Golden Age of Fly Fishing."

—Howell Raines

As far as equipment goes, buy the best you can afford. When you're just starting out, getting really good stuff is a waste. You can't yet use it to its fullest, so you're better off with a starter set that's more in keeping with your abilities and experience. Then as you get better, you can trade up.

By the same token, you want to avoid the really cheap rods and tackle. You're almost better off tying a string to a stick. At least then you have no illusions. Really cheap stuff is a headache.

For people who've been at it a while, there is a difference between great stuff and pretty good stuff. But it's expensive. It's up to you to decide whether the money is worth the marginal improvement in quality.

So many of our buying decisions are based not on economics, but on other intangible factors. When you cheap out and buy an inferior piece of equipment, what you are really saying to yourself is: "I don't deserve the best."

Forget that noise. You deserve it. You deserve the very best gear you can afford. You may even think, "What the hell," and pop for a really expensive rod, one you've always wanted but held back on for whatever reason. Treat yourself right. Treat your fishing with respect. Those are the keys to keep foremost in your mind when buying new gear.

Resolved: I buy the best gear I can afford.

March 17

"Sink into the day. Don't force it."

—Nick Lyons, on the secret of fishing

When you go fishing, sink into the day. Don't force it. Make an effortless effort. This applies in so many other areas as well.

Want to catch fish? Make an effortless effort.

Be a good or even a great fisherman? Make an effortless effort.

Learn how to fish? Make an effortless effort.

Learn about the rivers and different kinds of fish and lakes and clouds and insects and oceans and tides and birds? Make an effortless effort.

Fishing is paradoxical. It is not a pastime that gives itself over to effort and will. It is intuitive in nature. You cannot will yourself to catch fish or enjoy the process of it. You have to let fishing come to you.

But fishing will only come to you after you come to it. You have to make an effort, but it is an effort without striving or trying too hard. That is, an effortless effort.

And how, pray tell, does one do that? Well, there are no set rules. A good place to start is that old Bobby McFerrin song, "Don't worry. Be happy." Don't worry, be happy, no matter what happens, and you will be on the path to effortlessly rewarding fishing.

Resolved: I let my worries drift away when I fish.

March 18

"Each boat contains a minimum of nine guys and 14 cases of beer. The bottom of the lake is composed of a thick incrustation of old beer cans."

—Jean Shepherd, on a fishing trip

It's not going to be easy, but you're the man to do it.

First you call Max. He stays in touch with everybody. Every fishing party needs a guy like Max. He's the one with the boat.

Then you call Glaze. Glaze lives up at the lake and knows the scene firsthand. Glaze is a man you can count on, as long as there are no women around to distract him.

Wedge has to come, of course. Wedge is a staple at all these gatherings. He remembers everything you guys ever did together, way back to when you started doing things together.

Max calls Steve. Steve is always game for anything. He's in a basketball league at the Y, plays tennis, golfs, coaches soccer, takes his family on camping trips. You gotta have Steve.

Bob is more problematic. Bob is a real cool guy. He makes independent movies and rubs elbows with all those Hollywood big shots. But he lives in Malibu and that's a long way from the lake. He needs some persuading.

You call Bob. Max calls Bob. Wedge calls Bob. Steve calls Bob. Before Glaze can get to him, Bob gives in. He's coming, too.

So you got 'em all. Six great guys, a fishing boat, rods and tackle for everyone, and 112 cases of beer. Now what could be more fun than that?

Resolved: I organize a fishing trip with my buddies.

March 19

"I wanted to be like this—to be interested in and knowledgeable about one thing. I wanted to learn how to find fish, how to tell a good stream from a bad one, how not to frighten a trout in the water, what fly to use."

—Gretchen Legler

Want to become knowledgeable about fishing? Want to know this one thing really well? Then read, study, and learn about it. Read, study, and learn about it all the time.

The best fishermen are the most knowledgeable ones. Not necessarily in terms of book learning, but in terms of what they know. Water smarts, you could call it. They read, study, and learn about it constantly, every way they can.

They learn how to find fish, how to tell good streams from bad, how not to frighten trout in the water. And they learn all the time. Fishing is a lifetime education process.

You can learn about fishing in books and magazines. That's one way.

You can talk to other fishermen and study what they do and how they do it. That's another way.

And you can go out and do it. You can go out to a river or lake or the creek behind your house and learn while you're doing it. That's the best way.

There are lots of ways to learn about fishing, and the learning doesn't stop just because you've been fishing thirty or forty years. When the learning stops, you're through as a catcher of fish. Start today. Make fishing a continuing education process. Read, study, and learn about it.

Resolved: I make fishing a continuing education process.

March 20

"It is remarkable what a good judge of water can do."
—Alfred Miller

Some fishermen get so hopped up to fish a new piece of water that it's almost funny to watch. They pull up in their cars, grab their rods and tackles from the back, and rush down to the water with barely a thought about the best place to go or where the fish most likely reside.

Alfred Miller used to fish with a New York fisherman named Gene Russell, who had a different approach. Russell, explains Miller, "doesn't even set up a rod when he gets out of his car to fish a new piece of water. He just saunters along the bank for half a mile or so, smoking a pipe and looking; then he saunters back and either drives away or gets out his rod and goes to one, two, or maybe three places that he has mentally marked down during his stroll."

Now there's a thought: don't actually fish in the place where you stop. Mosey on down the road until you find a better spot.

Then when you find it, take your time. Check out one or two or three or four places before you rig up. Be a model of judicious restraint. Smoke a pipe as you saunter along the bank, mentally marking down prime spots and considering the possibilities.

Okay, so you don't smoke a pipe. But you get the point. A hasty attitude is hardly ever a good thing in fishing, and especially not when you're investigating a new piece of water.

Resolved: I take my time when I check out a new piece of water.

March 2l

"I can put no faith in humans in the place they are; watercress at evening is my lot."

—Medieval poem

Most fishermen are pretty good Joes. Quick to share a beer and a laugh. Still, there's always some rotten fish at the bottom of the barrel. Some people you meet in fishing are real jerks. Petty, narrow-minded, suspicious of outsiders.

Who needs that stuff? Life's too short. Avoid negativity and negative people in fishing.

Some old fishermen are just bitter. They've been fishing since before Noah. Nothing you ever do is going to impress them because they've seen it all a thousand times before.

Other, more competitive types can't handle it if you're catching fish and they're not. They'll find some reason to put you down or try to lower you to their level.

Others see themselves as the second coming of Lee Wulff and can't stand anybody who doesn't conform to their elitist way of doing things.

You may know people like that. Hell, you may even fish with them. If so, why?

Who you fish with can mean a lot. Surround yourself with positive people. And if you can't find anybody like that, go out alone amid the watercress at evening. That's always a positive experience.

Resolved: I avoid negativity and negative people in fishing.

March 22

"Somewhere in the mind of every angler there is a mythical fish."

—John Gierach

What is a mythical fish? The fish the old man caught in Hemingway's *Old Man and the Sea*, that's a mythical fish.

For trout fishermen, as John Gierach explains, it might be an Atlantic salmon reeled in on a fly rod. For those who love the challenge of salt water it might be a bonefish or tarpon. Bass fishermen seem to crave bigger and bigger bass. Northern lake anglers dream about the musky.

The pursuit of a mythical fish is fishing's version of the Holy Grail. That fish is out there, somewhere, just beyond the line.

Gierach writes, "Whatever the mythical fish is, it has to get to you in a certain, indefinable way, and it's probably not something you're going to catch every day. Often it's something you may, for one reason or another, *never* catch. Maybe it's even better that way."

Maybe you'll never catch it. Then again, maybe you will. It's nice to think about though, isn't it?

You.

Your mythical fish.

Click! Someone snapping the picture of the two of you together.

That's all. Nothing more than that today. Just a mental picture of you grabbing hold of a dream and claiming it for your own. If that doesn't get you revved up for a day of fishing, nothing will.

Resolved: I dream a dream of a mythical fish.

March 23

"Men are not free when they are doing just what they like. The moment you can do just what you like, there is nothing you care about doing. Men are only free when they are doing what the deepest self likes."

—D. H. Lawrence

Do what your deepest self likes. Fish.

Nourish your deepest self. Feed it and nurture it. Fish.

Why is fishing so important? Because it touches the deepest part of our being, the deepest part of who we are or want to be. Neglect that, and you are neglecting something very vital.

Now some fishermen raise their eyebrows at talk like this. (Of course, some fishermen raise their eyebrows at *anything*.) Fishing is just fishing and that's all there is to it.

Nobody really believes that, though. If fishing is just fishing, why does it give us so much lasting pleasure? Why does it get inside us and stay with us? There's nothing else like fishing.

Stand on a rock on the edge of the Carquinez Strait and look across. It's like a lake or a wide river. Brown hills rise up on the other side. The water is bluish-gray and opaque, an image of the unconscious. Hidden below the surface is another world, foreign to us, a dreamlike world of mystery and intrigue and the most exotic creatures imaginable.

How do we tap into it? The same way we tap into the deepest part of ourselves. We rig up and cast in a line.

Resolved: I do what my deepest self likes. I fish.

March 24

"My pappy once told me that the best time to go fishing was whenever you can get away."

—David Richey

The other day you snuck off in the morning and went fishing. How'd it go?

All right. Maybe *snuck* is not the appropriate verb. Lacks dignity.

Let's put it this way: you rearranged your schedule to allow yourself adequate time to pursue the ancient art of angling from the hours of 9 A.M. to 1 P.M., give or take a half hour or so.

Aw hell, maybe you just called in sick complaining of a nonexistent killer migraine. Anyway, you took the morning off and fished.

Now here's today's plan: take the afternoon off and do the same.

Hold it, hold it. Quit yer bellyachin'. It worked all right the first time, didn't it? Felt pretty good, didn't it? Well, this time just switch 'em up. Instead of rearranging your schedule—or whatever—in the morning, rearrange it for this afternoon.

What's that? You've got an important meeting you just can't get out of? C'mon, be creative. Your Aunt Zelda in Wichita just keeled over at the premature age of sixty-one. Funerals are always excellent excuses for hasty departures from work.

The point is: go! Work can always wait. And the great thing about afternoon fishing is how easily it slides into evening and night fishing.

Resolved: I take the afternoon off and go fishing.

March 25

*"I've always thought of my life as a river. Sometimes I feel a
destiny in its course, unpredictably predictable in its twists and
turns."*

—Ailm Travler

Well, you tried. That's the important thing. You took yesterday's advice to heart and took the afternoon off to fish.

You even used the suggested excuse—that your Aunt Zelda
in Wichita had unexpectedly passed. Then you bailed out of
work and burned rubber for the Stanislaus. You were on the
river hunting for trout with the sun still hanging high in the
sky like some giant yellow smiley-face.

Then you got to thinking, "Wichita's a long way. A person
needs time to do a funeral right in Wichita." So you called in
to tell work that you'd be gone for at least another day or two.

Unfortunately, by that time your brother had already called
in looking for you and revealed that (A) there was no Aunt
Zelda to speak of in the family, and (B) even if there was
someone to speak of by that name, she would've been the least
likely candidate to drop off because all your family was tra-
ditionally long lived, especially the women. So they fired you
on the spot.

That's depressing, naturally. Sure you needed the job
because you're flat broke and three months behind on the rent.
But look at it this way: you're fishing. It can't be that bad,
right? You'll have plenty of time to sign up for unemployment,
and after you do that, you can do more fishing.

Life takes funny twists and turns sometimes. But what
better place to ride them out than beside a trout stream?

Resolved: I think about my troubles some other day. Today,
I fish.

March 26

"After several days of casting I have become comfortable, even intimate with my rod, but I still discover something new about it every day."

—Le Anne Schreiber

Discover something new about your rod every time you fish. Here are two things Le Anne Schreiber discovered:

One day, completely by accident, she found that she was casting farther than ever. She realized that the added distance came from the way she snapped her wrist. "Before the cast," she writes, "I had been whipping my arm slower or faster, in a longer or shorter arc, to control the distance, but now I see it is in the wrist, not the arm and shoulder, that distance is determined."

Then she discovered something else about her rod. She had had a problem with slack that snarled her line when she reeled it in. She solved this problem by pulling the rod backward at the end of the cast. "Discovering this, I again remembered that I had known it; the motion was one I'd seen my father make hundreds of times, but I never realized it had a purpose," she says.

In both cases, she already possessed the knowledge to do something she had never done before. It was, as she says, "familar but forgotten knowledge, something I had read or, more likely, been told by my father in childhood." This is probably true for a lot of discoveries that people make while fishing. The knowledge is there, buried under the years; it's a matter of uncovering it. Once they do, it's like turning on a light.

Resolved: I discover something new about my rod.

March 27

"There is no use in your walking five miles to fish when you can depend on being just as unsuccessful at home."

—Mark Twain

Alaska.

    Idaho.

    New Zealand.

    Newfoundland.

    Great places, all. But you don't have to go to any of them to catch (or in Twain's case, not catch) fish. You can find great fishing close to home, wherever home happens to be.

    True, your favorite place may not have the lure of Costa Rica or the Bahamas. The tourist bureaus may not make fancy brochures about it. They may not advertise it in the back of the fishing magazines or devote five-page, full-color spreads to it.

    It may just be, when all is said and done, the place you like to fish. No more, no less.

    Fact is, you can get more out of fishing a place you know than a place that's foreign to you. You know the places to hit. There's less wasted motion. You know what to use, what usually works. And you never really know a place fully, anyhow. That's the beauty of fishing. There's always something to discover, something new, even in a place you've been a hundred times before.

    New and exotic locales have their appeal in fishing. But nothing can ever take the place of those old, familiar haunts.

Resolved: I go back to my favorite spot and fish the hell out of it.

March 28

*"But what if I fail of my purpose here? To dry one's eyes and
laugh at a fall, and, baffled, get up and begin again."*

—Robert Browning

Fishing is like playing the slots in Atlantic City. You've got to be willing to sit there. Some days, you've got to sit there a very long time. Some days, you sit so long your butt hurts.

But you can't really just *sit* there; you've got to work it. You've got to work it in the way you know how. Put your money in, pull the crank down. Put your money in, pull the crank down. Some people find it repetitious or boring. Not you. For you it's relaxing. There's a nice, easy rhythm to it once you do it for a while.

Playing the slots, you've got to be willing to put in your time. There is no other way. You've got to outlast 'em. You must know in your heart that sooner or later they're going to call your number. Sooner or later three of a kind will line up, bells will ring, and you'll be rolling in it.

It's the same with fishing. Those one-arm bandits under the water will break your heart. There are no instant results for fishermen, no guaranteed paydays. They have a name in Atlantic City for someone who expects to hit the jackpot every time out: sucker.

So that's today's message. Nothing more to it than that. This is a day of rededicating yourself to what slot players know.

Put your money in, pull the crank down. Try, try again. Put in your time. Outlast 'em if you have to. Have patience and faith. Sooner or later, if you do the work, bells will ring.

Resolved: I never give up on fishing.

March 29

"The best fisherman is the one who can cast accurately and judge the water carefully rather than cast all over the water without serious intent."

—Ray Ovington

Be of serious intent when you cast. Be purposeful. Cast with a specific goal in mind and let your actions work to achieve this goal. Here are more angling tips from Ray Ovington:

- Work the area near you first. Farther does not necessarily equate with better. It is more difficult to control the lure when you cast over a wide area.
- As with all things in fishing, take your time. "Do not cast too fast over a given spot," says Ovington. "Beating it to a pulp will tend to scare the fish." Let an area rest if you've been working it a while.
- Trout are like anybody else. They get tired of seeing the same thing over and over. Change your lure every few casts. Give them something new to look at. Maybe they'll like that one better.
- Slow the lure down. Put yourself in the place of the fish. If you were swimming around looking for something to eat in a cold, fast-moving river, would you take a fast-moving or slow-moving lure? You'd grab the slower one because it's an easier target.

These are classic spinning gear tips. But Ovington's principal message applies to every type of fisherman. Anybody can go out there and flail around. Be of serious intent. Cast with a goal in mind and let your actions work to achieve that goal.

Resolved: I cast with a purpose in mind.

March 30

"The curious thing about fishing is you never want to go home. If you catch anything, you can't stop. If you don't catch anything, you hate to leave in case something might bite."

—Gladys Taber

Don't go home. Make one more cast.

It's late. The light is fading. You've missed dinner. But you're not quite ready to quit just yet.

Don't quit. Make one more cast.

You've been fishing this one area for hours. Nothing's working. You have a sense, though, that something might happen if you hang in there a little while longer.

Follow that hunch. Follow that sixth sense. Make one more cast.

You will never know unless you make one more cast. This could be the one. This could be the strike you've been waiting for. Make one more cast and find out.

Lunch can wait. A beer can wait. Everything can wait. Make one more cast. There's always time for one more cast.

Your family is yelling at you from the car. They're ready to go. You nod and wave to them from alongside the stream and say, "One more cast." They yell back that you've been saying that for an hour and a half and you think to yourself, "yeah, that's right," and you make one more cast.

Let one more cast lead to one more cast lead to one more cast.

Resolved: I make one more cast.

March 31

"I can look back now and say I was born to fly cast. While it wasn't easy, I was drawn to it."

—Joan Salvato Wulff

Joan Salvato Wulff is the Babe Zaharias of fishing, one of the greatest fishermen of all time. That this fisherman is a woman makes no difference at all, although it did to her dad at one time.

Her father was named Jimmy Salvato. He owned a fishing and hunting shop in Patterson, New Jersey, in the late 1930s and belonged to the Patterson Casting Club. Like every proud papa, he wanted his son to learn to fish, so he took Jimmy Jr. with him to Oldham Pond and they practiced together. But he never took his daughter Joan, who was ten.

Joan didn't like this one bit. "I wanted to fly cast," she remembers. So she took her father's fly rod, went down to the casting club dock, and gave it a try on her own. But the rod separated into sections, and the tip flew into the pond water. Young Joan was aghast. She ran home in tears, afraid of what her father would do.

Fortunately, she rescued the rod with the help of a neighbor's rake before Jimmy Sr. came home for dinner. He did finally get the news (thanks to Joan's mom). The next Sunday, he asked his daughter to join him and her brother at the casting club. Thus began one of the most storied careers in all of fishing.

Memo to all dads with daughters: bring 'em along. Don't make Jimmy Salvato's mistake. It may surprise you how much they want to learn and be like dad, too.

Resolved: I bring my daughters fishing with me.

April 1

"The spirit that makes the great angler is compounded of terrifically intense concentration and a ferocious predatory urge to conquer and capture."

—Alfred Miller

Be a ferocious hunter. Fish with a predatory urge. Stalk your prey with the instincts of a killer.

Be like the angler who needed to reach a certain spot to fish in high water. He clenched his rod in his teeth and set out across a cliff that might have daunted experienced rock climbers. He used footholds and handholds, risking broken bones or drowning if he fell, and made his way across the wall to the place he saw.

Then he began to cast.

Before you catch fish you have to find them. Be like the angler who climbed down a cliff, swung across on a rope tied to a branch, and then friction-walked down a rock wall to a tree. The tree was only the beginning. From there he ventured down into a gorge to find a secret stream unsullied by other fishermen.

Don't kill yourself when you're fishing. That is not advised. But you may have to extend yourself. Rely on the experience you have and make calculated (not harebrained) risks. For that is what you are doing: hunting fish, though you may indeed put them back. But in order to put them back you have to catch them first, and you will not do that with the attitude of a Victorian lady asking her social circle to tea.

Concentrate on what you are about. Be ferocious in your pursuit. Stalk your prey with the instincts of a killer.

Resolved: I stalk my prey with the instincts of a killer.

April 2

"The fact is, you will always be told that it was better somewhere else."

—Carlo Uva

The fact is, it *is* always better in Montana.

Ever been? No? Well then, maybe it's time to go.

Try the Yellowstone River for starters. It's in Yellowstone National Park and offers lots of nice, easy-going cutthroat. There are some back-country trout streams in the park that are worth checking out: Lamar River, Trout Lake, Slough Creek, and Grebe Lake, to name but a few. The Grebe is home to the grayling, which is a hard fish to find elsewhere.

Montana is a lot like the West used to be: big sky, wild rivers, plenty of open spaces. Another place to go is Madison River with its rainbow trout that will fight you like a welterweight boxer. A couple of suggestions for the Madison are around Cliff and Wade Lakes and around Varney Bridge. The Gallatin River is nearby and worth a look-see also.

One more possibility is the Bighorn River below Yellowtail Dam. The Bighorn area is famous as the place where General Custer used to hang out, though he wasn't much of a fisherman and evidently not much of a general, either.

But don't trust these suggestions. Any place that you read about in a book is a place that other people know about, too. So you're better off getting a guide, or talking to the locals and going off and finding your own. And that's what's truly grand about fishing in Montana: you can go off and find your own.

Resolved: I go to Montana and spend some quality time fishing.

April 3

"All the past can help you."

—Robert Henri

Use what you have. Rely on your past to guide the present.

You've been fishing for a while. You've faced a lot of different situations. While no two situations are exactly alike in fishing, you have no doubt seen most situations before. Think back on a previous outing, and apply what you learned to your current situation.

Take it one step further: visualize a positive result based on the positive results you achieved in the past.

On the previous outings, how did you do? Did you obtain the results you wanted, i.e., catch fish? Use that knowledge—that visualization—in your favor. Re-create in your mind what happened on the earlier outings. See it again. See it as it happened: ending with you netting that big rainbow.

Such a positive visualization cannot but aid you in your current predicament (whatever it is). You've already achieved success in something very similar. That picture is clear in your mind. Now, bring that picture forward into the present. Apply it to the current situation in order to achieve the same success.

You're not operating in a vacuum. You have a library of positive mental images at your disposal. Rely on them the next time you fish.

Resolved: I visualize my past successes in fishing to help me face current predicaments.

April 4

"I brought home a set of fly fishing how-to videotapes. What better way to take up a sport than from a comfortable armchair?"

—P. J. O'Rourke

Learn to fly-fish the way P. J. O'Rourke did. Get yourself a set of how-to videotapes.

There were three tapes in P. J.'s set. "The first one claimed it would teach me to cast," he explains. "The second would teach me to 'advanced cast.' And the third would tell me where trout live, how they spend their weekends, and what they'd order for lunch if there were underwater delicatessens for fish."

Trouble was, the people who made the tapes assumed O'Rourke knew something to begin with. "I didn't even know how to put my rod together," he says.

What O'Rourke really needed, he says, was a fly-fishing video taught by Mr. Rogers. "This would give me advice about which direction to wind the reel and why I should never try to drive a small imported car while wearing waders."

O'Rourke learned that nymphs and streamers were not "naked mythological girls decorating the high school gym with crepe paper." And he liked naming flys: Wooly Hatcatcher, Royal Toyota Hatchback, Blue Wing Earsnag, and O'Rourke's Ouchtail were a few he came up with.

All in all, P.J. thought the videos were instructive. And if they worked for him, they might work for you, too.

Resolved: I check out a fly-fishing how-to video.

April 5

"I've never been in a boat with a man in my life, that I didn't learn something."

—Bill Dance

You always learn something when you go out in a boat with another man. Whether it's about the man or fishing or yourself or whatever, you always learn something.

There's no running when you're in a boat with another man. You're stuck together, at least for the duration, and the only place to go is over the side.

You can't get up and walk around and get away from each other for a while. You're there, so's he, and there's nothing you can do except live with it.

Some fishermen are quiet as mummies. Others, you can't shut up. Everybody is different. All in all, the quiet ones are probably easier to take than the ones that rattle on.

No subject is off limits when you share a boat with a man. Sex, money, sports, family. But mainly, when you're on a boat with another man, you talk fish. You leave that other stuff behind. It's you, him, the boat, the elements, and fish. That's all, and that's the way you like it.

A man who likes going out on a boat with another man likes the companionship and camaraderie as well as the fishing. He wants to share the good times with his brother or father or uncle or pal.

You always learn something when you share a boat with a man. Even if, as Bill Dance says, it's to never get in a boat with him again. But it's always something. Whether it's about him or the fishing or yourself.

Resolved: I go out on a fishing boat with a buddy.

April 6

"During my 87 years I have witnessed a whole succession of technological revolutions. But none of them has done away with the need for character in the individual or the ability to think."

—Bernard M. Baruch

Izaak Walton and Charles Cotton never fished with a graphite rod. But they were great fishermen.

Mel Krieger uses the most technologically advanced equipment on the market today. But you could send him out with a pole and a piece of string, and he'd be a great fisherman.

What makes great fishermen is the ability to think and adapt. That's what unites fishermen of the past and present. The gear has improved dramatically and will continue to get better. But it will never do away with the need to think.

You've got to find the fish. Figure out how to approach them. Read the water. Study the surroundings. Figure out what to use. If that doesn't work, try something else. Then something else again. Go to a different spot. Try a different angle.

Fishing is a kind of chess match between you and the fish. A lot of the challenge is mental. You give a pawn in order to take a rook three moves away. You work the board and your opponent slowly, steadily, patiently, until it's checkmate. The wonderful thing about wild trout is, they are great champions, too—Bobby Fischers of the water.

Take a thinking approach to fishing. It's not the gear or the whiz-bang technology that catches the fish. It's you.

Resolved: I take a thinking approach to fishing.

April 7

"An experienced, capable angler's stream sense becomes a part of his subconscious. Probably all he saw were a few places that seemed to say: 'Try me.'"

—Alfred Miller

Find a few places that say "try me."

This is what it means, in essence, to read water. Reading water is a matter of finding a few places that say "try me."

When you are uncertain where to go, or what to do next, stop for a moment and listen to what the water is saying. These places won't shout at you. They speak softly. So if you're rushing by or not listening, you may miss them.

Find a few places that say "try me." You'll know them when you see them, or when they speak to you.

Let your subconscious be your guide. In fishing, two plus two does not always equal four. The places that conventional wisdom points to are not necessarily the places to find fish. Those signposts can lead you down a blind alley.

Never overlook the external natural indicators. Always observe. Keep them in mind. But let your internal compass guide them rather than the other way around. Follow your own lead. Find a few places that say "try me."

Follow a hunch, even if where it goes is not immediately apparent to you. You don't have to be an expert or a grizzled fishing veteran to know where to look for fish. All you have to do is find a few places that say "try me."

That's all you're looking for. That's all anybody is looking for. When you find a spot like that, plant your flag and claim it as your own.

Resolved: I find a few places that say "try me."

April 8

"There's an alternative. There's always a third way, and it's not a combination of the other two ways. It's a different way."

—David Carradine

Today, make a fresh start.

Have a bad day yesterday? Couldn't catch a thing? Make a fresh start this morning.

Struggling this morning? It's not going the way you want. Relax. Make a fresh start in the afternoon.

Can't make it work in the afternoon, either? Make a fresh start tonight, in the dark, or come back tomorrow.

Getting frustrated or pissed off is probably not going to solve your troubles. A better way to go is to take a break from fishing and do something else, then come back and make a fresh start.

There are times when nothing goes right. And pushing doesn't help. Only seems to make it worse, in fact. The thing to do—although it's very hard to do—is to stop pushing.

You try it one way. It doesn't work. You try it another way. It still doesn't work.

You get away from it for a while and realize there's a third option. You come back to it, and this time, it works. There's always a third way, but sometimes you have to struggle a little before you can find it.

You know how to do it. You know what to do. All that is stopping you is yourself. Change your attitude. Unstick yourself. Out with your old, stale ways.

Resolved: I make a fresh start.

April 9

"Very curious. One day of trout fishing. Nevertheless, one day of trout fishing can be enough."

—Nick Lyons

One day. That's all you need. One day of trout fishing can be enough.

One day may be all you can spare. You can't get away for more. Well then, *take it*.

Don't wait until you can get a week or two weeks or even two days. Grab one day, if that's all there is to grab. Get away for one day this week, or one day this month.

Considering your schedule, getting away for a week may be fantasy. One day is more realistic. Chose reality over fantasy, and go for one day.

One day of fishing is always better than no days. And one day now is better than a week six months from now because you never know what will happen in six months. Something may come up and blow that long-anticipated fishing trip right out of the water. Better to grab the one day while you can, and let the future take care of itself.

One day of fishing can lead to two days, and two to three. You might have such a great time that you'll carve out more time for it in your schedule.

But one day can be enough. Just one day. Give yourself one day, and see what happens.

Resolved: I get in at least one day of fishing this month.

April 10

"The attraction of fishing is somewhere between the predictable and the unpredictable. To find it you have to feel your way along, ready to tuck yourself into the edges of the world as you find it, rather than the world that you packed for."

—Susan Williams, angler

Expect different pleasures, different experiences every time you fish.

It's easy to fall into a trap when you fish. Not a bear trap, but an expectations trap.

Say you go out one time and drain the lake. The hook barely gets wet before some twenty-pound bass is tugging on it. All the other boats in the lake pull up around you to watch. A camera crew films you for an upcoming TV special, "Bass Masters of the United States."

A week passes and you go out again, all fired up about what happened before. Not only are you fired up, but deep in your heart you halfway expect the experience to repeat itself.

It doesn't. The only fish you see are the dolphins pictured on the tuna cans you buy at the market. When you walk into the tackle shop, the other fishermen hide from you because they think you're bad luck and don't want it to rub off on them. The TV people edit you out of the "Bass Masters" special.

Everybody's luck in fishing goes from good to bad and all points in between, frequently on the same trip. But people get into trouble when they expect the same experience every time out, or a repeat of a past success.

Resolved: I stay open to new experiences in fishing.

April 11

*"O the gallant fisher's life
It is the best of any
'Tis full of pleasure, void of strife,
And 'tis beloved by so many."*

—Izaak Walton

One of the worst things you can say about another fisherman is to label him a "part-timer."

A part-timer is a guy who loved *A River Runs Through It*, buys all the latest gear, and then almost never goes fishing because he doesn't like getting his feet cold. A part-timer is a guy who really doesn't know what he's talking about but acts like he does. A part-timer is a guy who never goes in winter. A part-timer is a guy whose fishing library does not include *The Angler's Book of Daily Inspiration*.

You all know the type.

Never be a part-timer when it comes to fishing. Even if you can't do it all the time, give it everything you have when you can. You don't have to run away to Idaho and become a fishing guide to live the gallant fisher's life. It's a way of being, an attitude in which you give wholeheartedly of yourself and hold nothing back. You'll never be a part-timer with an attitude like that.

Make a full commitment to fishing, though you may do it only part-time. When you do it, really do it. Football players have an expression: "he left it all on the field." Leave it all on the field when you go fishing.

Resolved: When I fish, I give everything I have to fishing.

April 12

"Water is a thing so familiar to us all that we fail to appreciate its remarkable properties."

—David James Duncan

Two things to ponder the next time you're on a lake or stream (thanks to David James Duncan):

(A) More than 80 percent of the earth's surface is covered with water. That's 5 percent of the earth's total mass.

(B) Human beings are 70 percent water. Fruits and vegetables are even more. Their composition is 70 percent to 95 percent water.

According to scientists, H_2O makes the earth fit for human habitation. On the moon, conditions are more miserable than New York City in August: 120 degrees Celsius at noon to minus 150 degrees Celsius at midnight. But here on earth, oceans and lakes absorb heat from the sun during the day and release it at night, preventing the radical fluctuations that characterize the moon.

Water, not surprisingly, is at the center of many creation myths. As Duncan writes, "Tens of thousands of years ago our wise forefathers shared myths wherein water was said to be the primal, chaotic substance from which all forms proceed. It is clear that our forefathers have not been refuted, clarified or improved upon."

One thing is sure: it'd be hard to fish without water. Never take it for granted.

Resolved: I never take water for granted.

April 13

*"Children are never too young to begin study of nature's book,
and never too old to quit."*

—Dr. Charles L. Anderson

At what age do you start a kid fishing? Why not now?

Kids can definitely be a hassle and a distraction when you're doing anything, much less fishing. But it's better to start them earlier rather than later because if you wait until they're teenagers they'll be beyond all hope and make your life really miserable.

When they're young they will be more interested in playing around than actually fishing. That's okay. Let 'em play. Bring two rods—one for you, one for them to share among themselves. You maintain your post at the end of the jetty, hunting halibut, while they climb around the rocks looking for starfish or sea anemone. You keep one eye on them and one eye on the water.

Of your three kids, your daughter is older and more experienced. But she doesn't like handling the anchovies, and when she needs fresh bait she brings her rod to you. You give her your baited rod and you take hers. Meanwhile a pelican dives into the water looking for halibut, the same as you.

It's a great thing, fishing with your kids. Nothing like it. And the earlier you get them started and more accustomed to the experience, the better off you'll all be.

Resolved: I take my kids fishing when they're young, before they fall into the black hole of being a teenager.

April 14

It's a slow day, nothing else happening. Why not?

Pull them out from under the bed, or get them down from that shelf in the closet. Maybe you're the organized type and you've got them put away in a scrapbook, labeled and everything. More likely, they were tossed into a shoebox somewhere.

It's a great way to spend a little time, rummaging through your old fishing photographs. Lots of great memories in there.

Some people can chart the course of their lives through their fishing photographs. You're not just looking at fish. You're looking at yourself when you were eight, then again at eighteen, and twenty-eight, and so on.

Sure, it's a little sentimental. What's wrong with that?

You can take a trip around the world when you rummage through your old fishing photographs. You can visit the Louisiana Bayou, the Yellowstone River, and the mountains of New Zealand all in a moment's time.

Maybe you'll be so inspired that you'll want to go out and make new memories. Or you'll call up that friend you went to New Zealand with and see how he's doing. In any event, what's stopping you? Haul out those old fishing photographs and put yourself in a good mood.

Resolved: I put myself in a good mood and take a fishing trip down memory lane.

April 15

"Strike neither too slow nor too quick nor too hard."

—Dame Juliana Berners

The strike in fly-fishing is nearly a metaphysical act. Who can say why they strike a fish easily one day and not the next? Luck, bad timing, nerves, or just a rotten day—these are some explanations for it.

Interestingly, no less an authority than Ernest Schweibert says that a person's mood has a great deal to do with how successful he is in setting the hook. A fast-rising trout demands an alert fisherman. You might not react in time if you're feeling lethargic that day.

But you can go the other way. You can be wired from the two cups of coffee you had that morning and yank like an old-fashioned dentist pulling a tooth. You won't catch many trout with that approach.

A strike is a touchy-feely kind of thing. It's an act of delicacy and subtlety and sensitivity. Techniques vary according to conditions. No wonder fishermen run into problems with it.

Some fishing notables seem to think that a change in habit from one day to the next can affect your ability to set the hook. As Ed Engle puts it, "A day spent fishing hair bugs to slow-taking, hard-mouthed bass followed by a day on a trout stream fishing #22 midge imitations to quick-taking, relatively soft-mouthed, selective trout can be a disaster."

In striking as in so many other things in fishing, attitude means a lot. Look to yourself and your own frame of mind if the fish are slipping away too often.

Resolved: I strike neither too slow nor too quick nor too hard.

April 16

"Kneeling in the water, I scoop the rainbow into my hand. Pink and vulnerable, it's like a newborn baby."

—Allison Moir

Want to get the most out of your fishing? Imagine this is the last time you'll ever fish this spot.

Your attitude immediately changes. Bored? Restless? Frustrated? Tired? No way. This is the last time you'll ever fish this spot, and you're going to milk it for all it's worth.

All the questions you tend to ask yourself on a day of fishing get resolved easily and quickly. Should I skip dinner and fish? Do I hike upstream or down to see what's there? Do I stay a little longer? Do I stay an extra day? Do I check out that pool across the river?

You bet. When it's your last day at a place and you may never return again, you always decide in the affirmative. Yes is the only answer. You get off the fence and you plunge in.

It's like it's your last day on earth, your last day alive. Your senses become charged. You take nothing for granted. The air, the mountains, the sky, the river, the rainbow as pink and delicate as a newborn baby—every bit of it is special, a gift from God, and you want to cherish it all.

The truly wise see every day as a gift, as possibly their last. A day of fishing is a gift, too. See your next day of fishing as the last day you'll fish that spot, and watch your complacency disappear as fast as a captured trout that's just been released back into the water.

Resolved: I view my next day of fishing as if it's my last.

April 17

"All there is to thinking is seeing something noticeable which makes you see something you weren't noticing which makes you see something that isn't even visible."

—Norman Maclean

It's not how hard you fish, it's the decisions you make while you're fishing that determine success.

You can fish a spot hard. You can fish it till you're blue in the face. But despite all that effort, if you make bad decisions, success, like the fish, will likely elude you.

Conversely, you can be a veritable Jimmy Buffett on a trout stream. You can sip margaritas and learn to mimic the squawking of the stellar jay. But if you make the right decisions, success will be yours despite your apparent lack of initiative.

What are the right decisions? That part is up to you, based on what you know and what works for you. Do what comes easiest to you. That may be the best way to go.

Fishing is a thinking person's sport. The decisions you make mean something. Therein lies a great deal of its pleasure. In simple terms, your presentation of the fly may be perfect, but if you're not casting over fish, you're going to be pretty frustrated by morning's end. Similarly, even if your casting loops aren't poetry in motion, if you've made a better decision on where to fish, you'll probably have more success.

Think about it. Is all your effort in fishing being put to a constructive end?

Resolved: I take it easy. I think about what I'm doing before I do it.

April 18

"The degenerate lifestyle of western fly fishing guides is well
documented. . . . All they talk about, all they care about, is
moving water and wild trout."

—Randy Wayne White

That's a good rule of thumb for picking a guide: find one that
only cares about moving water and wild trout.

Get a guide who takes you seriously as a fisherman. You
don't want somebody who snickers every time you make a
comment, especially if you're paying that person hundreds of
bucks a day for the privilege of his company.

A good guide will put you in a position to succeed. That's
his primary job: putting you in a position to succeed. That
means knowing where to go and once you're there, setting you
up in the right spot based on your casting abilities. A good
guide can work a drift boat the way Willie Moscone handled
a pool cue. A sockeye in the side pocket, yes!

The reason you've hired the guide is that he knows things
you don't, so it's always nice to actually listen to him. You can
learn a lot when you do that. Guides are good even if you
think you know a river like the back of your hand. They might
show you a part of your hand that you've missed.

Nobody wants you to catch fish more than your guide. The
more fish you snag, the greater your enjoyment. Thus, a bigger tip. Guides are professionals, but on the whole they do
what they do because they love it. And a good guide will
transmit this love of the outdoors, this love of wild places and
wild trout, to all those around him.

Resolved: I hire a guide one of these days, even for a river
I know like the back of my hand.

April 19

"Nothing gives me more pleasure than doing something right onstream."

—John Randolph

Do something right onstream, and feel how much pleasure it gives you.

John Randolph compares a great cast in fishing to when a baseball player hits a home run, or a basketball player shoots a jump shot that swishes through the net, or a golfer strokes a long putt across an undulating green that rolls into the bottom of the cup. "My heart thumps a little louder," he says. "I can feel anticipation in my arms and up the back of my neck. The rise to the fly is an affirmation. What follows is a fulfillment."

Do something right onstream, and find fulfillment. Feel your heart race a little faster. Feel the tingle on your arms and the back of your neck, and be affirmed.

Get into the habit of doing something right onstream. Start your day that way. One right thing leads to another and another. You can develop good habits—habits of doing the right thing—just as you can form bad ones.

Have confidence that what you are doing is right. That is the first step. Trust yourself. It's better to do something technically wrong with a feeling of sureness than to do something technically correct with a feeling of doubt.

Do something right onstream. That will cut the legs out from under whatever doubts you have. By building on those positive feelings of achievement, you will achieve greater and greater things.

Resolved: I do something right onstream.

April 20

"Knowing fish is a process. I have been acquainting myself for 40 years."

—Lorian Hemingway

Be the one who asks questions.

The fisherman who stops asking questions is the one who has come to the end of the process. He's reached an impasse, whether he knows it or not. His learning curve has flattened. He's plateaued out.

The fisherman who is still asking questions has no illusions about knowing it all, or even a quarter of it. His mind is open. He's willing to learn new things. He knows there are always new things to learn.

Being the one who asks the questions is a way to assess others and plumb their knowledge. You can find out what they know and use it yourself. They know little about you and what you know because they haven't bothered to ask. But you know a lot about them, and this puts you in a stronger position.

This comes in handy in fishing, where knowledge is truly power. A person who asks questions can find out things others may not know and beat them to the spot before they get there. Of course you must be wary that the answers you're getting are legit, but that's another issue.

Asking questions is no sign of weakness. On the contrary, it's a sign of a person gathering strength, marshaling resources. Knowing fish is a process that never ends. Follow your curiosity always and never be afraid to ask questions. If there is one true path to wisdom, it is this one.

Resolved: In fishing, I keep asking questions.

April 21

"It's a real late run for the steelhead. You're just in time."

—A guide, to Pam Houston, before a
midnight run of steelhead

Here's an idea: you're never early or late when you go fishing. You're always right on time.

You know how it goes. Doesn't really matter when you get to the river; it's never the right time, say the locals.

"You shoulda been here last week," they tell you. "Man you really missed it." Or, "You're too early. This ain't the right time yet. September or October, now you're talkin'."

The best time to go fishing is the time you're fishing. Forget arbitrary definitions of early or late. Fishing is a party, and the party doesn't start until you get there.

There may be more optimum times for certain fish and certain runs at certain locations. That's a given.

But if you buy into the idea that you're late, you may rush what you're doing and in fishing that's never good. And if you think you're early, you may get discouraged more easily and give up.

Take the attitude that this is the best time to fish and make the best of it. You can have a bad time even when the fish are running and the time is supposedly ideal, and you can have a great time when nobody else is catching anything and it's not the right season.

A lot of this early and late talk is a form of negativity and you're better off without it.

Resolved: The best time to go fishing is the time I go fishing.

April 22

"Our idea of fishing is to put all the exertion up to the fish. If they are ambitious we will catch them. If they are not, let them go about their business."

—Don Marquis

Take control of the situation, then let it come to you.

However you define *control* in fishing, do it. Get on top of it. Take command. Then let it come to you. In this case, "it" means fish.

The ideal position is to be in such command that you can ease off, cease striving, and let events flow to you because they inevitably will. That is what control means.

You do not consciously direct the fish to come your way. That's ludicrous. But you know—*you just know*—they will.

So much of the time people feel as if they're running a race in which they're constantly falling behind. Whatever they do, it's not enough. They're going as hard and as fast as they can and yet they never seem to get ahead. The goals they've set for themselves remain just out of reach.

When you're in control, you're in synch with yourself. The sense of being hurried or pushed is gone. You're moving at exactly the pace you want. You're keeping up with the flow of events and you feel good about that.

You control the things you can control. Then you let the things that you cannot control come to you. For a fisherman, it's fish. He's done everything he can, he's in charge of his universe—all that he can be in charge of—and now it's just a matter of letting the rest of it fall into place.

Resolved: I take control, then let the fish come to me.

April 23

*"I'm a goin' fishin',
 Mama's goin' fishin',
 An' de baby's goin' fishin' too."*

—Taj Mahal, blues singer

Fish at your own pace. Whatever your pace is, fish at that pace.

Some may think that you go too quickly, or too slowly. But if it works for you, go at that pace.

It's never a good idea to rush in fishing. You rush, you scare the fish. You won't have too many friends in fishing if you scare the fish.

But tempo, like so many other things in this Einsteinian universe, is relative. One man's fast is another man's turtlelike slow. It's all a matter of what you're used to and what works for you.

You're bored with a spot. You're tired of working it. You want to go somewhere else. But your buddy thinks you're being impatient, that you'd better slow down and relax.

You're both probably right.

There is no supreme authority in fishing except the fish. They're the final arbiters. If something needs to happen with you in fishing, the fish will tell you. Slow down, move along, improve your techniques? The fish will tell you.

When you listen to the fish, if something needs to change, you'll change it. If you don't listen and don't change—well then, you're in a whole heap of trouble.

Until the fish tell you otherwise, fish a stream at the pace you like, in the way you like to fish it.

Resolved: I fish in my own way, at my own pace.

April 24

"I never get lost because I don't know where I'm going."

—Ikkya, Zen master

Get lost. No really, get lost.

Forget where you're going. Chart the time by the movement of the sun. Stroll lazily along a lazy trout stream. Meander with the meandering waters. Wander where your inclination leads you.

Goals are good in fishing and life. It's good to set a high target for yourself and hit a bull's-eye. There's a lot of satisfaction in that.

But there's also satisfaction to be had in setting your goals aside for a while. Goals can limit you. The ultimate purpose of goal-setting is to surpass the goal you've established and thus expand your personal horizons. Even so, by setting the goal in the first place you've defined yourself in a certain way. This is who you are, you are saying, and what you think you can do.

Getting lost is letting go of all that, at least for a while. When you get lost, you let go of who you are, as strictly defined by the goal-setting side of your personality. In the process you may find a new side to yourself, one that you didn't know existed, or had forgotten.

There is an added benefit for fishermen in occasionally getting lost. You wander around seemingly without a clue, then suddenly, there it is. A new, great place to fish. Then you're not lost anymore. You know you're right where you're supposed to be. And you hope nobody ever finds you.

Resolved: I get lost along a stream.

April 25

"The charm of fishing is that it is the pursuit of what is elusive but attainable, a perpetual series of occasions for hope."

—John Buchan

To fish is to hope.

Sometimes you can be out all day and nothing happens. Nothing happened in the morning, nothing happened in the afternoon. Now it is evening and nothing is still happening.

But do you go home? Do you chuck it all and call it a day? "Something may bite," you tell yourself. "Just wait."

Or the reverse: you've had a great day. Things are popping. You've pulled out twenty-three-pound salmons on back-to-back casts. But you're not content and you won't be until you check out this one little spot downstream. Why? Because you believe that the next fish will be your biggest yet, possibly the biggest of the entire trip.

And who knows, it may. Every fisherman is an optimist at heart. Every time a fisherman casts a line into water, he makes a statement for optimism, hope, joy. There are days of disappointment and no fish, certainly. Days when the getting wet, the hiking, the crawling through bushes and tree branches, the broken lines, the long stretches of boredom, the heat and fatigue and headaches, the perpetual harassment by bugs hardly seem worth the trouble.

But even on those days, this profoundly exhilarating thought powers you: your next cast will change everything, your next fish will be your biggest ever.

Maintain a hearty optimism when you fish. Sometimes on a long, bug-ridden day, it's all you've got.

Resolved: I make a statement for hope and optimism. I fish.

April 26

"That day together on the river was like a thousand other pages from the book of any angler's memories. There was the clasp and pull of cold, hurrying water on our legs, the hours of rhythmic casting."

—Sparse Grey Hackle

Relax. You're doing exactly what you should be doing.

Should is a terrible word when it comes to fishing and almost everything else. Delete *should*. Make it: you're doing exactly what you want to do.

Sometimes you think when you're fishing, "I should be somewhere else." Or, "I'm not doing this right." Or, "I'm spending too much time on this. I should be doing something else."

There are always plenty of fishing shoulds to torture you, if you let them. You're better off dumping the whole lot of them in the trash.

There's no other real way to determine what a person wants than by what he does, and this is what you want. You're on the river. And you're enjoying the hell out of it.

Take some deep breaths. Cool off. Tell those negative voices in your head to back off. Let all those shoulds that torture you in your everyday life take a vacation.

For now, you're fishing. Take satisfaction in that. You're doing pretty much what you want, in a place you picked, using methods that work for you. In what other areas of life can you claim as much?

Resolved: I relax and enjoy fishing.

April 27

"Any person can be a successful angler if he stops occasionally, observes the natural way of streamside life, then learns to use the knowledge he has gleaned to his best advantage."

—Robert Zwirz and Morty Marshall

Be open to change. Be open to change your plans at a moment's notice.

Everybody starts a day of fishing with certain expectations, certain plans in mind. And they may seem like pretty darned good plans at the time.

You may have had your mind on this certain spot on Hat Creek. It's all you've been able to think of for the last month. Then you find that about 145 other fishermen were thinking the same thing. Kiss your plans good-bye, and push on.

It is no small thing to change long-held plans. You've invested so much mental fuel in them that you can't possibly change. It's a waste, a loss, a failure of some kind. So to avoid feeling bad, you *make* yourself feel bad by hanging on too long, or stubbornly sticking with the plans no matter how terrible a time you're having.

It's not a loss to change your plans. It's not a failure. Far from it. You've adapted. You've turned your knowledge of a changed reality to your advantage. You have a better idea and you're moving on. You've opened yourself up to the possibility of something new happening, something that you did not expect but that may, after all is said and done, be the best thing that could have happened. That is a victory by any standard.

Resolved: I drop my streamside plans at a moment's notice when something better comes along.

April 28

"No man is really happy or safe without a hobby. Anything will do so long as he straddles a hobby and rides it hard."

—Sir William Osler

Want to enjoy fishing more? Get better at it.

It's true in fishing or hunting or writing or acting or cooking or whatever you want to name. The better you are, the more fun you have.

You don't have to go psycho. You don't have kill yourself. All you have to do is get better.

Getting better is so much fun because you can see the progress for yourself. You can see that you're not standing still, that you're going up the staircase.

Another reason it's so much fun is that you get strokes from other people. They see how much you've improved, and they let you know it.

When you get better at fishing, you do it more. The more you do it, the better you get. That's a fun cycle to be in. Once you get better, you can get really, really good. You can really ride it hard. That's fun, too.

Of course, the principal reason it's so much fun to get better at fishing is the fish. Although there is such a thing as beginner's luck in this sport, the better and more experienced you are at fishing, the more fish you tend to catch.

Want to have more fun fishing? Make a pact with yourself to get better.

Resolved: I get better at fishing.

April 29

"I find inspiration in situations where I lose myself, which comes when I'm in a group doing something, or I'm in a place where I really can't figure anything out and I just kind of give up."
—Willem Dafoe

Find inspiration where you can.

Find inspiration in the leap of a coho. Find it in the shiny silver of a Canadian steelhead. Find it in the fighting strength of a king salmon.

Find inspiration on this page or in this book. Find it in Thomas McGuane or Nick Lyons or E. Annie Proulx. Find it in a casual remark from a friend or stranger.

Find inspiration in a beautifully tied fanwing. Find inspiration in the fact that you tied it yourself and that you're developing real skill at the fly-tying art.

Find inspiration in a split-cane rod or any tackle that is made with care and loving attention to detail. Find it in a well-tied knot.

Find it in the crisp Sierra morning air. Find it in the warming sun. Find it in the cold, cold water. Find it in the delight of a child landing her first fish.

Find inspiration alone or with others. Find it in the simple fact that you are free and tromping through the woods.

Find inspiration where you can. Find it in Mount McKinley and find it in the mayfly. It's there. In small and large things, in the ordinary as well as the extraordinary. It's there in the simple and obvious, and it's there in things that are neglected and forgotten. You don't have to look for it. Open yourself to the possibility of it, and it will be there.

Resolved: I find inspiration in fishing where I can.

April 30

Let fishing define your life for a change.

You've let work define your life. You've let family define your life. Now let fishing define your life. Tie yourself into the world of water and the animals it contains.

Bring fishing forward in your perception of things. Fishing has occupied a seat three rows back for long enough. Invite it up to the dais. Give it a place of honor in your life.

Put fishing in the present tense. Make it current. Make it a thing you do rather than something you've done in the past and expect to do sometime in the future. Think of yourself as a fisherman.

A fisherman fishes. Want to fish this weekend? Do it. Want to go to Alaska? Do it. Want to take a sabbatical from work and bonefish in the Pacific? Do it.

A fisherman does these things because that's who he is and what he does. He does not defer forever. Not to do these things, not to fish, would be to violate his nature and he won't allow that to happen.

Define your life by fishing, if only as an experiment. Let fishing be at the forefront of your decision-making process and see if it changes the decisions you make.

Resolved: I let fishing define my life for a change.

May 1

"First a man tries to catch the most fish, then the largest fish, and finally the most difficult fish."

—Ed Hewitt

Numbers are the easiest measuring stick of performance. Catch six or ten or twelve fish, and no one could dispute that you've had a great day.

The next way to judge is size. You may have had a miserable day, but if you haul in a big one, the day is instantly redeemed. Everyone admires size. A really big fish is a masterpiece.

But the truest test for the fisherman comes when he hooks a really difficult fish. If it is both big and difficult, he is really onto something special. It's a challenge unlike almost any other in his life. It demands all of him, everything he has, even things he didn't know he had in him.

A difficult fish tells you what you are made of as a fisherman. It tests your skills in the most vivid and immediate way. It gives you a mental and physical grilling. You think you're good, bub? Let's find out.

It's between you and the fish. A simple drama of life and possible death played out in a primitive arena of water and earth and sky. Action is now. Consequences are immediate. You make a mistake, you pay. The fish earns its freedom. Often fate intervenes and decides the contest.

A fight with a difficult fish will make you a better fisherman and a better man. You never forget it. You come away in admiration of your opponent, hoping like hell to see him again or one like him. Always seek difficult fish.

Resolved: I hunt difficult fish.

May 2

"I saw the whole process, not as a frantic whipping and thrashing, but as one liquid motion, seamless and intact."
—Lorian Hemingway

Lorian Hemingway made a breakthrough in her fly-casting technique by watching a naked man do it on a river. Fly cast, that is. Let Lorian explain:

"It was then I saw the naked man in the raft drifting past, fly rod poised in mid-air," she writes. "Ordinarily, naked would have been enough, but as I watched more closely I noticed he was throwing his rod tip up to twelve o'clock and then waiting for a beat before following through with the forward cast. During that beat the line straightened out behind him, unfurling slowly from the arc it made as he brought the rod forward."

Why the man chose to fish naked is a question that was never answered. But Lorian did not question; she watched. She continues, "I watched the man cast another perfect length of line and discovered my arm moving involuntarily, following his motions. I watched his wrist. Hardly a bend in it as he pointed the rod arrow-straight in the direction of the unfurling line." Watching him helped her straighten out her own technique. She learned to unwrinkle her casting and think of it as one motion, not a series of herky-jerky movements.

So take a tip from Lorian. Keep your eyes open for naked people while you're fishing. You never know what you might learn from them.

Resolved: I see a naked man (or woman) on the river, I pay attention.

May 3

Leave all the doors open.

Not the doors to your car or your house, but the doors to your fishing life.

One example: a lot of highly experienced fly-fishermen look down on the roll cast as something for beginners or rank amateurs. They learned it themselves as kids. Now they prefer overhead or sidearm lay-down casts.

Fact is, the roll cast can be a very effective technique in certain circumstances. Smart fishermen keep it in their repertoire and polish it for those times when they need it.

The roll cast is a door, one of many in fishing. Shut the doors and you shut yourself in. You close yourself off. You'll never be as good a fisherman as you can be, never learn as much as you can, if you shut the doors.

A lot of learning is relearning. Relearning things you've forgotten or you once knew but that have grown rusty over time. Maybe you stopped using these doors for a while and boarded them up because you didn't think you'd ever need them again.

It turns out you were wrong. Everything you've experienced in your life has meaning and purpose and may come back to you at a later date. Keep the doors in your life open and well oiled. You never know when you may want to walk through them again.

Resolved: I keep my fishing doors open.

May 4

"I never lost a little fish. It was always the biggest fish I caught that got away."

—Eugene Field

Never lose a little fish. If you're going to lose a fish, make it a big one.

If you think you lost a five-pounder, make it a twenty-five-pounder. If you think you lost a twenty-five-pounder, make it a sixty-pounder. If you think you lost a sixty-pounder, make it a whale.

Fishermen are renowned for their exaggerations. Why fight the stereotype? Exaggerate like hell when you lose a fish.

Look, if you come back and say you lost a fifteen-pound fish, everyone will think you're lying and immediately knock it down to a measly three pounds. (*Measly* here is a relative term.) So it doesn't make any sense to say you lost a fifteen-pounder, even if you realistically think that's what it was. Throw realism over the side. Realism has nothing to do with a good fish story.

If you think you lost a fifteen-pound fish, tell people you lost, oh say, a thirty-five- or forty-pounder. The reason being, no matter what you say, people will think you're lying and knock down the poundage in their minds. So if you give them an exaggerated figure and really pile on the BS while you're at it, they'll only chop it down part of the way—say to fifteen pounds, which is your honest assessment of what that slippery little rascal weighed.

Did someone say "little?" Nah, nah. It was huge, that fish. The biggest I ever saw, it nearly knocked me off my feet. . . .

Resolved: When I lose a fish, I lose a big one.

May 5

It's May. Can you make a similar commitment? No? Why not?

All right then. May's out. Too busy. What about June? Even worse? How about July? August? What are you saying . . . *never*?

There is a virtue in observing regular habits, great virtue if one of those habits is fishing. A man who fishes every week has his priorities in place. It's like going to church. It's something that needs to be done.

Once a week may be asking too much for many people. It's hard enough to get away once a month, let alone once a week. Okay then, make it once a month. Heck, make it once every two months—whatever you can do. But make it regular, that's the point. Make fishing a regular part of your schedule.

Once you make it an unassailable part of your schedule—and you stick to it like the good gentleman Palmer Baker describes—you will be one small step away from making it a more *frequent* part of your schedule. You will have established a beachhead from which more fishing trips may issue, more often.

So what's it gonna be? Okay, so this month is bad. When can you start?

Resolved: I find a way to make fishing a regular part of my schedule.

May 6

"Salmon are my totem. My original call of the wild. They are role models for three of the traits I value most: tenacity, courage and passion."

—Jessica Maxwell

Hang onto your best conception of yourself as a fisherman.

You're going to have bad days. You're going to have stinking rotten miserable days. Hang onto your best conception of yourself no matter what kind of day you have.

Fishing, and fish, can be downright bewildering at times. It, and they, will administer tests to you in which you will not always receive an A. In fact, you may not get a passing grade at all. You may flunk.

Hang onto your best conception of yourself. Don't let one day or one trip, or even several days and a succession of trips, defeat you or discourage you permanently.

Separate performance from who you are. Did you do your best? Did you give it a fair and full shot? Then you have done all you can do and there is no reason to get down on yourself.

You may need to fish more. You may just need to relax. There may be things you can do to help achieve the results you want, but certainly the person you are—the man making the attempt—is not at issue here. Remember that. The fact that you are making the attempt at all says much about your tenacity, your courage, your passion.

Everybody fails. What defines a man—and a fisherman— is how he responds to failure. Hang onto your best conception of yourself, and come back strong.

Resolved: I hang onto my best conception of myself during the down times.

May 7

Maintain a youthful attitude when fishing.

Be receptive to change. Be flexible. Don't be an old grouch. Your granddad was an old grouch. Don't be like him.

A person with a youthful attitude will try new things. He will experiment. It doesn't have to be done that way just because that's the way it was done in the past. A person with a youthful attitude is willing to rattle the cup and see what rolls out.

If the numbers are good, cool. If they aren't, well, roll again.

Age has nothing to do with this. A sixty-year-old fisherman can have a youthful attitude, while a twenty-year-old may not. And some teenagers with fishing rods can be grumpier and more stuck in their ways than arteriosclerotic old men.

Nobody likes to fish with a grump. Nobody likes to fish with somebody who's always complaining about his wife or his job or his back problems, or who only wants it done his way and no other.

Does fishing itself promote a youthful attitude? Not for everybody, that's sure. Some fishermen are so dang grumpy, all that fresh air and sunshine seem to have no impact on them at all.

Bring a youthful attitude to the trout stream along with your rod and tackle. Your fishing will go better because of it.

Resolved: I bring a youthful attitude to the trout stream.

May 8

*"Fishing is not a lazy or 'contemplative' sport. Serious fishing,
for difficult fish, often requires both mental and physical
application. Only patience, skill and a thorough understanding
of both fish and fishing will make you consistently successful."*
—Tom McNally

Apply yourself. That is how you catch game fish.

Anybody can get lucky and throw in a line and hook a fish.
But luck alone will not catch game fish. You need to apply
yourself.

Apply yourself both physically and mentally. Having one
but lacking the other, you will catch fish, but not game fish.
You need to harness all your skills, all your experience, all
your know-how, to hunt and capture game fish.

Game fish have seen your like before. You're not going to
catch them off guard. They're ready for you. They've seen
almost every trap you can set for them.

You will not catch a game fish by being lazy. Hunting game
fish is serious stuff. You've got to put on your game face to
catch game fish.

You need the patience of Job to catch game fish. You need
skill and energy and devotion. You need to learn about your
prey—what makes them tick. This won't come with a snap of
the fingers. You need to apply yourself over time, and keep
applying yourself.

Apply yourself today, tomorrow, next month, next year, the
year after next. The meek need not apply. Only the steadfast,
only the truly diligent, will catch game fish. And they're the
only ones that deserve to.

Resolved: I apply myself to the serious pursuit of game fish.

May 9

"When I go fishing, I deliberately go to a place I don't know yet.
I want to make it hard for myself, mysterious, a shape-shifting
journey to another world."

—Ailm Travler

Go to a place you've never been and you will inevitably discover something new.

It may be about the river itself or the lake or the ocean. It may be about the fish that live there. It may be nothing more than the burnt-orange tint of the sky at sunset. But you will discover something.

Going to an old, familiar place is easier. You know what to do and what not to do. You know where to go and what to avoid. You know the good places, at the best time of day. You know all this because you've been there and done it before.

It's unsettling to go to a new place. The comfortable knowledge is gone. It is another world, familiar in its way but also mysterious and unknown. There is no memory to rely upon, no experience of place. You're rootless, a stranger in a strange land.

You apply your old habits to this new place and sometimes they don't work. It's frustrating. You long for that old place where your time-tested methods have proved so successful.

Make it deliberate. Make it part of your fishing routine. Go to a place you've never been. Test yourself. Be a searcher after experience as well as fish. Find out what you really know. Find out how good you really are. It's a sure bet you will discover at least one new thing—about the river or the fish or the sun or yourself.

Resolved: I deliberately go to a place I don't know.

May 10

"So fresh and exciting this walk up the road with haversack on my back. I belong to no one but myself. I have no road but this one."

—Sylvia Ashton-Warner

Start positive. End positive.

Make the bookends of your day positive. Do something good for yourself at the start of the day. Do something good for yourself at the end.

Sometimes this is not so easy to control. A tree falls over in the night, pinning your boots underneath. It is impossible to budge the tree or your boots. So you hike out to the stream barefoot, like a modern-day Huck Finn, and bloody your toe on a rock.

Still, you have the power to end the day well. Nurse that toe back to health with ample shots of Jack Daniels, while lounging comfortably around the fire. Next morning, try it all over again. With boots.

If you start your day badly, know that it will not end that way. Take comfort in the knowledge that no matter what happens during the day, it will end happily. And if events at the end of the day slip out of control, know that next morning you will set things right again.

A positive view of the outcome of the day tends to keep things on an even keel. You are less likely to indulge feelings of frustration, to plummet like a kamikaze pilot headlong into a negative spiral, if you know something positive awaits you later on.

Resolved: I start positive. I end positive.

May 11

*"We may say of angling as Dr. Boteler said of strawberries:
'Doubtless God could have made a better berry, but doubtless
God never did'; and so, if I might be judge, God never did make
a more calm, quiet, innocent recreation than angling."*

—Izaak Walton

Set it aside and fish.

Your teenage son has purple hair and a ring through his nose. There's a lock on his bedroom door, and you haven't been inside his room in years. Set it aside and fish.

Your company is downsizing. Rumor has it that the first ones to get the axe will be middle managers in their fifties. You are a middle manager in your fifties. Set it aside and fish.

The cat needs dental work. Apparently pet dentistry is a coming thing in the vet business. Set it aside and fish.

Your car needs a tune-up. Your bathroom faucet leaks. Your living room carpet is older than you are. There's a crater-size crack in the tile in your kitchen floor. The roof is leaking and water is dripping down into the walls of your house. Set it aside and fish.

The rumors were true. You got the axe. Set it aside and fish.

You read about Dr. Kevorkian in the newspaper. You think, "Hmm." You call the Michigan phone directory for his number. Set it aside and fish.

Sometimes things can seem pretty awful. Sometimes they *are* pretty awful. But there is an easy way to make yourself feel a whole lot better.

Resolved: I set it aside and fish.

May 12

"'Patience,' Cacciato said. 'That's what my dad told me. Have patience, he says. You can't catch fish without patience.'"

—Tim O'Brien

You've got to show patience when you're fishing. But you've got to show patience when you're not fishing, too.

If you don't have patience when you're away from the stream, you're probably not going to have much of it when you're on it. Patience is not a quality that will magically descend upon you when you put on your waders.

That is not to say you have to become a sort of fishing Gandhi. But you do need to find ways to put the brakes on before you reach the stream or while you're preparing for it. This could be as simple as not speeding when you're driving to the river. While on his way to a match, the golfer Sam Snead gripped the steering wheel lightly in his hands. This reminded him to take it easy and hold the golf club lightly, as if holding a small bird in his hands.

Use this technique—or something similar—to teach yourself to slow down, to relax. Really taking your time and checking out the water before grabbing your rod and tackle is another method. A fisherman who is impatient and overly hasty and rushing to get down to the stream will likely show the same qualities when he is finally there. Patience is built over time, through small steps. Find ways to slow yourself down, and make them part of your fishing routine.

Resolved: I take my time on the drive to the river.

May 13

"Fishing, like nothing else, had always provided a line that connected her, not only to fish and rivers and valleys, but to history and family as well. It grounded her in place and time."

—Elizabeth Storer

Your dad fished. Your granddad fished, too. Maybe your granddad taught your dad, who taught you. Fishing connects you to them. Every time you pick up a rod, they go with you.

Fishing connects you to the land and water as well. You know the land because you've fished it. These places are not abstract to you. You've come to know them over time. They're not simply destinations on the map, places to fish. They feel like home to you. When you go to one of these places, it's like going home.

You first went when you were a kid, using spinning gear. Your dad took you and maybe your granddad was alive then and he came along, too. Years went by. Your granddad passed on. After the funeral you went back. In your twenties, a fly-fishermen, alone this time. Every cast you made was in silent, singing tribute to the old man's grand and generous spirit.

Fishing is one way we connect with the world. Not only with the rivers and the valleys and fish, but also with our families and our past. It's not an escape, as some might contend. It's a journey toward what's real and lasting in our lives.

Resolved: I call my dad or my granddad, and I talk some fishing.

May 14

"Nothing, but nothing, fights like a Pacific king salmon hooked en route to the spawn, especially on light tackle."

—Jessica Maxwell

They call it the king because it is. It's the Elvis of salmon.

Other names for the Pacific king are the chinook or quinnat. The Chinook Indians lived in the Columbia River Valley in the Pacific Northwest. Chinook salmon are found in the Northwest, Alaska, and along the Pacific Coast.

The king is one of five species of Pacific salmon; coho, chum, pink, and sockeye are the others. All make that incredible, mysterious pilgrimage from ocean to fresh water for purposes of propagating their species. Unlike seemingly every other fish species on the planet, the tightly regulated Pacific salmon fishery is thriving and not at risk.

At sea, a king is as silver as moonlight; in its spawning colors, it turns a deep, gorgeous, almost glowing red. Silvio Calabi says "a large pair of spawning king salmon can look like tarpon that were caught in some mysterious nuclear accident."

The king is the biggest and hardest salmon to catch. It's the big daddy of salmon. The kings of the kings are bigger than your typical female Olympic gymnast; they weigh more than one hundred pounds and are five feet long. As is fitting for an animal of its magnitude and pugilistic powers, the king salmon inhabits mainly big, two-hearted rivers. And only big, two-hearted fishermen land them.

Ever caught a king salmon? Well, why not? Unlike Elvis, they're actually out there. Your time has come. Make a date with destiny.

Resolved: I plan a trip to Alaska. The target: king salmon.

May 15

Nobody wants to be fishing more than you. Quit wanting. Fish.

Nobody thinks about it more than you. Quit thinking. Fish.

Nobody deserves that cool, split-cane rod more than you. Buy it.

Nobody works harder and deserves a break more than you. Take a week off to fish. Hell, take two weeks.

Nobody has a better time at the lake than you. Go have a good time.

Nobody knows the river the way you do. Nobody knows trout the way you do. Get reacquainted with them both.

Nobody loves fishing with his family more than you. Take them along.

Nobody wants to fish for salmon in Alaska more than you. Quit wanting it. Go to Alaska. And watch out, salmon.

Nobody wants to haul in a tarpon off the coast of Bimini more than you. Go do it.

Nobody has more things they want to accomplish in fishing than you. Now's the time.

Whatever you want to do in fishing, whatever your dreams are, they will only come true if you make them come true. Quit wishing. Fish.

Resolved: I quit wishing. I fish.

May 16

"Talk about the joys of the unexpected, can they compare with the joys of the expected, of finding everything delightfully and completely what you knew it was going to be?"

—Elizabeth Bibesco

Start with this assumption: you know what is going to happen before you even set out on a day of fishing. That is, you are either going to catch fish or not.

You know the results before they occur. You do not know how, or how much, or what exactly will occur during the day. But you know the end result of your actions. You will either catch fish, or you will not.

Why, then, do you let one of these eventualities—the not catching fish—bug you?

If you knew you were always going to catch fish, in precisely the way you expected, what would be the fun of it? The challenge? You know that on some days things are just not going to go the way you plan.

You know that. It is as certain as the sun rising tomorrow. You can anticipate it. Therefore, why not take control over these events in your mind? Knowing the results of a day of fishing ahead of time, frees you from worrying about them. Less worry means greater enjoyment.

Go out to the lake with big expectations and those expectations will surely be dashed upon the rocks. Go out to the lake knowing that the results of the day are foreordained— you will catch fish or not—-and this will lend you a kind of control over your world.

Resolved: I know I will either catch fish or not, and I relax about it.

May 17

*"To me heaven would be a big bull ring with me holding two
barrera seats and a trout stream that no one else was allowed
to fish in."*

—Ernest Hemingway

For Hemingway, heaven on earth consisted of a bullring with
a trout stream nearby. What's yours?

A wild Alaskan river with the salmon running? A bass-fish-
ing boat on a serene blue mountain lake? A backcountry
stream in the High Sierra, where you fish and lay out in the
sun and swim in granite pools? A trip to the Florida Keys, by
day fishing for tarpon, at night chatting up a lovely senorita
in an open-air bar while the warm Gulf winds caress your
forehead? (Or maybe the lovely senorita is caressing your
forehead. Anyway, you get the idea.)

Chances are, as you construct this lovely fantasy in your
head, you know all the elements. It's not wholly fantastical,
not pure heaven. As with Hemingway, your heaven on earth
is composed of things you know and have experienced.

And that's great because that means it is attainable. Right
here. Right now. In this flawed life, on this dying planet. You
may, in fact, have already found paradise and simply want to
go back. Well then, what's stopping you?

What we want frequently reflects what we have. And if we
do not have what we want yet, it is well within our grasp. We
simply have to open our eyes and hearts. Heaven is here
before us.

Resolved: I picture heaven on earth, and then I go visit it.

May 18

"The current tugs at my legs. It occurs to me that if I fall, I will not have the strength to regain my footing. I concentrate on remaining upright, leaning into the current, angling slowly across the river towards shallower water."

—Mallory Burton

It is impossible to resist the negative for long in fishing.

Inevitably you will find yourself wading across a strong current, and see yourself falling.

Imagine the opposite. Force that negative picture out of your head and see a different one. See yourself staying upright, leaning into the current, angling slowly across the river to shallower, slower-moving water.

It is easy to get down on yourself in fishing. There is so much time, so many obstacles. It's largely a solitary pastime. The decisions you make are frequently yours alone. It is easy to think you are doing something wrong. If you make a wrong step, you suffer the consequences.

Try this, for a change: all positive thoughts, all day long. Assume the best in every circumstance. Concentrate on remaining upright. If something does happen that's not immediately to your liking, see it as an opportunity to learn. See every mistake as a chance to grow and hone your skills. Resist the negative. Turn a negative into a positive.

A positive frame of mind builds confidence. A consistently negative one destroys it. Achievement is the lasting path to self-esteem. But you will fail if you think you are a failure. And you will succeed—you will make it across the current—if you see yourself as a success.

Resolved: All positive thoughts, all day long.

May 19

"Ever let your hook be hanging; where you least believe it, there will be fish in the stream."

—Ovid

Ovid was a Latin poet who lived two thousand years ago. But he knew the one indisputable verity of fishing: you'll never catch a damn thing unless you hang your hook out.

It's true in fishing and it's true in life. You may think you have the greatest idea in the world. But you'll never know until you put it out there and see how it flies. You can hide your light in a box and hope for it to be discovered. But unless you're Emily Dickinson, that probably won't happen. You have to get into the mix and drop your hook in a likely stream.

There's a further insight in Ovid's thought. You can't predict where or when you're going to catch fish. You may have ideas, based on previous experience or knowledge. You may suspect, based on reports you've heard.

But as is so often the case, the fish may not be apprised of the same reports you are. The only way to know about fish, finally and concretely, is to let your hook be hanging. Sometimes you will find fish in the place you least suspect. You can surprise yourself and others, even a miracle can occur, as long as you let your hook be hanging.

In fishing, writing, business, art, science, government—all forms of human endeavor—a thing that seems impossible at first becomes realistic once a person accomplishes it. But it only becomes possible if first he lets his hook be hanging.

Resolved: Time's a wastin'. I hang my hook out.

May 20

"First and last, thanks to the Keeper of the Silence, who touched wild water seldom, but wrought great works when he did."

—David James Duncan

Be there.

This is the first and last rule of fishing and perhaps the only one: be there.

Be there, and you will learn. Be there, and you will know everything you need to know when you need to know it. Be there, and everything will become clear.

Why do fishermen devote their lives to such a pursuit? Be there, and you'll know.

What is it about dropping a line in water that makes a man come back to it again and again and again and again? Be there, and you'll find out.

Why are fish such endlessly challenging game? What do they know and how do they know it? Be there, and seek answers on your own.

What is it about the natural world that speaks to people so directly, in a way that cities and towns do not? Be there, and you will understand instinctively.

Why do some people think of fishing not as a sport or a pastime, but as a kind of religion? Be there, and you will become a believer.

There are a lot of questions in fishing. Be there, and you will find answers.

Resolved: I'm there.

May 21

*"In the school of life many branches of knowledge are taught.
But the only philosophy that amounts to anything, after all, is
just the secret of making friends with your luck."*

—Henry Van Dyke

Make friends with your luck.

Some days it will be good. Some days it will be bad. Make friends with it in any case.

Anybody can get chummy with their luck on good days. That's no great shakes. But you must accept your luck and make friends with it on the bad days, too.

Don't be someone who thinks he should only have good luck, then retreats into a miserable funk or rod-breaking frenzy when he does not. Bad luck in fishing is as inevitable as a broken line. It happens. You're better off making friends with that knowledge, rather than fighting it.

A person who makes friends with his luck is far more adaptable on a trout stream. His attitude is flexible, open, and adventurous. He accepts the recalcitrant fish and tangled lines and Amazon-like bushwhacking as part of the deal. He owns up to the knowledge that he—not his luck—may be responsible for the fix he's in. That he controls the situation he's in, and he has the power to change it. Leave your destiny in the hands of luck or fate or the gods of fishing, and you're leaving it in the wrong hands.

Take charge of your fishing. Control *that*. Your luck will even itself out over time.

Resolved: I make friends with my luck.

May 22

"Larger even than my memories is my anticipation of rivers yet fished."

—Charles Kuralt

Want to get psyched about fishing? Check out a guidebook to the next place you want to go.

It really doesn't matter where you're headed, there is probably a guidebook about it. If you're planning a trip to a place that doesn't have its own guidebook, man, that's really cool.

A good guidebook gets the juices flowing. It's got pictures of beautiful rivers and streams, pictures of trout leaping out of their skins, and best of all, pictures of guys standing in those rivers catching those leaping trout. It's got descriptions of where to go, and even if you don't hit those exact places, it will get you started in the right direction. You throw it in the trunk of the car and look at it when you need it, if at all.

A good guidebook not only helps you when you're there, it inspires you to get there. That may be its most important mission.

A guidebook is the first of many things you and your buddy will share on your trip together. You pass it on to him, he passes it back to you. You thumb through it on the drive. A guidebook is frequently a passport to the unknown. "Check it out," you say. "Let's do it." It's the essential talking part of every trip, a way to build that lovely sense of anticipation, if it needs building. And it's a crucial element of preparing for the really great part of fishing—actually going.

Start with a guidebook. Then go.

Resolved: I check out a copy of *Trout Streams of the Eastern Sierra*.

May 23

"I want to walk around in the woods, fish and drink. I'm going to be a child about it and I can't help it. I was born this way and it makes me very happy to fish and drink."

—Jim Harrison

Be a child about it. Walk around in the woods, fish, and drink.

There's an old story about two guys who were going fishing. They pulled their car over to the side of the road to ask an old man directions to Oakley Creek.

"What are you fellas doin'?" asked the old man.

Fishing, they replied. Trout fishing.

"Got any whiskey with you?" the old man asked.

No, the men replied.

"A little tobaccy?"

No, don't smoke, said the men.

"Well now," said the old man. "I thought you guys said you were going fishing."

Drinking and fishing go together like soup and crackers. You fish some, you drink some. You drink some more, you fish some more. All that fresh river water only goes so far. Sooner or later a person has to have something a little stronger.

Be happy. Walk around in the woods, fish, and drink.

Resolved: I walk around in the woods, fish, and drink.

May 24

"Frustrated—as were other fishermen on the stream—but curious, I gave up fishing to watch."

—Larry Koller

When you get frustrated fishing, a good thing to do is stop and watch the fish.

Put your rod down and walk away. Disengage yourself from your ardent desire to catch fish. Become an observer. See what you can learn without a rod in your hand, or desire in your heart.

Get a good vantage point and take a look. What are they doing? Ignoring the duns and taking only the stone flies? Some trout will inspect a fly before taking it, the way a jeweler will inspect a rare stone. They're so persnickety, you may never fool them.

One thing is sure: you will never fool them unless you pay close attention. Attention must be paid.

Stopping to watch the fish takes you out of your own head. You scrutinize the fish and let your mind wash over something else for a while. It's a way to give yourself a reprieve.

Sometimes your frustration has less to do with your fishing than other things that may be going on at that moment. While you're stopping and watching, these things may rearrange themselves into a better place in your head.

Fish are not subject to the whims of fishermen. When you stop to watch them a while, you acknowledge their separate reality and learn. You let your own curiosity blossom. Let your curiosity grow in the place formerly occupied by your frustration, and watch what happens.

Resolved: When I get frustrated, I stop and watch the fish.

May 25

"Fishing is not a sport but a pursuit that engages our total selves."

—Nick Lyons

Today, give more than you planned. Give everything you have, then give some more.

Astonish yourself with the breadth of your capacity. You think you can do only so much. You have done only so much on past days. Today, do more.

Engage your total self. Drive farther. Hike longer. Fish longer. Be on the river by dawn. Leave after dark. Fish a new place. Fish until you can fish no more.

Then take a break and fish some more.

Ever notice how the winner in a running race always seems to have something left at the finish? The other competitors struggle and collapse and barely make it across. But the winner busts the tape in a surge of energy. Though he ran as hard and fast as he could, his finish suggests that he could have gone still faster, still harder.

Be like the winner in a running race. Know that you can do more than you currently do, you can surpass your limits, you can break the tape and keep on surging.

If you fall short of your goal, so be it. At least you have tried, and tomorrow you may yet surpass it.

Resolved: I give everything I have, then I give some more.

May 26

"The first virtue: patience. Nothing to do with simple waiting. It is more like obstinacy."

—Andre Gide

The first virtue in fishing is patience. But patience is not simply a matter of waiting around for something good to happen. That's too passive—and frustrating.

Try another tact: be aggressively patient when you fish. Be obstinate. Refuse to give in.

Be a darned bulldog. Get hold of a trout pool and never let it go.

Be like a wall or a rock. Refuse to be moved. Let nothing short of an earthquake budge you from that spot. Then, if an earthquake does occur, ride it out. Pick up the pieces and go back to your spot.

Take the attitude that you will do it until you get it right. Even if it takes thousands of attempts and all your life. Be in it for the long count. If you get knocked down, get back up. Get knocked down again, get back up again. Be the Smokin' Joe Frazier of the trout stream.

Imagine yourself as a cranky Father Time. You've got all the time in the world and you can wait those fish out. Then when you finally hook one and begin to play it, the fish will just see who's on the other end of the line and give up.

Resolved: I become the Smokin' Joe Frazier of the trout stream.

May 27

"Men fish most for themselves."

—Richard Baxter

Fish for yourself.

You spend so much of your life pleasing others, or trying to. Your boss, your customers, your wife, your kids, your friends, your coworkers—enough already. When it comes to fishing, please yourself.

Some may call that selfish. For you it's simple survival. You need to fish or you're going to go out of your mind. Grab the rod and tackle and say good-bye to pleasing other people.

Fish wherever you want. Fish the way you want. Fishing is one area in life where you can do it your way. Fish according to your own methods and practices, the ones that give you the most pleasure and satisfaction.

Fish as long as you want, or as little as you want. If somebody comes along and says with a disapproving wrinkle of his nose that you're not doing it right, whack 'em upside the head. Then tie him to a tree and let the buzzards have him.

Fishing is not about pleasing other people. It's about pleasing yourself.

It's about finding room for yourself in a world that's too crowded and too busy. It's about letting go of the things that govern your daily life in order to find the other more lasting things that have to do with fish and water and earth and sky.

Find your place amid the truly real things in life. Fish for yourself.

Resolved: I fish for myself.

May 28

There's a great story about Edward Ringwood Hewitt, the granddaddy of eastern fly-fishing. An author of angling books and a big kahuna in the New York Angler's Club in the 1930s, Hewitt was famous as a daring innovator, a man who never hesitated to experiment. Fishermen from around the country made pilgrimages to the Neversink River in the Catskills to seek his advice and learn at the feet of the master.

One evening Hewitt was watching his fellow fly-fishers flail around miserably and catch nothing. Finally he picked up his rod, strolled down to the water, and landed a few choice fish in a snap. Asked how he did it, Hewitt explained that there were a variety of aquatic insects on the river. Everybody had been matching the larger ones. Yet these were bitter and the trout didn't like them. The fish preferred the small, dark insects, which were very sweet and much tastier.

But how did you know that? they asked him.

"I tasted them," replied Hewitt.

Follow the lead of one of the deacons of fly-fishing. Consider it part of the learning process. Never shy away from the challenges of fishing. Expand your gastronomical repertoire.

Resolved: I eat bugs.

May 29

"To many fishers, a good knot is a thing of beauty and a comfort to the mind."

—Silvio Calabi

The ability to tie knots is the mark of a good fisherman. A person who fishes a lot ties knots a lot, and he's usually pretty good at both.

Dexterity with a knot often means dexterity with a rod and reel. But knot-tying is more than a utilitarian concern. There's an aesthetic quality to a superbly tied trilene or needle knot, a kind of perfection.

Nothing gives away a beginner quicker than an inadequately tied knot. Here's a challenge: put down this book and tie a blood knot, one of the most useful and solid knots in fishing. After you do it once, do it again. Repetition is the key to knot-tying. Get so good that you could tie it blindfolded.

The best and most obvious way to perfect your knot-tying skills is to fish. Practice is boring and abstract. But when you're on the water, you're motivated because your knots can make the difference between holding a fish on the line, or losing it.

There's a point about knot-tying that goes beyond aesthetics or practicality. It has to do with a person's approach to fishing. If you are going to do a job, why not do a good job? Why not do it to the best of your abilities? If you're going to tie a knot, why not tie the best damn knot you can? Take pride in your knots and you will take pride in yourself as a fisherman.

Resolved: I learn to tie knots like a pro.

May 30

"A skillful angler ought to be a general scholar, and seen in all the liberal sciences."

—Gervase Markham

Every fisherman likes to talk fishing. Almost as many read about it and quite a few write about it. But singing? Old Gervase Markham thought a fisherman's liberal arts knowledge should include music, too.

A fisherman, he wrote, "should not be unskillful in music, that whensoever melancholy, heaviness of his thought, or the perturbations of his own fancies stirreth up sadness in him, he may remove the same with some godly hymn or anthem."

Certainly every fisherman has experienced heaviness of thought and perturbations of fancy after walking away from a stream empty-handed. Finding yourself in this sad state, you may have thought about snapping your rod over your knee or throttling someone's neck, but you have probably never considered singing "Michael, Row the Boat Ashore" or "Amazing Grace."

It seems funny to suggest, but do you think it's worth a try? Just humming these time-honored spirituals (or others like them) has a surprisingly tonic affect on a troubled heart, even a heart made uneasy by so innocent a pastime as fishing. They lift the spirit and inspire even a nonbeliever.

On that lonely and melancholy walk back to camp after a day of frustration, hum "Amazing Grace" softly to yourself. It may lift you out of your momentary frustration and help you realize the true nature of your situation—how lucky you are, how truly sweet this life is, how wonderful it is to be out in the woods and fishing.

Resolved: Okay, I give it a try. I hum "Amazing Grace" the next time fishing brings me down.

May 31

"For the next fifteen minutes the world shrank to a fish and a hook and a line and a reel and a man with a purpose."

—Elizabeth Storer

Be that man. Be the man with a purpose. Let your world shrink to a fish and a hook and a line and a reel.

It is amazing how quickly it happens. You wait seemingly forever. Nothing happens. Then boom! The fish strikes and your world is instantly transformed.

That is why people fish: to be at the center of the vortex, in the eye of the hurricane. Where everything outside is stripped away. Where nothing else matters, and you are living completely in the moment.

When it happens to you, stay calm. Stay calm as the center breaks apart. Stay calm as the world around you goes nuts. The best fishermen maintain this almost Zenlike calm in the face of a running fish and a rod bending almost to its breaking point and a line stretching down into nowhere and the loud, thundering current and an aching, straining back and the thousand other elements that come into play *right now* when you hook a real fighter.

Be purposeful. Be calm about your purpose. It's not easy to do. The blood pressure goes off the meter and your heart leaps with every leap of the fish.

To the extent that you can, step out of the situation even as you are engaged in it. Maintain the coolness of an observer though you are fully participating. Rely on your instincts and training. This will help you make clear decisions and remain true to your purpose.

Resolved: I stay calm amid the storm.

June 1

"Fish or cut bait."

—Saying

So how ya doin'?

In January you resolved to make this the best year of your fishing life. It's now June, the start of the sixth month. How are you faring?

You say you're fishing more than ever and you've got a big Alaska trip planned for next month? Excellent!

Uh, what's that?

Not exactly, you say. What you really meant was that you haven't gone fishing all year, but you did manage to see a cable rerun of "The American Sportsman" episode that took place on the Kenai peninsula?

Sorry for the misunderstanding.

Well, look. That's why today is such a big day for you. There's still plenty of time left, plenty of chances to drop your hook in water. Summer hasn't even started yet.

And fall. Ah, the fall. September and October may be the best time of all to fish. So there's no reason to throw in the towel yet.

All you need to do is rededicate and reaffirm. It can happen, if you make it happen. The best year of your fishing life. Starting today.

Resolved: I rededicate myself to making this the best year of my fishing life.

June 2

An essential part of fishing is knowing how to wait, and patience helps you do that. But how to develop patience?

Sometimes it seems like time stretches out forever in fishing. But that's only because you don't know when a fish is going to strike. You'd have a different, and more charged, sense of time if you knew when it was going to hit, even if that moment was an hour or two away. Your job as a fisherman is to compress the time between strikes, to limit your wait before receiving your reward at the end.

But sometimes the strike never comes. (Or it's a puny little bull trout not worth mentioning.) Where's the reward when that happens?

The key is in how you define *reward*. Define it solely by the number of fish you catch and you will feel rushed and anxious. You will fix your sights on the end of the process and ignore or diminish what leads up to it.

You will always be an impatient fisherman if you see the rewards coming at the end of the process. See your reward in fishing as simply being there, in getting a seat in the amazing natural show unfolding in Dolby sound all around you. See the process itself as the reward. Once you do this you will enjoy it more and be able to endure it longer.

Resolved: I see fishing as its own reward.

June 3

"The rod was fishing me, not I the rod."

—Lee Wulff

People tend to believe that the more you pay for something, the better it is. But Lee Wulff didn't think so.

Wulff, who knew fishing rods the way Stradivarius knew violins, was living in Greenwich Village when he bought a new Payne rod. He paid top dollar for it and fully expected to perform wonders with it.

A funny thing happened. No miracles ensued.

Instead Wulff found himself thinking more about the rod than what he was supposed to do with it. He worried about getting dings in it or wrecking it. He saw his rod as an investment, not a tool. It worked on him mentally to the degree that it interfered with his fishing.

So he got rid of it. He sold it to a friend and bought a far cheaper Heddon. "My fishing became a happier thing," he reported afterward. "I cast with abandon, caught more fish."

Keep this story in mind if you ever run into someone who's worried about scratching his expensive new beauty or seems more concerned about impressing you with his gear than with catching fish. The claims of advertising notwithstanding, it's not the rod that matters, it's the fisherman who wields the rod. A K mart special that catches fish is a great rod.

If your rod ever starts fishing you, junk it or trade down. Like Lee Wulff, your fishing will be a happier thing.

Resolved: I fish my rod, not the other way around.

June 4

"I vow to give fly fishing one season, from June to September, one season of valiant, unwavering interest."

—Allison Moir

Give fly-fishing one season. One season of valiant, unwavering interest.

Maybe—like one or two others—you saw *A River Runs Through It* and your curiosity has been piqued ever since. Give yourself a season to find out what it's like for real.

Maybe you mainly use spinning gear, but you're feeling the urge to progress, to try something more challenging. Take a stab at fly-fishing and give it one season.

Maybe you're a bass fisherman and you consider fly-fishers a bunch of snooty, elitist jerks. Still—apart from the quiche-eaters who do it—the thing does seem sort of interesting. Give it one season and check it out on your own.

What's three months in a life? What else do you have to do this summer? Few things in life are as rewarding, or as stimulating, as learning to catch wild trout using nymphs and flies.

One season, that will be enough if you give it your all. It's not a matter of giving fly-fishing the time. It's a matter of giving yourself the time.

One season. It's not much really, when you consider what you have to gain. You may not become a fly-fisher for life if you give it one full season. But then again, you may. Take the risk. Give your all to fly-fishing for one full season.

Resolved: I give fly-fishing one full season.

June 5

"I have waded the Snake River in the rain and looked up as the sun came out to find a rainbow arching the river; soon afterward I found a rainbow on my line, netted him and let him go—two rainbows in one hour."

—Charles Kuralt

What a day! Two rainbows in an hour. Think of all the things that had to fall into place for this to occur.

First Kuralt had to cut some time out of his schedule. Now retired, Kuralt was a veteran TV newsman whose "On the Road" reports brightened many a "CBS Evening News" broadcast over the years. Then he had to get to Idaho and find his way to the glorious Snake.

Of course Kuralt was a fisherman. So he already had his gear. And he wouldn't have been thrown off by a little rain in the forecast.

He waded out into the river. The rain in the forecast became rain in reality, but he kept casting.

Then the rain stopped and a rainbow appeared like in a storybook. A band of yellow, red, and green arching over the river. There were still gray clouds over the eastern mountains. Through it all Kuralt kept fishing. Then another miracle, this one in the form of a rainbow trout, materialized on his line.

These sorts of miracles are commonplace in fishing. They are a result of a complex, mysterious chain of events that dates back eons and cannot be fully understood or charted. But this much is known: you will never know all the miracles that fishing can bring until you make time in your schedule and go to Idaho.

Resolved: I fish the Snake River.

June 6

"I am, Sir, a Brother of the Angle."

—Izaak Walton

Get a gang and go fishing. A gang is a whole bunch of folks that includes your kids and a couple of their friends, maybe a buddy or two of yours and their kids, and one or two neighbor kids who are just tagging along for kicks.

The youngest ones carry the Cokes. That's the rule. They can't be trusted with the fishing rods, and they have to carry something.

The teenagers, they're bad enough. You have to watch 'em like a hawk to make sure they don't poke anybody in the eye with a rod or walk into a tree.

Give the girls some casts. That's another rule. The boys don't get to hog everything all the time. Girls are part of the gang.

There are so many people, everybody should fan out along the shore and form different groups. People can move around as they like.

It's true, when you fish with a gang, all the kids scare the daylights out of the fish. No sane fish would hang around a group like that. Oh well.

Sometimes fishing is the last thing on the agenda when you fish with a gang. It's more about catching lizards or skipping rocks or exploring the underbrush or sitting in the sun with your fellow brothers of the angle and drinking and talking.

But hey, you don't think you're appreciated in this life? Pull in a good-sized striper and listen to the cheers.

Resolved: I get a gang and go fishing.

June 7

*"Fish that's just been caught is as sweet as corn right off the
stalk."*

—John Hersey

After you get a gang and go fishing, invite the neighborhood
over for a fish fry.

Trout, abalone, stripers, catfish—whatever you're serving,
put it on the grill and cook it up. Dinner at Le Cirque can't
beat a backyard fish fry.

Invite the neighbors, or as many of them as you can stand.
You supply the fish, they supply the salad and corn on the cob
and garlic bread. Everybody brings drinks.

One good thing about a neighborhood fish fry: you have a
whole new audience for your stories. You can tell the story of
how you boated that big cutthroat and people are happy to
hear it. Each time you tell it the fish gets bigger and bigger
and the struggle gets mightier and mightier, of Charleton Hes-
ton proportions. But nobody minds, everybody laughs and
goes along with it because the fish tastes really good and
they've got a couple of glasses of Sangria under their belts and
what do they care?

A fish fry is a feast, a ritual as old as man. Odysseus's crew,
on it's way back from the war in Troy, ate fish and feasted.
The Vikings ate fish and feasted. Polynesian kings on their
Lahaina thrones ate fish and feasted. Native Americans ate fish
and feasted and shared their blessings with starving European
settlers who had come to their land.

The next time you catch a whole bunch of fish, invite the
neighbors over and eat like Polynesian kings.

Resolved: I invite the neighborhood over for a fish fry.

June 8

"Fish in the water represent pure potential. If the water is not clear, we do not know if they exist at all."

—Howell Raines

Howell Raines compares fishing to pulling a rabbit out of a hat. "We have reached into a realm over which we have no explainable mastery and by supernatural craft or mere trickery created a moment that is as phenomenal on the hundredth performance as on the first."

So true. It doesn't matter how many fish a person has pulled out of the water. There is something magical, and mysterious, in the act. It's like connecting with the life force.

Fish represent potential—the unseen. When you land one it emerges from the unseen realm into the seen, from potential to reality. A fish in water is a dream. A fish in a net is a dream achieved.

"It's a kind of creation," as Raines points out, "a birth that brings these creatures from the realm of mystery into the world of reality."

Fishing is a way to tap into your own potential as well. One of the best avenues of self-exploration. You find out a lot about yourself when you fish. Rod and reel are tools not only for fishing, but for exploring the unseen parts of your being.

Make a commitment today to maximize your potential. Turn dreams into fact. Not only in fishing, but in life.

Resolved: I get the most out of fishing that I possibly can.

June 9

"Every day I see the head of the largest trout I ever hooked, but did not land."

—Theodore Gordon

If something ails you in fishing, face it. Confront it. Look it squarely in the eye. This is the only hope you have to overcome the thing that is bothering you.

Unhappy with some element of your technique? Dissatisfied with your casting? Wish you fished more? Disgruntled with your fishing partner? Think you need new, or better, equipment? Still pining about the one that got away?

Whatever is nagging at you, the only way to get on top of it is to see it for what it is. Identify it. Isolate it. Even if you are never able to get rid of it entirely, you can control its influence.

By identifying it, by taking its measure, you simultaneously limit its power. When you can't put your finger on a thing, it's harder to control. It's amorphous and its influence spreads like an oil slick. It starts as a small thing that insidiously grows to ruin the entire fishery.

Get a positive ID on the thing that is bothering you, and you can stop it cold. You assign a boundary to it, a fence that limits its destructive power and its ability to spread. You separate it from the other parts of your fishing that are healthy and good.

Identify what's bothering you. Work on *that* while continuing to enjoy the things that you do well.

Resolved: I never let a little thing bug me too much.

June 10

Tired of the crowds? Tired of meek hatchery fish? Tired of puny dried up streams made dirty by cities and factories? Like Herman Melville and Ernest Hemingway and Jack London, go to the sea.

There is a mystery in the sea that a river or lake will never possess. Its vastness overwhelms. When you lose sight of shore you are truly alone, surrounded and engulfed by an immensity far greater and stronger than you.

If you do not respect the sea's power, you will be humbled by it. And sometimes even if you do respect it, you are humbled by it.

William Humphrey writes, "We have polluted it, depleted it, we have all but exterminated the leviathans Melville fished for in it, yet it endures, outwardly unchanged. The ocean withstands our imposition. In its ceaseless motion lies its permanence."

Those ancient leviathans may be off limits, but there are still tarpon and tuna and sailfish and bonefish and marlin and barracuda and shark. Need a new challenge? Want a break from inland waters? Want to try your hand at something different, and test your abilities on a grand scale?

Go to a vastness that overwhelms. Lose sight of shore. Go to the sea.

Resolved: I try a change of pace. I fish salt water.

June 11

"There are four legs to stand on. The first, be romantic. The second, be passionate. The third, be imaginative. And the fourth, never be rushed."

—Charles Olson

Treat fishing as you would your lover or wife. Charles Olson suggests these four ways:

1. Be a hopeless romantic. There is more to fishing than the size of your tippet. Revel in the process of it, not solely the results you obtain from it.
2. Be passionate. Pour yourself into it. Give yourself totally. Hold nothing back. Your lover will respond in kind.
3. Engage in flights of fancy. You do not have to do it the same way every time. There are other ways that are equally and perhaps even more stimulating. Experiment. Find new ways of doing things.
4. Lastly—and this, above all—take your time. Fishing is like any lover. It does not want to be rushed. It does not want to be a temporary stopover on your way to more important things. It wants to feel like it is the most important thing in your life.

Romance. Passion. Imagination. Taking your time. These are the secrets of fishing, and of making love. It is probably wise, however, not to share this comparison with your wife or lover. She may not take it too well when you explain that making love to her is like catching a trout. You may find yourself sleeping in the garage.

Resolved: I love fishing and my spouse, but not at the same time.

June 12

"People say they have theories, know where to find fish. I never know when I'm going to catch a fish."

—Tommy Martin, bass champion

A theory never caught a fish. Only a fisherman can catch a fish.

At one time scientists believed that the sun revolved around the earth. That was a theory. At another time scientists believed that the earth was flat and that if you sailed far enough across it in one direction, you'd fall off. That was another theory.

At one time the medical community believed that dirty hands had nothing to do with the transmission of disease. They resisted the idea that a surgeon wash his hands after operating on a patient.

There are plenty of theories in fishing, too. Some are good, some are not. All are limited.

A theory is only that—a theory. Put your faith in a theory, and a rude awakening awaits you when you finally introduce it to reality. A theory is a hothouse plant. Keep it inside under controlled conditions, and it will survive and even thrive. Plant it outside the greenhouse, let it live on its own in nature, and it will wither and die.

If a theory helps you catch fish, great. If it doesn't, dump it like last week's trash. Despite what they say, people don't really know when or where they're going to catch fish. Let others do the theorizing. You have no stake in theories. Your stake is in catching fish, that's all.

Resolved: I never let a theory get in the way of my fishing.

June 13

"'Oh it's a big one,' he shouted, 'I think it's a big one.' And when he finally reached down to lift the fish over the side, I could see that it was a big one, wet and silver-scaled with great black stripes."

—Charles Kuralt

Set your sights on the big picture, the big score, the big fish.

Anybody can catch a small fry. You're not just anybody. Go for the big ones.

A big fish requires a big effort, but it's worth it. A big fish ought to take a big effort. There's a rightness and symmetry to that.

Sometimes a little fish can take almost as much effort as a big one—and what do you get in return? Little fish, like little projects, fritter away your energy and time. The effort is always worthwhile when a big fish appears over the side of the boat.

Every fish has value. A little fish can outfight a big fish. But on the whole, everyone would rather catch a big fish than a little one. A big fish always has meaning. A big fish implies high adventure; it demands a story. It assumes a modicum of difficulty. Most important perhaps, it speaks volumes about the person who hauled it in. Now *that's* a fish and *that's* a fisherman.

A big fish somehow feels different—the intensity of the strike, the pull on the line, like you have hooked into some mammoth creature of the deep.

You will not always catch big fish. But you must always, always pursue them.

Resolved: Always, in the back of my mind, I hunt big fish.

June 14

"My birthday began with the water."

—Dylan Thomas

Today's your birthday. Happy birthday! What are you going to do to celebrate?

(Okay, maybe today isn't your birthday. But there is no denying that at some point this year, you will have a birthday. At which time the same question must be posed.)

For fishermen, the answer is simple: go fishing. Or if you cannot fish exactly on the day of your birth, make arrangements for same.

Nobody can begrudge you this simple wish. When you're young, birthdays are happy and carefree. As you get older they are occasions more for reflection and taking stock. There is no better way to celebrate one's birthday than with a fishing rod in one's hand, and no better place than on a wild mountain trout stream.

As you ponder your passing years you observe the timelessness of the river and the mountains and the sky, and there is solace in that. At night you raise a toast of Jameson's to your lips, and howl at the stars.

You were conceived and grew in water. You spent the first formative months of your life in the watery sac of your mother's womb. You resembled a fish at first, with gill-like appendages that later became ears. You came from water and now, on the day you celebrate leaving it, go back to it.

Resolved: I spend my birthday on the water.

June 15

"These were the enchanting words: remote and difficult."

—E. Annie Proulx

You do not need a four-wheel drive to go to remote and difficult places; what you need is a fishing car. A fishing car can be a truck or a car or even a 4WD. But it is never new and almost always beat to hell.

E. Annie Proulx's fishing car went eight hundred miles on no transmission fluid. But it only had an eight-inch clearance from the ground, and it nearly sank in the rain-engorged spring logging roads of backwoods Maine. She says, "I have never seen a car so hung up. Only the tops of the tires showed. Sven had to crawl out the window because the lower edges of the doors were deep in the ground. All the way, from the front bumper (somewhere down there) to the exhaust pipe, the fishing car was interred."

But they got it out. That's the true mark of a fishing car: it's a survivor. It always makes it.

There are maps and sunglasses and tapes and matches crammed into the glove compartment. McDonald's milkshake cups, socks, shoes, gum wrappers, beer cans, newspapers litter the floors. The windshield wipers don't work; the side door is crushed in and held together by duct tape. But it runs and runs and runs, long past the time those newer, wimpier vehicles have given up, groaning and weeping in misery.

Want to go to remote and difficult places? There is only one way. Get yourself a fishing car.

Resolved: I clean out my fishing car and get it ready for my next trip.

June 16

"There is a peculiar pleasure in catching a trout in a place where nobody thinks of looking for them, and at an hour when everybody believes they cannot be caught."

—Henry Van Dyke

Fish run in schools; so do fishermen. Catch a trout where nobody has thought of looking for them.

Defy the conventional wisdom of the stream. Pay no heed to the nattering nabobs of negativism. Go down a path of your own choosing, one that leads you away from the pack and possibly toward fish.

Nobody has all the answers. Very few even ask the right questions. When you see a man seated on the bank in conversation with a fish, the two of them politely sharing biscuits and tea, follow that man. Until such time arrives, trust your own judgment. Listen to your own streamside counsel.

Many people will tell you why your plans cannot succeed. They will explain that the odds against you are impossibly high. They will think you're foolish and want you to give up, as they themselves have given up. Your decision to give up will vindicate and support their own.

There are plenty of fish out there, in places where no one suspects. But you must be willing to strike out after them, to look for them where no one else is looking, at hours of the day and night when everyone else thinks you're out of your mind. How satisfying it is to catch one this way!

Resolved: I look for fish where nobody else thinks they are.

June 17

"The unique ardor of the trout fisherman is best complemented by blaming failure, not on his own ineptness, but on the devastating cunning of his wily antagonist."

—Harold F. Blaisdell

Do the best you can. Who can fault you for that?

Fishing is a sport that makes a mockery of conscious striving. Trout and their watery brethren love to frustrate people who give it that old college try.

Most fish are uneducated and never went to college. Perhaps that is why they do not understand such concepts and tease the people who hold them dear.

At any rate, your response is clear: do the best you can. There is honor and dignity in that, and you owe yourself nothing less. It is the one sure way to find out if you can do all the things that your heart believes you can. You leave too many unanswered questions if you give anything less than your best.

What's the sense in saving it for another day? Give it all up, see what you have. How else will you know?

When you try something for the first time, do the best you can. When you go somewhere new, do the best you can. When you decide to go upstream in search of fish, do the best you can. Over time you will come to know your limits and how to extend them. Doing the best you can will make you do better, in fishing and everything else.

Resolved: I do better.

June 18

"Every now and then, I saw a dimple on the water when a trout rose to swallow a fallen bug. I had to swallow my desire to run to the car and grab my rod. The sitting still was an act of discipline."

—Bill Barich

Sitting still *is* an act of discipline, especially on the first day of a fishing trip. The juices are flowing. All that pent-up energy and desire have to be released. You'd run over your own grandmother if she got between you and the stream.

Bill Barich offers a more tempered approach: "The notion was to be calm instead of frenzied, as I usually am on the first day. I concentrated on the creek, its flow, the channels where fish were feeding, trying to commit the details to memory. It takes a long time before you begin to see things with any degree of actuality."

Barich saw things with such actuality that he didn't even go fishing right away. He drove to the lodge and checked in.

Being calm is always good in fishing but especially on that excitable first day. Why not hold those impulses in check for a while? Swallow your desire to run to the car and grab your rod. Concentrate on the creek, what the fish are doing. Commit the details to memory and maybe come back later in the day when your chances are better.

If you're like that the first day, think how laid-back you'll be on the second and third days. Butterflies will alight on your hand, birds will perch on your shoulder. And the trout? Well, they'll probably be as ornery as usual, but at least you'll be in the right mood to face them.

Resolved: I take it nice and easy on that first day.

June 19

"One of the few advantages of maturity is that petty failures no longer make you break rods, get drunk and curse at strangers."
—Bill Barich

Control what you can control. Then let the rest of it go.

Can't control the wind. Can't control the rain. Can't control the fish. Can't control your line breaking or some of those other petty failures that fishermen endure.

If you can't control it, what's the sense of getting upset about it? Of fighting it? Railing against it? Trying to manage or manipulate it? It is beyond manipulation, beyond control. The only reasonable thing to do in the situation—if you can be reasonable, which is sometimes hard—is let it go.

Let go of the things you cannot control, and move on. Many a fisherman has gained this hard-earned maturity only after a long struggle.

When you seek to control what you cannot control you turn your power over to it. You lose control. The wind is the wind. But it comes to occupy a place in your mind far greater than its actual nuisance power, which can be considerable. It becomes a monster. And it controls you.

Focus on what you can control. Match the hatch. Attend to your rod and tackle and make good casts despite the conditions. Control yourself and your own mind. Control your actions. Let those petty failures and all the rest of it go.

Resolved: I let go of the things I can't control in fishing.

June 20

"Faith without works is dead."

—James 2:26

Do the work. Put in the time.

There is a craft to fishing. It takes considerable skill to do it well. You will never fully learn the craft and develop the skills unless you put in the time and do the work.

Fishing is not work. It's meant to be fun. But like any other discipline, to be good at it you have to work at it.

You have to read about it. You have to practice. You have to listen and watch others. Mostly, you have to fish. That all requires time and an unwavering commitment to your craft.

Look at the best fishermen. They've been doing it all their lives. They do it because they love it, but they've also put in a good chunk of time working at it. There's no way around it. You've simply got to get down to the stream and do it.

Did you expect a shortcut? Take a magic pill and instantly become Joan Wulff? Doesn't work that way. You can get something out of fishing as soon as you drop a hook into water. But to get good and stay good you've got to put in the time and do the work.

Resolved: I have faith in myself and my fishing. I keep working at it.

June 21

"Being outdoors on a sunlit day is the only self-justifying state of existence I know."

—Le Anne Schreiber

Here is an excellent, sunlit resolution: fish more this summer than any other summer before.

Hold it.

On second thought, that may be too ambitious an agenda for this time of year. Ambition is an emotion better suited for fall or winter. Ambition does not belong in the tackle box of the summer fisherman.

The whole idea of fishing is to get away from things for a while and relax. By quantifying the idea—more fishing than ever before—you put subliminal pressure on yourself. It becomes a goal and sets you up for disappointment if you don't achieve it. It makes you fix on the thing rather than the doing of the thing, which can spoil your fun.

It's like focusing on the number of fish you catch, rather than the fishing itself. You judge your day solely by results, and lose the point of it.

Summer is not a time for resolutions. Summer is a time for lazing around, getting away from it all, playing hookey. Time to pack up all your cares and woes. Time to fish without goals in mind. Time to shirk responsibility for a while.

Okay then, make it this: lots and lots of fishing this summer. But no pressure.

Resolved: I fish a whole bunch this summer.

June 22

The famous One Fly Competion in Jackson Hole, Wyoming, requires fishermen to fish with only one fly per day. It's a two-day contest. Participants earn points based on the number and size of the fish caught (and released). Each fisherman registers his fly with contest officials in the morning, and that's what he uses all day long. If he loses his fly in the brush, tough luck. He's through for the day (he can keep fishing, just not for points).

Now in ordinary circumstances, a fly-fisherman uses a variety of flies. Conditions change and he changes his flies accordingly. Something works for a while, then doesn't. Or nothing works at all and he keeps trying until he finds what does. In fly-fishing as in life, you want to keep your options open.

But have you ever noticed that if you give a small child a lot of choices, he or she doesn't know what to do? You can run into the same problem fishing. It's possible to have too many choices, to place too much importance on the type of fly you're working. As has been noted elsewhere, it's not the fly that catches fish, it's the fisherman.

Why not hold your own One Fly Competition? You and your buddies, one fly, all day long, see who wins. You will be amazed to learn how well you can do with less.

Resolved: All right, we give it a whirl. My buddies and me, one fly, all day long.

June 23

"Stalking is another of the fundamentals upon which one may judge the quality of an angler."

—Alfred Miller

Fishing is a religion, and as with many religions, sometimes a believer must get down on his knees. He must stalk the fish. He must climb and wade. He must bushwhack through the underbrush (though quietly). He must get down and crawl.

It is said that Ray Bergman wore out the knees of his waders from constant crawling to get to places that he would have never reached on his two feet.

The story is told of another fisherman who fished on his knees on an upper stretch of the Nissequogue River on Long Island. He made his way up the stream for a quarter of a mile, inching forward on his knees.

Sometimes you need to do things like that to get to the best places to fish. They are accessible no other way. Many fishermen are lazy by nature and prefer not to work that hard. These fellows may not catch many fish, either.

There is a spiritual component to all this. When you crawl on the ground or fish while kneeling (so the fish don't see you), you show the proper humility. It is, as one Englishman put it, "an attitude of reverence to the fish." You may want to remember this the next time you fish. Go down on your knees before the fishing gods, and they may show you mercy.

Resolved: I fish on my knees, if necessary.

June 24

"I open the door to my father's office. Once it really was an office, piled with paper and books, but long ago it was turned into a fly-tying and rod-building room."

—Gretchen Legler

You want to be a writer? Get a quiet place to write. Want to paint? Get a loft or studio. If you want to do anything with a real commitment, you need a physical space to do it in.

So what's different about fishing? Nothing. You need a room of your own, a place where you can tie flies.

Gretchen Legler describes what it was like to visit her father's fly-tying room: "When I open the door a smell rich and thick meets my nose—a smell of the skins of birds and old, old smoke. The walls are still thickly covered with plastic bags of fly-tying material hanging from hooks; peacock herl, rabbit fur, skins of mallards and woodducks, tinsel and bright yarn, packages of turkey quills, pheasant necks, swatches of deer hair."

To a kid a room like that is magical, full of strange, incredible objects. Hooks, glue, tweezers, tools, fly-tying vises. And the flies themselves! "Elaborate streamers, tiny imitation mosquitoes, deer-hair grasshoppers of varying sizes, scrubby-looking nymphs and elegant Royal Coachmans," were what Gretchen found in her father's room.

Think about how you can develop a room like that. Maybe in the garage or attic. A room somehow removed from the rest of the house, a room to store your rod and tackle properly, a room to tie flies.

Resolved: I give myself a fishing room.

June 25

"I fished with a man who knew all the secrets. Fish lay where he said they should lie and took hold as he said they would take, and one remembered and fished it that way for oneself until the knowledge was properly one's own."

—Roderick Haig-Brown

This is the way it works, the way of the world. You fish with somebody who knows, a man who knows all the secrets. For most young fishermen, it's their father. He knows all about fishing because he's been doing it a long time. He knows things you never even thought about.

He passes this knowledge on because to keep it to himself would be a selfish act, and you try your best to absorb it. It's not easy, it takes time. Fishing is not a thing that you suddenly know how to do, like solving a math problem. Much of what a person learns seats itself in the subconscious. You learn things slowly over a period of months and years, and gradually this knowledge becomes your own.

Eventually you become the man with the knowledge, the man with the secrets. Your duty as the keeper of the secrets is to share them with your son or daughter, just as your father shared them with you.

When was the last time you took your kid on a fishing trip? Well, it's summer. The weather's warm. The kids are out of school. It's time to go again.

Time to pass on more secrets. Time to share the knowledge. Time to prepare your kid for the day when he or she becomes the keeper of the secrets.

Resolved: I take my son or daughter on a start-of-summer fishing trip.

June 26

Forget art. Do everything as well as you can.

Do it, don't overdo it. You don't have to create a masterpiece when you go fishing. A good, honest job will suffice.

Run from pretentiousness as if it were a man with a gun. Pretentiousness has no place on a trout stream. A fisherman who's a jerk is still a jerk.

In architecture as well as fly-fishing, form is function. You're thinking about the wrong thing if all you can think about is the beauty of your casting loops. A god-awful, ugly-as-sin cast that hooks a fish is always better than a picture-perfect cast that doesn't.

Some people think of fly-fishing as an art. Who the hell knows? But until you see a trout sipping chilled Chardonnay at a Soho gallery or applauding at the opening of the latest Harold Pinter play, it is probably best not to worry about things like that too much.

Let the aesthetes fret about art. No pencil-necked aesthete ever caught a fish in his life.

Art is for snobs. Fishing is for people who like to catch fish. Never forget it.

Resolved: To hell with art, I'm fishing.

June 27

"We do not understand the earth in terms either of what it offers us or of what it requires of us, and I think it is the rule that people inevitably destroy what they do not understand."

—Wendell Berry

Show a righteous indignation about all the forces that threaten fish.

Show a righteous indignation about the destruction of fish-and-game habitat virtually everywhere on the planet.

Show a righteous indignation that wild, free-running rivers and creeks have been destroyed by dams.

Show a righteous indignation about man's callous degradation of fish spawning grounds, like the sacking of temples of worship by jack-booted armies.

Show a righteous indignation that coho salmon populations are endangered off the Pacific Coast and so many other species on all coasts have been lost entirely.

Show a righteous indignation that once-pristine lakes and waterways are now fouled with oil, garbage, and other forms of pollution.

Show a righteous indignation that even the ocean, the mighty ocean, is being suffocated by pollution.

Show a righteous indignation that where fishermen once fished happily in the rivers that flowed through their towns and cities, many of those same rivers are now dead or entombed under concrete.

Show a righteous indignation that the forces that threaten wild fish and wild rivers and clean skies and open spaces are forever on the march and must be stopped.

Resolved: I show a righteous indignation about all that threatens fish.

June 28

"When I return to my seat I pull from my red backpack a book my friend gave me, The River Why by David James Duncan. It is a book about fishing for people who don't fish."

—Gretchen Legler

There are people who love fishing but don't like to fish. Instead they like to sit under a tree and read while other people fish. And then they like to eat the fish that other people catch.

The River Why is an excellent book about fishing for people who don't fish. It's a man's journey of self-discovery. Self-discovery is a big theme in books for people who like to read and eat, but not fish.

Another excellent fishing title for nonfishermen is *Trout Fishing in America*, by Richard Brautigan. Brautigan is a 1960s-era beatnik-hippie who records his impressions of life and people as he goes on fishing trips.

Norman Maclean's *A River Runs Through It* may be the best-known nonfishing fishing book of all time. It inspired a popular movie starring Brad Pitt. *Blues*, by John Hersey, is as much about philosophy and history as it is about bluefish.

Women generally take a different slant on fishing than men. Less technical, more introspective. *A Different Angle* is a collection of works on fly-fishing by women writers. Included are Joan Wulff, Gretchen Legler, Le Anne Schreiber, and the wondrous E. Annie Proulx.

These are only suggestions. There are many more great titles to choose from when you decide to go fishing but don't want to fish.

Resolved: I read *The River Why*.

June 29

"Then, mirable dictu, I hooked a fish."

—P. J. O'Rourke

Having a hard time of it? Nobody had a harder time of it than P. J. O'Rourke.

"When I stepped in the river, my act came to pieces," he explains. "My line hit the water like an Olympic belly flop medalist. I hooked four 'tree trout' in three minutes. The only thing I could manage to get a drag-free float on was me after I stepped in a hole. And the trout? The trout laughed."

Then something happened. Something miraculous. He hooked a fish.

He goes on, "I lifted my rod—the first thing I'd done right in two days—and the trout actually leaped out of the water as if it were trying for a *Field & Stream* playmate centerfold." His voice rose three octaves in his excitement. It was a rainbow trout, at least five or seven inches long. To P. J. it resembled a marlin. "I haven't been so happy since I passed my driver's license exam," he says.

Whether you're a hard-core vet or a neophyte like P. J. O'Rourke, catching a fish is always something of a miracle. It always takes you by surprise, even when you expect it. It always grabs you in some way.

Doesn't matter how cynical you think you are. Doesn't matter how skeptical you've become about life or anything else. Doesn't matter how many times you've done it before. Catching a fish is a simple miracle that makes you happy.

Resolved: I make myself happy. I fish.

June 30

"If the building of the bridge does not enrich the awareness of those who work on it, then the bridge ought not to be built."

—Frantz Fanon

Every time you fish is an opportunity to enrich your awareness. Of yourself and the world around you.

Every time you fish is an opportunity to learn. About fishing and fish. About water and trees and rocks and earth and sky.

Every time you fish is an opportunity to get to know an old friend, or a parent, or a child. No better way to get to know a person, or become reacquainted with one, than on a fishing trip.

Every time you fish is an opportunity to discover something about yourself that you did not know.

Every time you fish is an opportunity to go to a place you've never been.

Every time you fish is an opportunity to become a better fisherman. An opportunity to test your abilities in different environments and in different ways.

Every time you fish is an opportunity to grow as a human being. It may not just be an opportunity, but an obligation. What's the point of fishing if you're not learning from it? What's the point of doing anything if you're not using what you've learned to build a bridge to the world at large?

Resolved: Every time I fish, I view it as an opportunity.

July 1

"The trout do not rise in Greenwood Cemetery."

—Saying

Get up and tackle the day.

Don't wait for the day to come to you; go out and meet it on the front lawn. Invite it inside for a cup of coffee and a doughnut. Hello!

Quit waiting for tomorrow. Tomorrow never comes. Today is the day. Bring it on.

You have no choice. Today is going to happen whether you like it or not. Whether you're ready or not. So get up and face it. *Now*. Get on top of it before it gets on top of you.

A day is like a wave. It will break over you and knock you over if you're looking in the other direction. Why not grab a board, see the wave forming, get into position, paddle like hell, jump to your feet, and ride?

Great things lie ahead. Great fishing—and surfing, too! Get up, get out of bed, and go after it.

Listen. This may sound morose, but it's true: you're going to be dead a long time. You're going to sleep the big sleep for *centuries*. So as Sparse Grey Hackle says, "You had better do your fishing while you are still able."

Do you feel all right? Are you able? Well then, bring it on.

Resolved: I get up and tackle the day.

July 2

Every fisherman has his own fishing secret, something that works for him alone. These secrets sometimes have nothing to do with how to tie a bomber or other technical issues.

There's a poignant scene toward the end of *The Godfather, Part II*, in which Fredo Corleone is talking to his young nephew about fishing. They're sitting on a dock in Lake Tahoe.

"Wanna know how to catch a big fish?" Fredo asks. The boy nods yes, and Fredo confides in him in a knowing, big brotherly way. He says that every time he wants to catch a big fish, he says a Hail Mary. He says it has never failed him. He says whenever he goes fishing, other people are amazed as he pulls all these fish out of the water. But they don't know his secret: saying a Hail Mary before each one.

Now this did not save poor Fredo, who was shot dead a few scenes later, but what's wrong with having a fishing secret of this kind? It doesn't have to be religious in nature. It can be the Hail Mary, a piece of a Yeats poem, a saying, an inspirational thought, the University of Southern California Trojan fight song—whatever.

If it speaks to you, it has value. If it gives you comfort or pleasure or satisfies you in some way, there is a kind of truth in it. Never be afraid to whisper it softly to yourself while fishing.

Resolved: I hold my personal fishing truths sacred.

July 3

"I learn by going where I have to go."

—Theodore Roethke

How do you learn to fish? How do you learn *anything*? By going where you have to go.

You have a certain idea of what you need to do and what you need to learn. These expectations can be flat-out wrong. Go where you have to go, and you will find what you really need to learn after all.

Want to fish in New Zealand? Learn by going. Want to try for tarpon off the Florida coast? Learn by going.

Let your desires lead you. Your desires will make you go. Once you are there you will learn all you have to learn.

You can learn before you go. You can talk to your friends and read about it in books. All that is valuable. But it will never be as valuable as what you learn with your own eyes, on the stream itself, doing the things your desire tells you to do.

Mastering fishing can seem like a mountain at times. It is so intimidating, there is so much to learn. Because the mountain is so big and vast, you shy away from attempting to climb it at all. Never let learning intimidate you in this way.

Go where you have to go, and you will find what you need to learn.

Resolved: I learn by going. To New Zealand, Florida, or wherever I desire.

July 4

"It is impossible to avoid the conclusion that the fishing habit, by promoting close association with nature, by teaching patience and by generating or stimulating useful contemplation, tends directly to the increase of the intellectual power of its votaries and through them to the improvement of our national character."

—Grover Cleveland

Today's a holiday, a day off. What better way to spend a day off than fishing?

It's Independence Day, the Fourth of July. Declare your independence from your regular routine, and fish.

Make your own sort of fireworks show. Pull a wild rainbow from a stream.

It is the patriotic thing to do. Your country needs you to fish. A former president even said so. Fishing promotes a close association with nature. It teaches patience and thoughtfulness.

Not only that, it increases your brainpower. Now *that's* a new one.

Because fishing does all these things (and more), it improves a person's character. One person can make a difference. He can do good work. He can exert a positive influence on his children, his friends and family, his neighborhood, his city or town, his state, and yes, even his country.

Consider it not only a pleasure to fish today, but also your duty. It is your duty to skip out on the usual Fourth of July barbecues and go find some untouched mountain stream where the trout are rising.

Resolved: I celebrate my independence today. I fish.

July 5

"Trout are like dreams hovering in the elusive unconscious. In capturing one, if ever so briefly, before release, there is that sense of revelation occurring when one awakens in the night, snatching a dream from the dark portals of sleep."

—Kitty Pearson-Vincent

Do something you've never done before in fishing.

It could be something small, or something large. It could be a thing you've thought about doing for a long time, or maybe it's just come up recently. Whatever it is, take it out of the realm of dreams and do it. It's time.

Maybe you've secretly been afraid of it. Afraid of failing, or whatever. It's time to put the fear behind you.

If you can't immediately do this thing you're contemplating, well, that's the way it goes sometimes. But at least you've faced it. You've taken that hazy, unconscious thing hovering in your mind and made it concrete. Sooner or later, if you keep after it, you will accomplish it.

Fix on a far target. Hit it, then move on to a new target, one that is even farther away and more difficult than the original. This is how every fisherman learns and improves. He never gets comfortable with doing the things he knows. He keeps doing things he's never done before, keeps seeking revelations, ever pushing his boundaries outward.

Resolved: I do something in fishing I've never done before.

July 6

"Experience is knowing that you've made this mistake before."

—Saying

Learn from your failures as well as your successes.

Lose a fish? Strike too fast? Learn from it. A failure is only a failure if you regard it as one.

Everybody makes mistakes. The only real mistake you can make is thinking you have nothing to learn from your mistakes.

Bobby Jones, the famous old-time golfer, said that he learned more from the balls he skulled than the ones he hit well. The same applies to fishing. You can learn more from the fish you don't catch than the ones you do.

Why aren't you catching fish? What are you using? Where are you fishing? How did you approach? What's the time of day? Every situation in fishing is a kind of outdoor classroom, suitable for learning and growth.

Nothing is wasted, in fishing or life. Something that you did or thought twenty years ago can pay off for you today. That's true for your mistakes, too.

One could even argue that there is no such thing as a mistake—that everything happens for a purpose, although we may have trouble divining its meaning at first. Look always for the greater meaning underlying your mistakes, and your fishing will rapidly improve.

Resolved: I regard my mistakes as opportunities for learning.

July 7

"It's hard to imagine any water being clearer or colder than the North Umpqua in the springtime."

—Richard Hoyt

Feel the cold. It's great, isn't it?

Okay. It's bone-chilling cold, and that's never entirely great. But the fact that you are feeling the cold, the fact that you are out on the North Umpqua in your waders, the river flowing between your legs—that's great, isn't it?

Now tilt your cap back and lift your head. What do you feel now? Does that feel good or what?

After a while you wade to shore, take a break. Maybe eat an orange and lie back in the sand. Then you can really feel it. That hot, hot Oregon sun shining down on you like a heat lamp.

Here's another great thing about fishing: it's not an in-between sort of experience. It's a journey between extremes. The burning heat of the sun, the freezing cold of the water. Nothing wishy-washy about it. It's one or the other, and often both at the same time.

Health nuts like to swim in ice-cold water, then jump out and go directly into a steaming hot sauna. Moving between the extremes of hot and cold is good for the blood circulation, they say, good for the body and soul.

What about you, felt the extremes lately? The numbing coldness of a snow-fed river, the searing heat of a late afternoon sun? Fishing can be an uncomfortable physical experience at times, but at least it's not wishy-washy. And its extremes will make you feel alive.

Resolved: I imagine the cold, cold waters of the North Umpqua. And I go.

July 8

"I said, 'What a beautiful place!' He replied, 'Trout can only live in beautiful places.'"

—Charles Kuralt

Want to find trout? Go to a beautiful place.

Go to hard-to-find places. Go to places where you travel down dirt roads for miles and miles and you're still not there. Go to places where there are no dirt roads—no roads of any kind. Go to places where you have to hike up along ridges and down into canyons.

That's where you'll find trout. At the bottom of the canyon, a day's walk from the trailhead. A river will slice through the granite walls like a silver ribbon. It will be as pretty as a postcard.

Trout are like rich people. They're snobs. They live in the fishy equivalents of Martha's Vineyard and the Côte d'Azur. Go to these high-rent places and you will find them lounging around the pools, dining according to fancy and whim, turning their noses up at anything that does not please their overly refined aesthetic sensibilities.

Seek beautiful places, and therefore, trout. Every other piece of advice on where to find trout is rubbish. You do not need a guidebook. Just look for beautiful water. You'll find them somewhere in the vicinity.

Turn your thinking around. Instead of thinking trout first, think beauty. Let your appreciation of beauty and nature lead you to trout. For a trout must love beauty even more than caddis flies. Why else would it live in such places?

Resolved: I seek beautiful places, and therefore, trout.

July 9

"This is another picture of me fly fishing. . . . My fly rod is tucked under one arm, and in my other hand I am holding a shining, flickering cutthroat trout upside down by the tail. I learned all this from my father."

—Gretchen Legler

Among the things Gretchen learned from her father was how to resuscitate a dying fish. She was fishing one day with her father and husband, and after waiting all morning to get a strike, her husband hooked a big fish. He played it too long, however, and nearly killed it.

Her dad stepped in. Gretchen watched as he moved it "slowly back and forth in the water, forcing oxygen into its gills." The fish swam off upstream as if born again.

Another thing Gretchen's father taught her was about strike indicators. Unsure how to fish a small trout stream in southern Minnesota, she asked for his advice. He told her to use wet flies. "He sent me a gift of a small packet of fluorescent green and orange 'strike indicators,' bits of colored foam tape you tear off and stick on your leader when you are using a nymph," she recalls. "You watch the strike indicator and when it stops moving, odds are your nymph is being nibbled by a trout." Her dad's tip helped her catch fish.

It's easy to turn the old man off. Your father, the fishing expert. His advice is frequently repetitive, overbearing, and dogmatic. But he does know about things like strike indicators and how to revive a dying fish. So cut the old man some slack. Throw him a bone. Listen to him once in a while. He'll feel better and who knows, you may even learn something.

Resolved: I listen to my dad's fishing tips.

July 10

Let the day stretch out in front of you. Let it stretch out in front of you like a long, flat Nevada highway.

When you're fishing, imagine you're a retiree with time to kill. (Maybe you *are*. In which case, good for you.) You've got nothing to do and plenty of time to do it in.

Never tell anybody that you're coming back from a day of fishing at a specific time. Leave it hazy and uncertain; give or take an hour or three. If you say you'll be back at six, you put implicit pressure on yourself to produce results. Deadlines imply results.

That's partly why you fish. To leave clocks and deadines behind. You don't want time to pull you anywhere. That happens enough as it is. You want to follow the day wherever it leads you, for however long it takes.

It's summer. The days are longer and warmer. Perfect for ambling about and fishing and coming back after dark, or maybe not at all.

Some say this is wasting time. They don't know what they're talking about. Wasting time is doing work that nobody cares about, including yourself, and which has only one purpose: making money. That's a real waste of time.

Fishing is never a waste of time. It's good, productive soul time. And it's best when you can ease your usual grip on time and deadlines.

Resolved: I come back from a day of fishing whenever I feel like it.

July 11

"I don't like to go fishing by myself. I want to go out with someone to strap it on his backside."

—Ricky Green, bass fisherman

Forget solitude.

Forget communing with nature.

Forget all that mystical mumbo jumbo from *A River Runs Through It*.

Sometimes the best thing to do is go out with someone and strap it to his backside.

In plain terms, that means catch more fish than he does. More fish and bigger fish. And more bigger fish. He catches a twelve-pounder, you pull in an eighteen. He catches the biggest bass on record in the morning. You break his record in the afternoon.

Is it pretty? Nope. Is it enlightened? Nope. Is it fun? You bet.

A big fish is money in the bank. It's bragging rights. It's being able to say over beers at Cliff's that you caught the biggest fish of anybody that day.

Of course, you gotta remember: he who lives by the bass-catching stick dies by the bass-catching stick, and all that. Today you're slapping it to his backside, but tomorrow your rear end is shiny and red as a vine-ripened tomato.

Still, it's a good game to play and no harm between friends. Whoever gets the most fish, wins. Whoever gets the biggest, wins. It's every man for himself, and may the best man win.

Resolved: I strap it to his backside.

July 12

"Most people would just as soon eat barbeque without licking their lips as catch fish without wiping their hands on their pants. It takes the fun out of it."

—Roy Blount Jr.

Always be a fisherman who wipes his hands on his pants. What's the point of fishing if you can't get all dirty and grungy and smell like hell?

There's a famous postcard that reads, "Old fisherman never die . . . they just smell that way." That just about sums it up for most fishermen.

It's the same with a fishing boat. A fishing boat should never be clean. Maybe when it starts out in the morning, but never by the end of the day. If it's not completely filthy by then, chances are you were doing something in the boat, but it wasn't fishing.

A fishing boat, as Roy Blount Jr. says, should be grubby. "You could spill a couple of beers, some ketchup, a can of oil, or some of that soggy fuzz that worms come in and it wouldn't be noticed," he rightly points out.

Things are lost in the bottom of a fishing boat and never seen again. And when they are found, no human hand wants to touch them.

You like to fish for much the same reasons you liked to play in the mud when you were a kid. It's an excuse to get dirty. You never truly appreciate being clean unless you get dirty from time to time. Fishing gives you a chance to get grubby and feel good about it.

Resolved: I always wipe my hands on my pants when I fish.

July 13

Ever thought of developing an itinerary for your next fishing trip?

Some fishermen may rankle at this idea. They don't want to plan, they just want to fish. And let everything take care of itself.

But maybe you're not fishing as much as you'd like on your trips. You're getting sidetracked with errands, or whatever, and not spending nearly enough time doing what you came to do.

A fishing itinerary might help. Write down where you're going each day and how long you expect to fish. You don't have to be too precise, a rough guide will do.

The purpose of such an itinerary is simple: fish more. Form a plan about what you want to do, and you are more likely to do it. You don't leave things to chance. You don't forget things and let them fall through the cracks.

You've written it down on paper. You've thought about it. You've invested some time in it, talked to your fishing partner about it. You will almost certainly follow through on it. An added benefit of an itinerary is that you are more likely to try new places. You've created the time in your schedule to explore, and so you do.

If you rebel at the thought of being tied down on something as free and easy as a fishing trip, be sure to allow time in your schedule to do nothing. Every good fishing trip should have plenty of time for that.

Resolved: I develop a fishing itinerary that includes going to new places.

July 14

*"So I have always been grateful to fishing, happy with it as a
part of my life, unable to explain its allure and unwilling, ever,
to justify or apologize for it."*

—Nick Lyons

Be satisfied with who you are. Feel satisfaction in the fact that
you are a fisherman.

Quit apologizing for it, if you do. There's no need. You don't
have to explain yourself to anyone. Hell, you're fishing! What's
wrong with that? What's better?

Yes, you practice catch-and-release fishing. But sometimes
you also kill fish and eat them for breakfast. Somebody got a
problem with that?

People have been fishing for thousands of years. And they'll
be fishing a thousand years from now.

Some of the biggest conservationists around are fishermen
and fishing groups. They want clean rivers and wild fish, and
they're working to preserve them both.

Some of the critics of fishing seem to think that fish magically appear in plastic-wrapped packages in their supermar-
ket freezer section. But no, people actually had to kill those
fish, too.

Leave the apologies to others. You are who you are—and
that's great in itself. You're a fisherman. You're fishing. What
could be better?

Resolved: I take satisfaction in who I am.

July 15

"Tight lines, and if they're not as tight as you wish, you will have a memorable time of it all the same."

—Advice to an angler

Make peace with your habits. Adjust fishing to your habits, not the other way around.

Say you're at the top of your game in the morning. That's when you have the most energy and feel the best. An obvious strategy is to hit the stream early.

But suppose you're not bright and bubbly when you wake up. Suppose you need at least two, and possibly as many as four, cups of coffee—black, thank you—before you even begin to resemble a creature other than Bigfoot.

Well then, adjust your fishing accordingly. Go out later. Chances are you'll be coming on strong when those morning types are fading. Fish in the early evening or after dark, when they're tuckered out and curled around the fire.

The point is, know what works for you. Fishing won't suddenly make you a new person. On your next trip, along with your rod and tackle, you must also bring *yourself*. And with yourself comes all your personal baggage—habits, desires, needs, experience, hopes, etc.

But whoever you are—whatever baggage you bring to fishing—it's workable. That's one of its marvelous features. Your lines may not be as tight as the next guy's. But you can have a memorable time of it all the same.

Resolved: I accept the way I do things and make them work for me.

July 16

" 'Let out a little more line,' Jack says, so gently it's as if he is talking to himself."

—Pam Houston

When you're not sure what to do, in fishing or life, let out a little more line.

When you feel like you can do nothing right, when everything you do seems wrong, let out a little more line. You may just be pinching yourself too tight. Cut yourself some slack.

When you're casting with a fly rod, let out a little more line. That's what Pam Houston's friend told her when she was having problems, and it worked. She improved.

So will you. You'll get that fish. Just let out a little more line.

Quit being so hard on yourself. You're a pretty good fisherman. You do pretty well, considering. Let out a little more line and see how you do then. With a little more line, you may achieve wonders.

It's possible, you know. Wonders are attainable. But you'll never know for sure until you grant yourself a little more line. A person with a little more line will go a little farther, and that extra distance can make the difference between wondering what could be in your life, and truly knowing.

Forgive yourself. Permit yourself a little more line. Then take the dare, shoot for the moon, do something impossible.

Resolved: I let out a little more line—and see what I can do.

July 17

"I am alone. Peace wraps me like an airy miracle. Slow and light."

—Margot Page

Before you leave for home after a fishing trip, take a moment. Take a moment to take it all in.

The river.

The mountains.

The trees.

The sky.

The birds.

And of course, the fish. Walk down to the river and say good-bye. Until next time, fellas.

Go alone. You have your own personal relationship with the fish and everything else. Say good-bye on your own.

A moment for yourself is the best possible way to end a trip. No doubt you're running behind. No doubt you have lots of driving ahead of you. No doubt you have to get home.

These things can wait. Take a moment to think about what you felt like when you arrived and how much better you feel now. Think about what a great place this is and how well you fit into it.

You're never sure how you stand with the rest of your life. But with fishing, you are. You have obstacles, you face them. You immediately know how you fared. There are no gray areas. Fishing is very simple and pure that way.

Now, turn and go. Don't look back. Maintain that vision of clarity and keep it sacred until the next time.

Resolved: I take a moment at the end of a trip to gather it all in.

July 18

*"Whatever our point of view or frame of reference, the world is
richer and more amazing than we realize. All frames of
reference are limited. All points of view can be supplemented by
further experience under new and various conditions."*

—Donald Granger

When you face a problem in fishing, the natural response is
to solve it or try to.

Problems will not go away on their own. They must be
addressed or they will get worse. That's conventional thinking anyway.

Here's another approach: let a problem lie. Leave it alone.
Trust that the answer will present itself over time, if an answer
is to be found at all. There are problems without solutions after
all, and despite what many good-intentioned people think,
there are problems that do not need solutions.

This is not a matter of ignoring a problem so much as giving it a rest. Even that presumes you'll return at a later date
in a conscious attempt to solve it. This may be a good tactic
to adopt generally, but not in every case.

Some very ticklish problems permit no ready answers. They
seem beyond the capacity of the will, governed by factors outside an individual's control, such as the passage of time and
the birth of new conditions.

So if you're struggling in fishing, the best answer may be
to stop struggling. Change your perspective and thus let your
problem go. You may find that the thing that's bothering you
may be a creature of your own making.

Resolved: I quit struggling with my fishing and let the
answers present themselves.

July 19

Go outside. Spend the whole day outside. And bring your rod.

Get out of the office. Quit staring at four walls all day. Put down the book and turn off the TV. Leave behind that cooped-up, claustrophobic, straitjacketed indoor life and go outside where the sun is shining, birds are singing in the trees, and fish are leaping out of the water.

That's another great thing about fishing: not only are you outside, but you are outside for a *long time*. You're not just taking an evening walk or a morning jog. You spend hours, if not days, out there—long, lovely stretches of uninterrupted time when it's just you and the singing birds and leaping fish.

You don't fish indoors. There is no such thing as indoor fishing. That's pretty darned cool.

Maybe in the twenty-second century after we've turned the ozone layer to rags and it's dark and gloomy and raining perpetually like in *Blade Runner*, fishermen will be forced to ply their craft in weirdly covered Astrodome-type fishing ponds. It won't be safe to spend more than ten minutes outside, and the only surviving fish will be hatchery fish.

What a thought. Fortunately that time has not yet arrived, if it ever will. Let's enjoy while we can. Go outside. And bring your rod.

Resolved: I spend the whole day outside fishing.

July 20

"Ezio Pinza had a great voice, but was not a very good singer. Maria Callas was a great singer whose voice was undependable."

—Myron Ernst

You can be a great fisherman without possessing great fishing technique. You can have very polished fishing skills but not be a great fisherman.

There's more to fishing than catching fish. There's more to fishing than how you wield your split-cane rod. Fishing is like anything else. It's what you bring to it as a human being that ultimately matters.

Who's the better fisherman? The kid who's thrilled to death after landing a catfish at a pond, or the world-weary tarpon fisherman who never seems satisfied with what he does? The man is technically superior and catches everything in sight, but he seems to have lost something vital in the process— something that the kid still has.

The trick in fishing or in anything else is to retain the innocence and enthusiasm of the boy while developing the skills and technical know-how of the man. Technique without soul signifies nothing.

Barbra Streisand once said that 85 percent of singing was personality and attitude, what you bring to the song as a person. The rest is voice.

There's a rough parallel with fishing. You don't have to be technically proficient to be a good fisherman or to get a lot out of it. Engage yourself fully in the whole experience. Your skills will then fall naturally into place.

Resolved: I keep the technical side of fishing in perspective.

July 21

"Everyone to his own. The bird is in the sky, the stone rests on the land. In water lives the fish, my spirit in God's hands."

—Johann Scheffler

Appreciate your own unique skills as a fisherman. There's nobody like you. Nobody can do what you do.

Who knows this patch of water as well as you? Who knows this land? Who has a commitment to it like you? Who has your sense of integrity? Who brings your knowledge and love and joy? Who can match your hard-won wisdom? Who else brings such a unique set of skills, experiences, thoughts, virtues, and abilities to fishing?

Other fishermen may have more fishing experience, but no one has done what you've done. Others may know more than you about fishing, but no one knows what you know in the way you know it.

You lack nothing. You have everything you need, right now, to become the very best fisherman you can become.

Jimmy Houston does not know what you know. Nor does Mel Krieger or anyone else. No one can match you. No one can duplicate you. You're *it*. They broke the mold after they made you.

People get discouraged because they tend to focus on what they lack. They dwell on their inadequacies compared to how they perceive others. Meanwhile, those people we envy spend their private moments worrying about measuring up to some other perceived lofty standard, and round and round we go.

Nobody quite attacks a stream like you. Revel in it.

Resolved: I appreciate my unique qualities as a fisherman.

July 22

"To capture the fish is not all of the fishing."

—Zane Grey

Today's urgent message: kick back. Set up two lines, get a beach chair and umbrella, and pack an ice chest full of cold ones. Let toting that ice chest be the hardest thing you do all day. It will be a lot lighter when you come back.

Unless it's too complicated to do two things at once, work on your suntan while you're fishing. You can stand up every now and then to check your lines. How do they look? Good?

Well then, sit down. You must be exhausted after all that effort. Here, have a beer.

Some people passing by might think you've fallen asleep. What do they know? You're just contemplating with your eyes closed.

Anything doing yet? No? No sense rushing 'em. They'll come around in time. If I were a fish I wouldn't want to be rushed either.

Other people might see you sitting and drinking and watching your lines and think you're doing nothing. What fools. Fact is, you're riding a tiny planet like a rocket ship through the vast, dark regions of space. Those same people probably think their puny actions are making the world go around. You have no such illusions.

Any bites yet? Nah? Well, there's time. Have another cold one and think about it.

Resolved: I kick back and go fishing.

July 23

"Electronics can provide an edge, not a guarantee. What matters is knowing what to do, then doing it."

—Jack Neu

Jack Neu set a record for largemouth bass caught in a single day. He knew what to do, and he did it.

Electronic fishfinders show bottom contours, water depth, water temperature, and they target fish. They do not, however, come with a money-back guarantee to catch fish. The best equipment in the world won't draw scratch if the person operating it doesn't know what to do with it.

Some fishermen think they can show up at a lake, flip the switch on their electronic gear, and automatically pull big fish out of the water. It'd be nice if it worked that way, but it almost never does.

Neu himself uses paper graphs. He says they contain more detail, showing the size of individual fish. Better still, because it's paper, you can lay it out across the dining room table and really dig into it, like you're exploring a treasure map. "You can get to know the bottom of a lake as well as the layout of your home," says Jack.

Whether you use electronic aids or paper graphs, your best tools are the knowledge and experience you bring to your craft. Good old-fashioned intuition still works. Rely on yourself first and last.

You know what to do. You have the tools. Now do it.

Resolved: I rely on my instincts and use electronic fishfinders only as a tool.

July 24

"There is more misconception, disagreement and prevarication about casting than any other part of the sport. For one thing, practically no fisherman knows how far he can really cast."

—Alfred Miller

Alfred Miller tells a nice story about a group of old-time eastern fishing club members who always bragged about how far they could cast.

One of the members got so sick of it that he went out secretly to the stream and staked off actual distances on the bank. At lunchtime, when the bragging started ("I made a medium cast, about 60 feet," said one), the fellow challenged them all to a casting competition.

The members dutifully trudged out to the stream, and of course, no one could even come close to a sixty-foot cast. While the one fellow felt proud of himself for exposing such braggadocio, everyone else felt like he'd lost a close relative. "Since it is obviously impossible to tell a fish story without mentioning a 60-foot cast," Miller writes, "the members lunched in gloomy silence until at last they rebelled, chucked the beggar out, and went back to making 60-foot casts at the luncheon table."

A long cast is like the big one that got away. Everyone knows that no one casts as far as he says in his stories. Realism is not the point; entertainment is. So cast as far as you please in your fishing sagas. But be on the lookout for any blackguard who may have staked out actual distances on the bank.

Resolved: I always cast 60 feet or more in my stories.

July 25

E. Annie Proulx tells a story about a fishing partner of hers, a fellow by the name of Sven, who ordered a bunch of flies in the mail. They were beautiful flies, expertly tied, and Sven laid them out on a black cloth and drooled over them like they were expensive jewels.

When fishing season finally opened, Sven put the folded cloth on the seat next to him in his car and tore out for God's green acres. Driving along the interstate he felt a sudden need to inspect his flies, so he pulled into a rest area and spread the black cloth out on the hood. "Beautiful," said E. Annie, who had seen the flies. "He was tempted to lick one."

A little way down the freeway, Sven began to look around. Where was the black cloth? It wasn't on the seat next to him. It wasn't on the hood.

Uh-oh.

Sven did a U-turn in the middle of the interstate, jumping the divider. By the time he got back to the rest area a tour bus was pulling out, towing his flies. They were embedded in the rear tires of the bus, as Proulx says, "ready to lure whatever road trout were out there."

Moral: always put your flies back in the car after you take them out at a rest area. Or do as Sven did. Furious about losing the flies, he bought a vise and learned to tie his own.

Resolved: I keep a close eye on whoever ties my flies.

July 26

"The place is a fisherman's challenge and a fisherman's dream: lovely, enchanted, and endlessly tantalizing. I love it."

—Robert Traver

Find a place to fish that is both a dream and a challenge. One without the other will not suffice.

Suppose you found a beautiful place to fish, but the fish were docile hatchery fish that were easily caught. Would that be a satisfying experience for you?

It's doubtful. It's fun to be successful. It's fun to pull fish out of the water. But if you're not being tested in some way, you will quickly get bored. After a while you will be searching for new spots where you can hunt more difficult fish.

This is a good thing to remember when you feel frustrated. Much of the pleasure of fishing is in the challenge. The two are interwined; without the challenge, the pleasure is muted or nonexistent.

Some fisherman may dream about finding a secret trout pool similar to the one that Robert Traver found on the Middle Escanaba: lovely, enchanted, and endlessly tantalizing. But unless it is also challenging like the Middle Escanaba, he probably won't go back to it. Achieving a dream affords real satisfaction only if you have surmounted obstacles to do it. The higher and larger the obstacles, the deeper your satisfaction.

Resolved: I accept the pleasures and the challenges of fishing.

July 27

"It was always excuses—this happened, that happened. Well, you know how it is."

—Ray Bergman

Yep, it's always something.

Some rocks chisel down your leader and it snaps at just the wrong time. You hook a fish, start following it, and fall into the river like a klutz. Several fish pull off the hook. See, your hooks were damaged by rocks and you didn't notice. And then you forgot to check your fly to see how the hook was doing, etc.

You don't have to look far if you're looking for excuses in fishing. They are all over the place. If you haven't offered a lame excuse at one time or another on why you are fishless, you're not a fisherman.

At least be creative about your excuses. Don't come back with those same old tired lines. Make it a whopper: "I had this huge trout totally locked up, and then this big grizzly suddenly appeared. We started fighting over it. . . ."

Don't be bashful. Give your excuse with real conviction, and others will be more inclined to believe you.

One last thought: you might try learning from what went wrong, rather than repeating the same error over and over and offering excuses about it. Keeping a close eye on your tackle is an excellent strategy to avoid making any excuses at all.

Resolved: Excuses schmuses, I catch fish.

July 28

"I went from five fish yesterday to four fish today, to five fish tomorrow. Now that's an uplifting thought."

—Fish Fishburne

Catch one more fish than you did yesterday.

If you caught one fish yesterday, catch two today. If you catch two today, catch three tomorrow. Catch four the day after that.

Numbers in fishing can be motivational, if you have that frame of mind. Catching one more than you did yesterday is goal oriented, but it's a realistic goal. You set your sights on a target and you try to hit it. It keeps you involved and in the game.

Of course, you will not always succeed. You may not draw scratch on some days. When that happens, start over the next day and just catch one.

Even when you have a great day, there are still probably one or two fish that got away. So catching one more will always feel attainable. It will always seem like something you can do, or at least try to do.

Thus engaged, you will push yourself and learn. The only way people learn in fishing or anything else is by extending themselves. Vowing to catch one more fish than you did yesterday is a way of saying, "I want to get better, I want to to improve my skills, I want to be a better fisherman."

Resolved: I push myself and learn. I catch one more fish than I did yesterday.

July 29

Beget contentment. Walk the meadows by some gliding stream.

Feeling gloomy and down on your luck? The world pressing in on you? There is no better prescription for what ails you than to walk the meadows by some gliding stream.

The secret to physical and mental health? It's no secret. Walk the meadows by some gliding stream.

Imagine yourself there, fishing rod in hand, walking the meadows by some gliding stream. Isn't that a better place to be than where you are now? Isn't that a better way to spend the weekend than what you've got planned?

You know it is. So pick up the phone. Call whoever needs to be called. Tell them an emergency has come up and you can't make it this weekend after all.

"Is it serious?" they'll ask.

"You bet it is," you'll reply. "I have to walk the meadows by some gliding stream."

Okay, maybe it's not such a good idea to say that. But you'll think of something and you know it'll be worth it.

Resolved: I cancel all my plans for this weekend and instead walk in the meadows by some gliding stream.

July 30

"He hadn't expected to be a great fisherman in a day. He understood that, like a good marriage, fly fishing looked easy from the outside."

—Elizabeth Storer

Relax. You're making progress.

You may not feel like you're making progress in fishing. You may feel like you're pushing a pea up Everest with your nose. But really, you're moving forward. You're making strides.

Fishing is not easy. Who said it would be? If you expected it to be easy, and you're disappointed because it's not, that says more about you than it does about fishing. You might want to take a hard look at how you're looking at things.

You say you've been at it how long? Well, you haven't even cracked the surface yet. There is a lot more to learn. Stuff about fish and insects and weather and reading water and casting and tying knots and on and on. You've got to look at fishing from the inside, not just from the outside. And if you don't understand that, it just shows how much more you've got to learn.

Rome wasn't built in a day, and all that. You can't expect to be a good fisherman overnight. The main thing is, don't be discouraged. Quit looking at the top of the mountain and thinking about how much farther you have to go.

Focus on that little pea. Put your nose to it and push. Then push some more. Keep pushing, and little by little, you'll get where you want to go. Before long you will be at the top of mountain, standing in the clouds, looking around for new mountains to conquer.

Resolved: I take satisfaction in the progress I'm making in fishing.

July 31

"Follow your bliss."

—Joseph Campbell

In life, in love, in everything, follow your bliss. Let bliss be your guide.

What do you like most about fishing? What moves you? What gives you the most joy? Whatever it is, that's your bliss. Track it the way a hunting dog tracks a scent. Stay on it and never get off it, no matter what happens.

Maybe it's not any one thing that moves you; maybe it's all of it. The whole experience of fishing. Well then, grab for that experience with everything you have.

Want to be a bass fisherman? Be one. Want to be a fly-fisherman? Be one. Want to be a big game saltwater fisherman? Go do it. Look inside you, see what stirs your heart and soul, and chase it like there's no tomorrow.

Who knows, there may not be a tomorrow. Life is short. You're dead a long time. Follow your bliss.

Cease planning. Cease waiting. Stop projecting ahead to things that may or may not occur. Think about what will happen if you don't do what you dearly love.

You will encounter bumps in the road. You will meet people who think you are crazy. You will encounter forces that oppose you. But it will all work out if you follow your bliss.

Ask yourself this: what gives you joy? If the answer is fishing, then follow it with all your heart.

Resolved: I follow my bliss. I fish.

August 1

"What is the best season of the year to go a-fishing? I think the best time is when you feel like it and can leave home and business."

—Charles Bradford

It's the first of the month, time for a fishing update. How ya doin'? Taken the ol' rod and reel out lately? What do you mean, no? What the heck have you been doing?

What's that—it's not the right time? What's wrong with now? The best time to go fishing is always the time you can go fishing.

It's summer, time to play. Imagine what you'd be doing now if you were at the lake. It's beautiful there. Beautiful and oh so warm. There you'd be—sitting in the boat, drifting around, soaking it all in, and every now and then snapping up a big hairy bass. Isn't that a pretty picture?

Now, compare that vision of loveliness to what you've got planned for today. What's to compare, right?

Summers are made for play. Fishing is a form of play. Remember how your parents used to tell you to go outside and play when you were a kid? Well, it's the same now, except that your parents aren't here to boss you around anymore (thank God) and instead of walking fences and playing kick the can, you want to fish. All that's left then is for you to give yourself permission.

Resolved: I go outside and play.

August 2

"I realized that fly fishing is about suffering and that it would always break my heart. I also know that for those of us who suffer our fly fishing passions, there is grace."

—Ailm Travler

Draw your conclusions from the many positives in fishing, rather than the one or two negatives.

Nothing is ever perfect. Nothing is ever completely right. Think about what is good and right about what you do, and draw your conclusions from that.

You have a great day of fishing. Everything goes wonderfully. But all you can think about is how the leader broke on that one big fish after you battled it for twenty minutes and got it within spitting distance of the boat.

That's a bummer all right. There's no way to put a happy face on that.

But don't let the one or two things that go wrong spoil all the things that went right. Many, many great things happened. A few things that would have made the day even better (like boating that big fish) did not. Keep it in perspective.

Think about what you have, rather than what you lack. Think about who you are, rather than who you are not. Think about all the qualities you possess, rather than the ones you do not. Think about what you did, rather than what you didn't do. Think about the fish you caught, rather than the ones that got away.

Resolved: I base my conclusions about fishing from the many positives in it.

August 3

"There's no rush, no time clock, no foreman here. Everything is still, except the rings on the surface of the water. It's just us and the fish."

—Elizabeth Arnold

Studies have shown that people begin thinking about Monday and the start of the work week on Sunday at about 5 P.M. Try to break that habit on your next fishing trip.

It's not just a Sunday-Monday occurrence. Your perception of time is always influenced by the next day. Thursday night is more relaxed than other weeknights because you know that tomorrow is Friday and you only have one more day of work. Friday and Saturday nights are great because there's no work the next day. Then Sunday evening comes along and the sobering realization that you have to go back to work in the morning sets in.

On your next fishing trip, stay in the day. If it's Friday, experience Friday for all it's worth. If it's Saturday, do Saturday. Then—the big test—when Sunday rolls around, live without regrets. Experience Sunday fully.

Before you can stay in the moment, you've got to stay in the day. The lovely thing about fishing is that you usually stay in the day and the moment without any conscious effort at all. But frequently on Sundays or the last day before you're set to go home, the mind wanders and you must reel it back in.

Put those depressing Monday thoughts off as long as possible. And if you stay late on Sunday and end up driving home in the wee hours of the night, you can always catch up on your sleep at work.

Resolved: I stay in the day when I fish.

August 4

"They say 90 percent of the fish are caught by 10 percent of the fishermen. I'm going to keep working until I'm in that 10 percent."

—Tyler Nelson

Be one of the chosen 10 percent. Be among the elite. Be a person who catches fish, rather than someone who watches other people catch fish.

How do you do that? You work at it. You work at it some more. And you keep working at it.

You fish when you don't feel like fishing. You fish when you feel like your brain has turned to sawdust. You fish when you feel like you're making no progress at all and never will. You fish when you're tired and unhappy and discouraged and feel like you're banging your head against a wall.

You get good at fishing the way you get good at everything else. There are no magic revelations, no shortcuts, no secrets. You get good by working at it, making small incremental advances over time, advances that are so tiny you need a microscope to find them. But they're there, and if you don't give up and you keep working at it, what you know and can do will finally become obvious to everyone, including yourself.

The other 90 percent of the fishermen on the stream think the reason you're catching fish and they're not is because of the flies you're using or your rod or some fool reason like that. But you know the truth of it.

You put in the time. You did the work. And you're still doing it.

Resolved: I put in the time. I do the work. I become one of the chosen 10 percent.

August 5

"I quickly learned that fly fishing means fishing edges—deep against shallow, swift against slow, light against shadow. There is a skill in finding edges."

—Susan Williams

Fish the edges. Always fish the edges.

Want to become a better fisherman? Fish the edges. Want to challenge yourself and grow? Fish the edges. You're falling behind as a fisherman unless you're fishing the edges.

Go early. Stay late. Try a new type of fishing, in a new place. These are ways in which you can fish the edges.

Go to Alaska or Wyoming or Nova Scotia. These are places (and there are many others) where fishermen are fishing the edges.

Go to the edge of your known world. Don't worry. You won't fall off. Have courage. Go to the edge of your skills. Go to the edge of what you know. Go to the edge of your capabilities with a rod and reel.

Go as far as think you can go. Then go a little farther. In this way, your universe will expand. You will come to the edge of what is known, and like Columbus, discover a new world.

Resolved: I fish the edges.

August 6

"Before focusing on her gear she sits very still to watch and listen. She frees all her senses, for immersing herself in the surroundings."

—Sally Stoner

Immerse yourself in your surroundings when you fish. Immerse yourself in the natural world that is unfolding all around you.

Fisherman, immerse thyself. That's a good rule before fishing, after fishing, and during fishing.

You cannot dabble in the natural world and be a fisherman. You cannot sample it here and there, as if tasting from an hors d'ouevres tray, and expect to enjoy it as much as a person who scoops it up with both hands and swallows it whole.

When a person is baptized, he or she is immersed in water. It is a ritual that signifies submission. Immersing yourself in the natural world when you fish signifies the same thing.

It is a sign of respect and humility and awe. When you immerse yourself in your surroundings, you sit and watch. You are still for a moment. You seek to understand and learn. You no longer see yourself as the sole actor on the stage, but as a small player in a much larger drama, a drama of heaven and earth. The river, the clouds, the three ducks swimming in the river, those deer tracks you saw on the way, the hawks circling overhead, the digger pines and tamarack trees on water's edge—these all are honored players in the drama.

Sit still, watch, listen. Immerse yourself in the natural world of fish and fishing.

Resolved: I immerse myself in my surroundings when I fish.

August 7

"And so with good talk and good fishing the day raced by."

—Max Shulman

Like many other fishermen, Max Shulman had always been attracted to deep-sea fishing. "But somehow I never got around to it," he explains. "It seems like every time I planned to go, something annoying would come up to prevent it, like a root canal or a job." But finally he made up his mind and lit out for Great Harbour Cay in the Bahamas.

There, he boarded a chartered fishing boat captained by a red-nosed man named Rummy Rafferty. "What excitement flooded my breast as I gazed for the first time at the incredible blues and greens of the Bahamian sea!" Max recalls. "How my pulses pounded and my eyeballs shone as the mate baited the hooks with mullet and balao and dropped them over the stern."

They went in search of marlin, and although Max got three "tremendous" strikes, he did not land one. How did he know they were marlin? Well, Rummy saw them. Which led Max to develop these immutable truths about deep-sea fishing:

"1. Fishing boats leak.
2. Fishing boat captains drink.
3. Any fish you lose is a marlin.
4. Fishing was always better the day before you got there.
5. Though deep-sea fishing is a very difficult sport, it can be mastered by any man or woman with average strength and inherited money."

Resolved: I deep-sea fish in the blues and greens of the Bahamian sea.

August 8

"Patience, movement, light tackle, a variety of baits. Follow these four suggestions, and you should catch fish."

—Bel Lange

A catfish is an ugly, but honorable, fish. He's a bottom feeder who will eat just about anything you throw at him, including clams, grass shrimp, worms, chicken livers, cut sardines, and anchovies. One California delta fisherman fishes for cats using Vienna sausages.

Its whiskers are called barbels. They can jab you and make your hand swell if you're allergic to them. Cats rely on their barbels to taste and feel. Their swim bladder can even produce sounds.

The best time to fish for catfish is at night since they're nocturnal feeders. But plenty are caught during the day, often in shady spots where they like to hang out in schools. Catfish are good eating. Better than trout, some say. Another of their virtues is that fishing for them is not exactly like running the Olympic marathon. Throw out the line, pull in the slack, and pinch yourself to make sure you don't fall asleep.

Catfishing is like any other kind of fishing: it takes patience. They're on their own schedule and that may or may not coordinate with yours. Don't hesitate to move, say the experts, if you haven't gotten a bite in a half hour or so. Mosey on down to another place. Sooner or later, you'll nab one.

Catfish are great kidfish. The first fish caught by many a young angler was a catfish. While they may look ugly to some, catfish are as handsome as marlins to those kids when they've got one on the line.

Resolved: My kid and I catch some catfish and eat 'em up.

August 9

"Fly fishing is folly; useless, unreasonable, irrational and without purpose."

—Ailm Travler

Okay, the morning was bad, a complete washout. Everything went wrong, nothing went right. Whatever the fish were looking for, you couldn't supply it.

So what do you do? You go back out.

Come in for a while. Have lunch, take a break. But in the afternoon, or early evening, go back out.

Still nothing changes. All day it's like that. You stay out there till the sun drops behind the hills and then you drag yourself back to the lodge, cold and wet and utterly miserable.

What do you do the next day? Same thing. Go back out.

And what if the whole weekend is like that? What do you do *then*? It's obvious. The following weekend, or as soon as you can, you go back out.

It's like that old line about being thrown from a horse. There's only one thing to do if you want to keep riding: get back on that horse.

Fishing is the same. Whatever happens, go back out. However down you feel at any given moment, go back out. Good things will eventually happen, but only if you go back out.

Resolved: I always, always go back out.

August 10

"For angling rod he took a sturdy oak; for line, a cable that in storm never broke."

—Sir William Davenant

For your fishing rod, go out into your backyard and pull a branch off a tree. For your line, use that ball of string in the garage. Dig up some worms, and you're set.

What's that? You need your high-priced rod and all your other gadgets or it's just not right? Okay, bring them along. But that won't make you any happier than the fellow who uses a tree branch and string.

Aldo Leopold writes, "I have the impression that the American sportsman is puzzled; he doesn't understand what is happening to him. Bigger and better gadgets are good for industry, so why not for outdoor recreation? It has not dawned on him that outdoor recreations are essentially primitive, atavistic; that their value is contrast-value; that excessive mechanization destroys contrasts by moving the factory to the woods or to the marsh."

Leopold wrote this in the 1940s, but it is just as true today. People equate gadgets with pleasure, technology with fun. But the real pleasures of fishing—indeed all outdoor recreation—are essentially primitive. In fishing as in life, simplicity is best.

One reason people like to fish and get lost in the woods is to reconnect to a wildness that is missing from their everyday world, yet still exists inside them.

A tree branch and string may be asking too much. But almost every fisherman could get by with a lot less than he does. Why not try it next time and see how it feels?

Resolved: I take a hard look at my gear with the idea of simplifying my fishing.

August 11

"We talked motorcars, politics, literature, women, racehorses, the parlous state of the world, but mostly we talked fishing, which has both of us in its iron thrall."

—Robert Deindorfer

You're crazy about fishing, right? Why not join a fishing or casting club and meet other people who are as crazy as you?

You will find people like yourself in a fishing club, people who love to fish and who love to talk about it. Some of them like to talk about it more than they like to do it, it's true. But they're mostly harmless and frequently entertaining.

Joining a club can give you access to a casting pool. You can practice your casting when you're tired of all the hot air.

Lots of real, honest-to-God fishermen belong to fishing and casting clubs. They go down to the casting pool and sharpen their skills prior to plying their craft for real on a stream or lake.

You may love to fish but have trouble finding people to fish with. You may have worn everybody else out. Consider joining a club and finding a partner.

Fishing clubs schedule fishing trips, book charters, and hold classes. They have dances and social affairs. It's not a bad group to fall in with, as long you're not a stickler for truth when it comes to the telling of fish stories.

This is another benefit to joining a club. You can polish up your storytelling skills, in addition to your casting. For you can get by in fishing without the latter, but you'll be completely lost without the former.

Resolved: I join a fishing or casting club.

August 12

"Instead of going to my cabin, I walked to Eastman Lake and sat on the shore for a few minutes, just staring at the moonlight on the water. Moonlight never gets old."

—Bill Barich

Instead of turning in for the night, go outside and take a walk under the moon.

Instead of closing your eyes right away, lie in your sleeping bag and watch for shooting stars.

Instead of sitting around a TV, sit around a big fire and tell even bigger fish stories.

Instead of commuting on freeways, drive along a two-lane country road with cows grazing on the hillsides. Then turn off onto a dirt road that leads to a fishing spot that only you and your partner know about.

Instead of moping around the house this weekend and feeling bored and restless, take off for the mountains.

Instead of work, work, work, play, play, play. Feed your soul for a change.

Instead of fishing to catch quantities of fish, hunt for that one difficult fish that challenges everything you have.

Instead of retreating into the conventional, do what you believe is right. Follow your plan for life, not someone else's.

Instead of thinking about fishing, fish.

Instead of dreaming about all the things you want to do in your life, start doing them.

Resolved: Instead of turning in for the night, I take a walk in the moonlight.

August 13

"The critical geometry in the camping trip is the other person."

—E. Annie Proulx

It's time to find some new fishing buddies.

There's nothing wrong with the old ones. They're pretty good guys. But one's always busy and can never get away. Another is broke. Another just got married and you know how that goes.

You can still fish with those guys, but it won't kill you to hook up with somebody new. It may be somebody you already know, it's just that you've never fished with him. You've talked about it but for one reason or another never done it. All you have to do is pick up the phone and call him.

Fishing with somebody new will shake things up. This new guy naturally does things differently. You can take him to your favorite places and he can take you to his. You can show him a few things and vice versa. You learn from each other.

Maybe he's got more experience than you. He's a stronger hiker, a more skilled caster. What's normal for him is a challenge for you. You realize after spending a little time with him that you've gotten a little comfortable in your ways and that this has not necessarily made you a better fisherman.

Sometimes it works out, sometimes it doesn't. But it's worth a try. When you do find a new fishing buddy, it's like discovering gold.

Resolved: I fish with someone I've never fished with before.

August 14

"Approach from the hay meadow side was easy and that bank was well worn with the boots of fishermen. Everyone fished there. But this approach was in plain view of the trout, and I never saw any there except small fish."

—Ernest Schweibert

Seek the path of greatest resistance. If the path you take is easy, it's wrong. If it's hard, it's right.

Wrong and *right* may be too strong. But the point is this: you will grow as a person and as a fisherman if you venture into areas that challenge you and make you uncomfortable.

That's not easy to do. It's far easier to go along as you are, doing the things that you do, in the way that you do them. You're a nice person. You make a nice living. You have a nice family. You enjoy your weekends. You fish from time to time.

It's very difficult to leave this comfortable setting and move into one that is harsher and more demanding, where you are challenged and threatened and attacked, where you're less sure of your strengths and more aware of your weaknesses, where the assumptions upon which you base your ordinary life do not exist, where you're not sure about *anything*.

It's like you've fished all your life in the little stream in the valley. You know it pretty well and you pull trout from it all the time. But to really test yourself as a fisherman and find out what you're made of, sooner or later you've got to go to the Madison or the Umpqua or Bristol Bay. By following the path of greatest resistance, you will grow.

Resolved: I seek the path of greatest resistance. I head for Bristol Bay.

August 15

"The chase is the thing."

—Silvio Calabi

The chase, not the capture, is the thing in fishing. Put your faith in the chase and you will have a lifetime of great fishing. Lust only after the capture and you are sure to be disappointed and bitter.

Fishing, as Silvio Calabi says, is "a game played out in chest waders on freestone streams around the world." The tools of the game have improved over the years, but the basic challenge remains the same today as it was for the ancients.

Sometimes you catch 'em, sometimes you don't. The thrill is in the chase.

In the old days fishermen returned from the river with heaping creels of fish. Nowadays fishermen let the fish go after they catch them. But the essence of the experience—the chase—is the same for both.

You chase them in rivers and streams. You chase them in lakes. You chase them in bays and inlets and straits. You chase them in the ocean. You chase them around the world, wherever they are. Fish can run, but they can't hide.

When you meet another fisherman, you instantly feel a camaraderie. He is a fellow initiate. He has played the game, shared the chase. He, too, knows its heartaches and joys and perpetual fascination.

To chase is to be alive. Never stop chasing. Chase after your dreams, chase after happiness, and chase after fish.

Resolved: I put my faith in the chase, and keep chasing.

August 16

"Striking and landing bass require delicacy and timing, of course, but the main thing is to get 'on fish'—to find out where they are congregating—and to figure out what to throw at them."

—Roy Blount Jr.

The keys to catching bass are the same for trout or salmon or any other fish. Get on them, then figure out what to throw at them.

If what you're throwing at them works, go for it. If it doesn't, throw something else.

You can consult a book and find out what to use. Or you can ask the locals. In Papua New Guinea, the fishermen reportedly use condoms to catch tuna. When the condoms fill up with water, the tuna strike.

Hey, if it works, why not?

Despite all the millions of words written about fishing, nobody really knows why fish go for certain things and ignore others. Some people have tasted insects in an attempt to find out, but it still remains pure speculation on their part.

Sure, there's delicacy and art to fishing. Sure, there's a spiritual side. But ultimately fishing is a utilitarian craft and every fisherman is as pragmatic as those Papua New Guineans. If it works, it's good. If it doesn't, it's not.

Get on fish.

Figure out what to throw at them.

Remember these two simple rules the next time you go fishing, and you'll do just fine. Oh yeah, and pack the condoms in case you get lucky in the lodge bar afterward.

Resolved: I get on fish, and I use what works.

August 17

"Half the beauty of fly fishing is not how many fish you can catch but seeing the beauty of a mountain stream."

—Bob Fisher

Enough with indoor living and indoor pleasures. It's time to go to the mountains.

Maybe you take a friend, or maybe you don't. For certain, if you go with somebody, he likes to hike and fish and drink and hoot at the stars. Because that's what you're going to be doing a lot of in the next five days.

You drive all night and skate right in past the ranger's station. Nobody's there because it's three in the morning and they've all gone to bed. You sleep at the trailhead by the side of the road.

You're up early, as early as you can muster. You've got your multipiece fly rod. You pack your pack, and you're gone.

The trail drops steeply down a ridge. It works on your thighs a little because you haven't done much hiking lately but it feels good anyway. You pass through corridors of pine and tamarack. You enter a sloshy, bug-infested meadow and walk a log across a creek. After a while the trail opens into a long, sunny stretch with a view across the canyon.

You hear the river before you see it. Then, coming out of the forest, you see it. It never fails to take your breath away. You hike upstream for a few miles until you find a spot that's far away from everything and everybody, and you take out your rod. You have arrived.

Resolved: I take a fishing trip to the high country.

August 18

"What a marvel shalt thou contemplate in thy heart and what sweet delight, when on a voyage, watching when the wind is fair and the sea is calm, thou shalt see the beautiful herds of dolphins, the desire of the sea."

—Oppian

Today, when you fish, you may see something you've never seen before. It's possible.

You may do something you've never done before. That's possible, too.

It's possible that you will learn something about fish and fishing that you had not known.

It's possible that you will pick up something new about rivers and current and eddies—and that this knowledge will make you a better fisherman.

It's a distinct possibility that while fishing you will learn other things as well. You may notice how the digger pines hang over the river at that one spot or how the wind picks up at a certain time every day—things you had not noticed before.

You may be stunned and humbled by the beauty of your surroundings. That's very possible.

It's equally possible, indeed likely, that something will surprise you today. You, who know so much. Surprised. Who'd have thought it.

It's possible that today you will reel in the impossible— the biggest fish of your life. It's possible, you know. Anything's possible.

Resolved: Today when I fish, I explore the possibilities.

August 19

"They felt the exhilaration of a singing reel, a bowed rod, and a leaping red-sided trout."

—Sally Stoner

Use what motivates you. Whatever it is, use it.

If catching big fish motivates you, use it. If seeing yourself in a photograph holding a record fish motivates you, use it. Make that image become a reality.

If numbers motivate you, think numbers. See how many fish you can catch and release today. See if you can top that number tomorrow and the day after that. If that is what moves you, use it.

If the exhilaration of a singing reel and a bowed rod motivates you, use it. If fishing gives you a kinship with nature and provides a spiritual connection with wild things and wild places, use it. These are great and wonderful things that motivate many fishermen.

If becoming a great fisherman motivates you, use it. If all you want is to be is competent or better than you are now, use it. Let your zeal for self-improvement spur you on.

Maybe you love the small details of fishing. Maybe you love tying flies. Maybe you take satisfaction in a well-tied knot. Maybe you love to spin marvelous casting arcs and you love it when people watch. Whatever it is that motivates you in fishing, use it.

Resolved: I feel the exhilaration of a bowed rod and a leaping trout.

August 20

"I will now choose among four good sports and honorable pastimes—to wit, among hunting, hawking, fishing and fowling. The best, in my judgment, is fishing, called angling, with a rod and a line and a hook."

—Dame Juliana Berners

Once you're there, be *there*.

It's okay if you want to be somewhere else. Perhaps your job is pushing in on you and you need to work this weekend. No sweat. Dig in and get it done.

Or perhaps you'd rather just stay home. You've been running around like crazy lately. All you want to do is order Chinese, rent a movie or two, and spend some quality time in the sack with your significant other. Cool. Sounds like a plan.

If you don't want to go fishing, don't go. Nobody is forcing you. You're better off staying home and doing whatever than dragging yourself out to the lake (man, what torture!) if you don't want to be there.

But once you're there, be there. You've made the choice. Now give yourself the space to enjoy it. Put aside the job. Put aside your weekday concerns. Let the family take care of itself for a while. While you're fishing, be with it. You'll get back to those other things.

A fisherman who is truly into what he is doing but can only fish once or twice a year will get more out of it than someone who goes every week but whose mind is on other things.

Resolved: When I fish, I'm truly there.

August 21

*"After she left me and I quit my job and wept for a year, I
decided I would only fish and drink. In the river was a trout
and I was on the bank, my heart in my chest, clouds above."*

—Jim Harrison

Dumped by your girlfriend/wife/partner? Sorry about that. But there's no better place to recover than on the banks of a river, consoled by clouds and trout.

Every relationship requires a mourning period after it ends. It takes time to mend a broken heart. While it's mending, you can get in some serious fishing.

So don't rush this mourning period. There are a lot of cutthroats out there after all, and you may need to go to several different rivers before you can ever think about facing women again.

Here's a thought: now that all your emotional scars have healed, why not invite a lady on a fishing date?

A fishing date can be pretty romantic. You're outside in a beautiful, nonthreatening environment. You pack a nice lunch—a bottle of Bordeaux, some smelly cheese—and lay out on the banks of the river.

You show her how to cast, of course. She's a gamer who gives it a real try. Then she watches while you send your fly line around in beautiful loops the way those little rhythmic gymnasts fling their ribbons in the Olympics. Then you pull a trout out of the river, and confirming what a sensitive, nature-loving guy you are, you place it gently back in the water.

You're in, buddy.

Resolved: I live the fantasy. I invite a lady on a fishing date.

August 22

"There is, I've learned, one constant in all types of fishing. The time the fish are biting is almost but not quite now."

—P. J. O'Rourke

It's always better on the other side. That's one of the axioms of fishing.

Another tried-and-true cliche: the fishing was always better the day before you got there.

The reverse of this, also a cliche, is what P. J. O'Rourke discovered: the fish are always on the verge of biting, but not quite yet.

There is nothing you can do about the cliches of fishing (or the cliche-speakers). They are inescapable. Wherever you go, whatever the time of year, you will run into someone speaking in cliches, passing them off as original thought.

As a fisherman, make a pact with yourself to find out the truth of what you hear. If it's better on the other side, then *go* to the other side. Find out what it's really like over there.

The same is true for the cliches about time. Get there earlier than you usually do if you can. Go at a different time of year. Or stay a little longer and wait to see if the fish ever start biting. (Probably not. The cliche-speakers are never wrong.)

But this really isn't about cliches or the people who use them; this is about you. This is about finding out for yourself what's true and what's not. Extend this thinking beyond the cliches of fishing into more meaningful realms. What is it really like in Alaska? Is it as good as they say in New Zealand? Find out the truth of what you hear for yourself.

Resolved: I go to the other side to see what's there.

August 23

"There is no danger from the fish, but anyone who goes on the sea the year-around in a small power boat does not seek danger. You may be absolutely sure that in a year you will have it without seeking, so you try always to avoid it all you can."

—Ernest Hemingway

Seek adventure, but not danger. Anyone who fishes—in small power boats on the sea or any other way—will meet with danger from time to time without having to look for it.

Danger frequently accompanies adventure. Every fisherman knows that. But you can have high adventure and still keep the risks low.

One way is to watch the booze. An alarmingly high percentage of fishing and outdoor accidents occur when someone is drunk or drinking. You stop using good sense and something bad happens. And when something bad happens, it always happens fast.

There's a thrill from danger, just as there's a thrill when you stand at the edge of a high cliff and look down. It's intoxicating. There's something strange and mysterious like a siren's song pulling at you and secretly whispering for you to jump.

There are plenty of thrills in fishing without all that. There's nothing thrilling about misjudging a strong current and getting swept off your feet and thrown into a rock-strewn rapid that is churning like the inside of a washing machine. Accidents will happen, but many are avoidable.

Today's lesson: use common sense when you're out there. Think safety first. Stay away from iffy situations, especially when you're alone. Watch the drinking. Enough said.

Resolved: I seek adventure, but not danger.

August 24

Forget Costa Rica. Go to Belize.

Better yet, go to Costa Rica first. Swing up into the mountains and catch some wild trout. Then go down to the water and snag a sailfish. On your way back, stop over in Belize.

Belize is a postage stamp of a country bordering Mexico and Guatemala on the east and the sunny blue Caribbean on the west. There are white sand beaches and rain forests. Accommodations are not what you'd call primitive—there are flushing toilets—but it's not exactly Club Med either.

The national fish of Belize is the snark. Actually, no. A "snark" is from a poem by Lewis Carroll, who didn't fish and probably never visited Belize, poor fellow. The fish in question is, in fact, a snook, which can grow to more than thirty pounds but is not the national fish of Belize, if such a thing even exists.

The snook is a fighter, known for its tenacity. If you want a fish to shake your line, the snook is the one. They like to hang out in shallow water around bridge pilings or in mangrove roots. But there are a myriad of other strange swimming creatures in the warm waters off Belize. You'll find tropical fish there that you won't find in an aquarium.

You heard it here first. Go to Belize. It's a scene you'll never forget.

Resolved: I catch a snook in Belize.

August 25

It was hard, but you did it.

Nobody else thought you could do it, but they were wrong. You did it.

You set a goal for yourself, and you did it. It wasn't easy either. You didn't sell yourself short. You aimed high.

Even you weren't sure at times whether you could do it. But you kept plugging, and you did it.

You didn't do it overnight. You didn't do it on your first try or even your thirty-first try. But eventually you did it.

You failed before you succeeded. But the failures were only temporary, and the success is lasting.

You had help, sure. Success has a hundred parents and all that. But it wouldn't have gotten done if you hadn't done it. Most things worth doing are like that. One person sees what needs to be done, and he or she does it. This time, you were that person.

Everybody had an opinion. They always do. One person thought this, another person thought that. Opinions are like noses. Everybody has one. Well, you listened and listened, accepting some advice and rejecting the rest. But mostly you followed your own inner counsel, and that is how you did it.

Resolved: Whatever I want to do in fishing, I do it.

August 26

"Finding a fish is the problem; the rest is patience."

—Alfred Miller

Puzzled over some element of your fishing? Trying hard to get it right but can't quite figure it out?

Let the answer come slowly.

You don't have to have the answer right away. What's the rush? Give yourself time and the answer will come.

People are conditioned to getting quick and easy solutions to everything. What's happening in the news? Flip on the TV. Hungry? Stick a frozen dinner in the microwave. Write a letter to a friend? Nah, too slow. Fax or call.

Think about when you were a schoolkid. You learned math with flash cards. When the teacher asked the class a question, hands shot up in the air. You were rewarded not only for giving the correct answer, but for saying it quickly.

But some problems don't lend themselves to quick and easy answers. It takes time to figure them out. The best thing you can do for a problem you're grappling with in fishing is walk away from it for a while.

You are a conscientious fisherman. You really do want to get over the hump and solve whatever problem you're working on. And you will, if you give yourself the time to do it.

Resolved: I let the answers come slowly.

August 27

*"There is always a feeling of excitement when a fish takes hold
when you are drifting deep."*

—Ernest Hemingway

Want to drift deep and feel the excitement when a fish takes
hold? Sign up for a charter.

Charters combine fishing with socializing. You can go in
large groups or small, but always with other people. Charters
are not a solitary fishing experience.

You can charter your own boat with a bunch of your
friends. No doubt your club sponsors charters. That's the reason many fishing clubs form in the first place—to get enough
people to book a charter.

Charters give you a chance to fish places you might not
ordinarily get to. You might fish a big inland lake, explore a
bay, or venture out into the ocean. There's safety (and solidarity) in numbers.

You also hunt different types of fish, depending on where
you are and the time of year. Salmon, halibut, sturgeon, rockfish, stripers—you name it. You can always find a chartered
fishing boat in search of your favorite fish.

Charters depend on fishermen. If there aren't enough
signed up, they may not go out. Charters are a kick in the
pants. You'll meet people. You'll have a shared fishing experience. And you may even catch some fish. That will make the
day worthwhile, no matter what.

Resolved: Some buddies and I sign up for a charter.

August 28

"Eastward I go only by force, but westward I go free."

—Henry David Thoreau

East is great. There's nothing wrong with East. It's better to go East and fish than to go to anywhere else and *not* fish.

But it's different out West, it just is. There's no Kenai Peninsula in the East. There's no Umpqua or Deschutes. There's no Henry's Fork. There's no Madison River or Yellowstone.

Go West, young fisherman. Go West.

This is not a regional or provincial issue. This is about fishing. Sooner or later, a person who is serious about his fishing must follow the compass in one direction: west.

When Westerners say the land is bigger out there, they're not kidding. So's the sky. There are still fewer people and more open spaces on the map. And there are more places to drop a line in water.

To paraphrase Dizzy Dean, the West ain't what it used to be, but then what is? It's still got plenty of what every fisherman is looking for: uncrowded water and wild trout.

Zane Grey, Ernest Hemingway, Mark Twain—they did their trout fishing in the West. Jim Harrison, Thom McGuane, Richard Ford—they now do theirs in the West, for what it's worth.

Once you go, you'll never look at those old familiar fishing places the same way again. And you may never want to come back.

Resolved: I go West and fish Henry's Fork.

August 29

*"I dropped the berry in the stream and caught a little silver
trout."*

—William Butler Yeats

At the start of the summer, you vowed to take your son on a
fishing trip.

Well Dad, how'd you do?

Good for you! You cut out early from work on Friday to
beat the traffic. You arrived around midnight and pitched a
tent at a campground within walking distance of the lake.
There were other fishermen around, but not enough to bother
you.

On Saturday you explored the edges of the lake in a boat.
It was way cool. It always surprises you how different the view
looks from the water than on shore. You're in the middle of
this watery expanse, with mountains surrounding you. People on the shore just don't understand it and they never will
until they go out on a boat and see for themselves.

It was just you and him, fishing. Nobody said much until
Nate pulled out a little silver trout like in the poem. You
snapped the picture and his smile was as big as the fish. He
got so hyped, you could hardly shut him up after that.

It was after dark when you finally brought the boat in. You
came back to camp wet and tired and happy.

When you drove home on Sunday, Nate slept like a baby
the whole way. You didn't mind. You rolled down the windows, turned up the radio, and sped down the freeway a
happy man.

Resolved: I take my son on an end of summer fishing trip.

August 30

"Only in the observation of nature can we recover that view of eternity that consoled our forebears."

—Thomas McGuane

Take your inspiration from nature.

Take your inspiration from the sun poking over the rim of the canyon, bringing light and warmth to the chill dawn.

Take your inspiration from a night full of stars and a toasty-warm sleeping bag.

Take your inspiration from a raccoon that visited in the night but went away empty-handed. (Hah! Too bad!)

Take your inspiration from the way the light streams through the pines and hits your bag, finally forcing you to get up and put your boots on.

Take your inspiration from the golden stream that you let loose after a solid night's sleep.

Take your inspiration from the rocks along the water's edge, polished smooth by current and time.

Take your inspiration from the cold, cold river water borne of glaciers, now flowing to the sea.

Take your inspiration from how good the water tastes and how cold it is on your face. Want to wake up fast? That'll do it all right.

Take your inspiration from the birds chattering in the trees and the river sounds all around you.

Take your inspiration from the river itself, forever changing yet always the same.

Resolved: I take my inspiration from nature.

August 31

"I became a fly fisher, not because of aesthetics or passion, or politics or trendiness, but because when I was growing up we had fly rods in the garage."

—Jennifer Smith

Want your kids to grow up to be fly-fishers? Store your fly rods in the garage.

That may be all you need to do. You don't have to rag on them or preach to them. Store your fly rods in the garage, and they may gravitate to them all on their own.

If you make a big deal about your rods and start laying down rules about them, the kids may revolt because that's what kids do. They may reject your fishing rods as a means of getting back at you, for whatever reason. They may become bullheaded and stubborn and act like they know it all (or at least more than you), which is another thing kids do.

See your fly rods as an everyday fact of existence, which is what they are. Put them on the level of an appliance, almost like the washer and dryer. They are always around because they are frequently in use.

When the time comes, your kids will get their own fly rods. If you've done your job right, they won't regard fly-fishing as a burden, something their dad is foisting off on them. They'll have a hands-on approach to it. They'll value it as much as you do.

Having fly rods in the garage sends a strong, clear message. You're a fisherman. These are your tools. You value them. They're part of your life. Your kids will pick up on that, and they'll learn from it.

Resolved: I store my fly rods in the garage.

September 1

"All of us have our own rivers, I remind myself, with their own beginnings and endings. I stand in awe of the wonder of circumstance and the mystery of our lives."

—Margot Page

There are no eternal truths anymore, just personal ones. Look for your own personal truths, in fishing and in life, and follow them.

Your truth doesn't mean much to the next guy. That's okay. His truth may not mean much to you.

But the fact that each of you has personal truths—you can respect that.

You may go down a certain path in life that others question. But it's your personal truth and you know the rightness of it even if no one else does. It's like that greeting card where a youngster stands at a crossroad. One road marker says, "Your Life." The other says, "No Longer An Option." Following your personal truth is no longer an option for you. You *must*.

Let your personal truths lead you down the Bio-Bio or ice fishing in the Yukon. Follow your personal truths on a trout fishing pilgrimage to Argentina or bonefishing at Christmas Island.

Some people may think you're crazy, while others envy you. You have the guts to do what they would love to do, but don't.

You're a lucky man. While others are blind to their personal truths or confused about them, you're very clear. Your personal truths lead you. They shine like a lighthouse on a foggy night at sea, showing you the way to go.

Resolved: I follow my personal truths, in fishing and in life.

September 2

"There are no second chances with an experienced trout. I might trick a six-inch native trout or even a ten-inch stocked trout, but to catch a veteran trout, twelve inches or more, I must be perfect, and I seldom am."

—Le Anne Schreiber

How do you outthink a veteran trout? Le Anne Schreiber has some suggestions.

First (and most obvious), be quiet on the approach. And be careful about shadows. "On sunny days I must notice where shadows fall," she says, "so I can hide my own among those cast by the trees."

Before she enters the stream, Le Anne sits on the banks to check out the insect population. She sees what's flittering above the water and turns over rocks in the streambed to see if any insects are there.

She feels she has one clear advantage over a trout: the knowledge that "he can't expect to expend more energy getting food than the food supplies; he must find some quiet spot and let the food come to him." So she scans the surface of the water for variations in flow—big rocks, fallen logs, anything that creates a pocket of still water where a trout can rest without battling the current.

Even when she does everything right, she still may not hook a fish. And this is what all fishermen must remember: perfection will not necessarily bear fruit. You can do everything just the way you are supposed to, and the trout may still ignore you. You must somehow find consolation in the fact that you have done everything you can, and let it go at that.

Resolved: I find perfection in heaven perhaps, but never in fishing.

September 3

Which kind of fisherman are you? Do you Fish, or Go Fishing?

Jean Shepherd's dad liked to Go Fishing. Jean explains: "He was the kind who would Go Fishing maybe once a month during the summer when it was too hot to Go Bowling and all of the guys down at the office would get The Itch. To them, fishing was a way of drinking a lot of beer and yelling. And getting away from the women."

To young Jean, however, fishing meant more. "To me," he says, "it was a sacred thing. *To fish.*"

Every fisherman understands the distinction. A guy who likes to Go Fishing does it every now and then, and when he does, it's accompanied by a lot of drinking and yelling, but no women. He's also a bowler.

A guy who Fishes, on the other hand, fishes a lot more than a guy who just Goes Fishing. He may drink as much but he's quieter about it and this makes him more serious somehow.

Here's an idea: how about going on your next trip with a person who's your fishing opposite? If you're a person who likes to Fish, you may need to lighten up some. Inviting a hooting, beer-guzzling Go Fishing type might help in this regard. On the other hand, if you Go Fishing, a man who Fishes could probably teach you a thing or three about the history and art and philosophy of fishing. Well, it's worth a try, no?

Resolved: I invite my fishing opposite on a fishing trip.

September 4

"Never hesitate to experiment. Try out ideas of your own. That is the way all sport fishing began and that is the way it will be improved."

—Joseph Cook and William Wisner, authors

Here's your mission for the day: make new mistakes.

New mistakes, you ask? Why make any mistakes at all?

Listen. That's unreasonable. Everybody makes mistakes. Everybody casts into the trees. Everybody reacts too quickly or too slowly and lets a fish slip away. Everybody fights a half-hour battle with an incredible marine creature that turns out to be a clump of seaweed.

It's unreasonable to expect perfection in fishing or anything else. In fact, if you're not making mistakes, you're not really trying. A person who makes mistakes is testing his abilities and expanding his personal boundaries.

The idea is to make new mistakes. Don't repeat the same old tired miscues. That may indicate you're following unconscious patterns that you're either unaware of or unwilling to break. The first step in breaking out of a rut is to become aware of it.

The things that hold you back in fishing today are probably the things that held you back in the past. They're nothing new. When you make new mistakes, it is a sign that you are advancing into unknown territory. You have become aware of your old ways of doing things and you want to end them or go beyond them.

Resolved: I make new mistakes in fishing today.

September 5

"Watching a good caster on a stream will teach you more in 20 minutes than you can learn reading 20 pages."
—Robert Zwirz and Morty Marshall

Go find another fisherman, someone who's really good. Take a break from your own fishing and sit down and watch.

He probably won't mind. He may even be flattered. Most good fishermen have done the same thing at one time or another. That's partly how they got so good. They sat down and studied other fishermen to see what they were doing and learn from it.

Forget analyzing the guy. Suspend the critical faculties for a while. Just watch. Pay close attention.

Observe the little things. If a person is off on the little things, he will have a hard time with the big things. A lot of well-done little things can net you a big fish.

Watch how he pauses at the end of each casting stroke. Watch how he controls his slack line. Watch how he moves his rod tip straight toward his target. Watch how gently he applies power.

When you are watching, try to take your ego out of it. See what he is doing and how it works for him. Try to look beyond the obvious.

A keen observer will not necessarily become a great fisherman. But every great fisherman is a keen observer of nature, fish, and other fishermen.

Resolved: I study other fishermen with a keen eye.

September 6

"The thrill of seeing a big fish in a magnificent jump, the thrill of a sharp tug on the rod, the sensation of success when you slip the net under a lunker—this is the outdoors and you are the prime actor in the scene, unhelped, unaided by another."

—Ray Ovington

Believe in your rod and reel. Believe in the strength of your tackle. Believe in your fishing abilities. Believe in your knowledge of water and the environment. Most of all, believe in yourself.

You can do it. Whatever it is, you can do it.

Everything is possible if you believe in yourself. Lacking that, nothing is.

Believe in yourself because you've faced this situation before. You know how to handle it because you've handled things similar to it in the past.

But you are more than a sum of your past. You have experience, imagination, and heart. Know that if you face a new challenge in a setting that's foreign to you, you can adapt to it. You can handle it and do what needs to be done.

If all this sounds terribly naive, so what? What's wrong with naivete? A little naivete can go a long way in fishing.

It's not your rod and tackle that catches fish, it's you. You are the prime actor in every fishing drama, nobody else. And when things get rough and hard to take, that innocent, almost childish belief in yourself is what will carry you through.

Resolved: As naive as it may seem, I never stop believing in myself.

September 7

"The spirit that makes the great angler is compounded of terrifically intense concentration and a ferocious, predatory urge to conquer and capture."

—Alfred Miller

What also makes a great angler is the ability to carry on.

You've hiked a river in search of fish. You're exhausted. You've been at it all day. You've caught nothing, or at least nothing to speak of. You've run out of ideas and energy. The sun is going down and it's turning dark. What do you do?

Carry on, of course.

That may mean, in this particular instance, staying on the river after nightfall, or what seems more reasonable, returning to camp to be consoled by your friend Jack Daniels. Nevertheless, it never means giving up. A person who carries on never, ever gives up. His surrender to those scaly underwater creatures is only temporary. He will be back tomorrow.

Carry on is the right phrase (and attitude) for fishing; *press on* is not. If you're pressing in fishing, you're expending too much energy and effort. You're pushing too hard. You may need to let events come to you, rather than trying to force them according to your dictates.

With fishing come setbacks. With fishing come disappointments and reversals of the most frustrating kind. Nevertheless, you must summon up the wherewithal to slosh your way back to camp in the darkness. Then, after a good night's sleep, get up the next morning and go after it again.

Resolved: Always, I carry on in fishing.

September 8

Follow the three Es, not the three Ds. That's the advice of Paul Morton, a communication consultant who conducts business and management seminars around the United States. His advice applies equally to the business of fishing.

In Morton's lingo, 3E means easy, effortless, enjoyable. Keep your fishing easy and effortless, the way it is meant to be. When you do that you're going to enjoy it more.

The thing to avoid is 3D, and it's easy to see why. It stands for difficult, distasteful, and depressing. Has fishing gotten too hard in some way? Is it putting a sour taste in your mouth? No wonder you're depressed.

Lighten up. Fishing is supposed to be fun. Remember the way fishing was when you were a boy. Return to that feeling and explore it anew. Sure, you know more now. But is all that hard-earned wisdom making your fishing more pleasurable, or less?

Maybe you need to tie a knot blindfolded. Or enter a distance casting contest. Or flycast a hole of golf. Or have an all-day, one-fly fishing battle with a friend. Or jump in a lake naked. Or get drunk.

Or all of the above.

When you fish, think of E for easy. Stay away from the dreaded Ds.

Resolved: I keep my fishing easy, effortless, and enjoyable.

September 9

"He was fishing for his soul, not his stomach."

—Robert Deindorfer

There's a story about a fly-fisherman who was exploring an isolated part of Asia when he came upon a beautiful, wild river. He unpacked his Orvis rod and promptly tried his luck.

His luck, as it happened, was not good. He drew nary a peck. Over time, the native people who lived along the river grew curious about the visitor's strange ways. Neither spoke the other's language, so they could only communicate through gestures.

The people were friendly and polite, but bemused. They could not believe how poorly the fly-fisherman was doing. To show him a better way, a couple of them ripped branches from a tree along the bank, tied lines to their crudely fashioned hooks, and began pulling fish out of the river left and right.

As their fish piled up, they excitedly pointed them out to the fly-fisher, who continued to draw nothing. Finally the locals offered him their entire catch, an offer he graciously refused. He could not make them understand that he was fishing for his soul, not his stomach.

The moral: to each his own. Both branches of fishing philosophy—utilitarian versus spiritual, bait versus flies—are valid, as are both types of fishermen. Just know that if you fish for your soul, sometimes your stomach will go hungry.

Resolved: I fish for my soul.

September 10

"There is no activity so conducive to the health and happiness of a civilized man as angling with an artificial fly."

—Hennings Hale-Orviston

You're a civilized man and you've been working hard, too hard. It's time for a break. It's time to go angling with an artificial fly.

Everybody needs a break now and then. Not only that, everybody needs periodic reminders about taking a break. How do you know when it's time to lay off work? Here are four signs:

1. You dream about your job at night, and it's a nightmare.
2. Your colleagues run from you at the coffee machine in the morning for fear of being verbally assaulted.
3. You plot on your lunch napkin ways to murder your boss.
4. You bring your sleeping bag to work as a means of getting through the afternoon.

Think of how many good ideas about work come to you when you get away from it for a while. And those ideas probably would not have occurred to you (or not as quickly) if you had dutifully stayed on the job. Getting away from work is good for work. It's even better when you get away to fish.

Need any more persuading? Uh, what's that? You say it was your boss who needed persuading all along?

Oh.

Refer to number three.

Resolved: Rather than commit a capital offense and spend the rest of my life in prison, I take the day off from work and fish.

September 11

"The trip to a day of fishing is invariably a great pleasure, but in some ways the trip back after some successful sport is greater still."

—Robert Deindorfer

Going is sweet. Coming back is even sweeter. A lot of people like to go because of the way it makes them feel when they come back.

You fish in the morning and into early afternoon, but you don't want to get back too late so you take off about three or four o'clock. Traffic isn't too bad as you wend your way out of tl. .nountains. You're kinda dirty and a little tired and you feel great.

You drive the first leg. Your buddy'll drive the second leg, when you get down out of the mountains and hit the valley where it's flat and dull and the traffic picks up. You like driving the first leg because it's still piney woods country. You're jacked up from fishing and cruising home.

While you're pumping the gas, your buddy fills up at the mini mart. Bag of tortilla chips, gum, Snickers bars, cans of roasted peanuts. You've worked up a real appetite the last few days.

On the way back, you talk about fishing and the things you did and the places you want to try in the future and when you think you can get away again. After a while you get tired of talking and turn on the radio. Iris DeMent is singing the Merle Haggard song "Big City." You're still on the road when the sun sets. Nobody says a word as the sky explodes like it's on fire and the clouds turn orange and pink and red.

Resolved: I go fishing, so I can feel the way it feels when I come back.

September 12

"There is not a fly fisherman on earth, no matter how skilled, who has not been humbled by a low-hanging branch or a submerged boulder."

—Judy Muller

When Judy Muller went to the Jackson Hole One Fly Competition one year, she saw (and heard about) some amazing retrievals. At the One Fly, contestants only get to fish with one fly per day, so they go to extraordinary lengths to hang onto them.

One woman swam under her boat to save her fly. When she emerged on the other side, her rod and fly were both intact. Not bad.

Equally impressive was a New Zealand guide who hung his fly up on a tree branch. He had to climb the tree ("a wobbly lodgepole pine," says Muller) and then edge out on the limb to untangle it. He did, and remained in the competition.

Still another angler used his guide as a ladder, climbing onto his shoulders to reach a fly stuck in the upper branches of another one of those irritating lodgepole pines that always seem to get in the way of a perfectly fine cast.

It is probable that you will not climb on your buddy's shoulders or swim under your boat to retrieve an errant fly. Your first reaction when you snag one is: "Damn!" Then you investigate.

Stay with it. Don't give up hope (at least not right away). Every fisherman would agree that it is nearly as satisfying to retrieve a fly that's been given up for lost as it is to hook a fish.

Resolved: I make an amazing retrieval of a fly today.

September 13

"To her way of thinking, the entire year was designed solely to summon September into existence: cool, crisp mornings turning to warm afternoons under a saturated blue sky."

—Elizabeth Storer

It's September. Is there a better time to fish?

The blazing heat of August is over. The cold and hard weather of winter are still too far away to think about. The leaves are turning. There's an edge to the air. Mornings are cool and the day warms up without overheating. Then at night, unlike summer, it cools down again.

In September the kids go back to school. The weekend campers have pretty much shot their wad and stay home. Summer is over and people have had their vacations and are back to work full time.

That means some of those places you had to fight for elbow room in last month are empty now (mostly empty anyway). It's back to basics: you and the fish.

The best things about September are "the fat, hungry fish," as Elizabeth Storer says, that move silently through the water like phantoms. But they're not phantoms at all. They're living creatures, and like all living creatures they like to eat and you've got just the thing to whet their appetites.

Summer would seem to be the most relaxing time for fishing. But many fishermen prefer September. Next week is the official opening of fall. How are you going to spend it?

Resolved: I take a long fishing trip this September.

September 14

*"We must touch his weaknesses with a delicate hand. There are
some faults so nearly allied to excellence, that we can scarce
weed out the fault without eradicating the virtue."*

—Oliver Goldsmith

Maximize your strengths as a fisherman. Do the things you
know how to do, and exploit them to the fullest.

Don't worry too much about your perceived weaknesses—
what you supposedly lack. All you lack to become a better
fisherman, if you lack anything, is resolve. Summon that, and
you will have it all.

Conventional wisdom looks at a person's character and
notes his weaknesses and strengths, as if they were two separate, indivisible things. In reality, your weaknesses are tied
to your strengths and vice versa.

Remember this if you ever get too down on yourself. Sure,
there are always things you can do better in fishing. There are
always more things to know. But that type of thinking inhibits
you because it focuses on what you can't do or don't know.
Your weaknesses are part of you. But so are your strengths.

Trumpet your strengths. They're your meal ticket. They're
what carry you, like a tennis player who runs around a ball
to hit his forehand. He may have a weak backhand, but look
at that rocketing forehand.

What you know and can do with a rod and reel is a lot.
Build on the areas where you feel strongest and most comfortable. Exploit them fully. Your confidence will grow and
your weaknesses will seem miniscule compared to your
strengths.

Resolved: I recognize my strengths as a fisherman and build
on them.

September 15

"There is great pleasure in being on the sea, in the unknown wild suddenness of a great fish."

—Ernest Hemingway

Take pleasure in your circumstances, whatever they are.

Conditions aren't perfect, you say? When *are* they perfect? Take pleasure in the conditions, whatever they may be.

Let the hurricanes blow. Let the thunder sound. Let the rain pour forth as in Noah's time. A great fish may strike at any time, and you must be ready.

What's that, now? You say you feel rushed, that you don't have nearly enough time to fish as you like? At least you're fishing! There are a lot of people who would trade places with you in a flash, who wish they were standing in your waders (not with you in them though). Take pleasure in the time you have, however short, and make the best of it.

Some fishermen like to gripe. They may not have a specific complaint, they just gripe on general principle.

Oh well, if that's your pleasure, gripe away. Take pleasure in your griping and know that you're lucky to have people who will listen (if indeed they haven't all left the room by now).

Whatever your pleasure, take pleasure in it. And if you're miserable, take pleasure in *that*. For inevitably, if you are like most fishermen, fishing will make you miserable. But your misery must always be tempered by the fact that you *are* fishing and that can never be entirely bad. What brings you misery also brings you unsurpassed joy. If this seems a contradiction, so be it. Take pleasure in the contradictions as well.

Resolved: I take pleasure in fishing, no matter how miserable I am.

September 16

One of the great things about fishing a certain spot on a river or a lake is that you can go back to it time and time again and still learn things about it.

There's a Rorschach test quality about fishing at such a spot. You see something different each time you look at it. And what you see depends a lot on where you are in your life.

When you were a teenager and fishing with your dad, you saw it in a certain way. After you became a man and started working the river on your own, you saw it differently than you did when you were younger. Then when you came back with your own family your view of it changed again.

And when you're an old man showing your grandson how to fish, you will have yet another perception.

The river has an objective reality. To a person with no stake in it, it's merely a stretch of water along the road. But for you it brings a rush of memories and feelings and longings of the deepest sort.

The place has never changed (not much anyway). But you have. What you saw as a teenager doesn't exist anymore—at least not in your mind. But what you discovered as an old man was there when you were a teenager. You just couldn't see it at the time. In this way and in so many other ways a river teaches you about yourself. There are always things to learn. There's no outgrowing it, it always grows with you.

Resolved: I remain open to what rivers and lakes can teach me.

September 17

"Water is made for fishing."

—Edna Mills

Get tough on your next fishing trip. Be purposeful. Take a narrow view when you fish.

Eliminate distractions. Before you proceed with an activity, ask yourself this: is it going to cut into my fishing time? If the answer is yes, be merciless. Cut it out. Or if that's not possible, take care of it quickly, then get down to the water.

You've worked hard to get some time to fish. Now take it. Save your apologies for later.

One of the joys of fishing is the lack of a clock. You take your time. There are no deadlines, no places you have to be. You dawdle and meander. What's the hurry anyway? The river will still be there. The fish aren't going anywhere.

The only problem with this attitude is that sometimes you really do have to get down to it. You've got to leave behind your everyday world with its problems and distractions and step into that clear, cold, rushing water.

The things that seemed so important to you before you started fishing will fall away to nothing once you make your first cast. You will tune into the fishing and tune out everything else. The hours will slip away, and when you return to your everyday world all those things that once seemed so important and so in need of attention will seem like the inconsequential nothings they are.

Resolved: I focus on my fishing and keep the distractions to a minimum.

September 18

*"Innocence is a wild trout. But we humans, being complicated,
have to pursue innocence in complex ways."*

—Datus Proper

Does something bother you about your fishing? Do something about it.

You're not fishing as much as you'd like? You're not as good as you want to be? You're dissatisfied with your equipment? You want to travel more? You want to fish new places? You want to find someone else to fish with? You need new challenges?

You can sit around and let that thing bother you, whatever it is. Or you can do something about it. It's your choice.

Fishing is simple, though people tend to make it complicated. There is a simple solution at hand. Do something about it.

What to do, exactly? That's up to you. But the situation won't get better unless you do something about it. You didn't expect someone else to do it for you, did you?

Your destiny is in your hands. You have the power to remake your world. Let luck take care of itself. You'll have good luck and you'll have bad luck. If you sit around waiting for your luck to improve, it never will. Do something concrete about your situation, and luck—good, bad, or indifferent—will seem far less important.

Resolved: If something is bugging me in fishing, I do something about it.

September 19

"Imagination is more important than knowledge."

—Albert Einstein

In a typical day of piscine hunting, you will inevitably face situations that are familiar to you. Since you've faced these situations before, you may also have come up with familiar solutions.

Today, try something different. Try a new solution to an old problem. When you meet with a challenge, approach it in a way you've never done before. Find an imaginative new alternative, different than what you've done in the past.

Your old methods may have worked pretty well. You can always go back to them if this new way fails.

But it may be an improvement. You must grant this possibility. It cannot be denied. In trusting your imagination, you may find a better way of doing things, one that makes your old methods instantly obsolete.

Experience is a record of the known. It points you down a path that you've already traveled. It is the safe choice that offers predictable rewards.

Imagination takes a much riskier path that is fraught with danger. Sometimes it leads nowhere. It frequently ends in failure. You must have courage to trust it over the long haul.

Give your imagination free rein today. Abandon the tried and true. Be an Einstein on the stream and explore new ways of doing things.

Resolved: I find an imaginative solution to a familiar problem.

September 20

"When I grow up, I want to be a little boy."

—Joseph Heller

Maintain a youthful attitude when you fish. Take risks and dare. Be willing to experiment and make mistakes. A young fisherman makes plenty of mistakes. But as he does, he learns.

Be adventurous. Stalk those fish upstream and down. Don't follow the dictates of conventional wisdom. Go where no one else thinks you can catch fish.

Be naive and optimistic, two more attributes of youth. An old fisherman knows better, so he does not try. A young fisherman does not know any better, so he tries. He may fail in his attempt, but he learns. As he learns, the world of fish and water gradually becomes more familiar to him. In time, it feels like home.

A young fisherman is constantly learning, no matter what his age. An old fisherman thinks he knows it all. Even Methuselah, if he had been a fisherman, could not have known all there is to know about fishing.

Imagination is youth. Experience is age. Choose imagination over experience. But be a sponge when it comes to useful information. Take what you can that's valuable from other fishermen, and leave the rest.

Maintain a cheerful, open attitude, whether you are twenty-five years old or seventy-five. No one is crankier than a cranky fisherman. Know that if you have not caught anything yet, very soon you will. And if you don't catch any today, know that you will tomorrow.

Resolved: I maintain the optimism of youth when I fish.

September 21

"You have to be something of a detective to fish for bass."
—Larry Bower, bass fisherman

You have to be something of a detective to fish . . . *period.* Whether it's for lake bass, river trout, or deep-sea marlins, you need a Sherlock Holmesian bent for detail and a roving eye for any clues that will lead you to fish.

In the case of bass, knowing the lake is essential. Most experts say that the places where people usually look for bass are not necessarily the places where bass hang out. Bass love the shade. You can catch tournament-winning largemouth and smallmouth bass by casting along the boat docks. Unlike mad dogs and Englishmen, bass like to stay out of the noonday sun and loiter in the shade of the docks.

Other good spots to look for bass (thanks to the detective work of outdoor writer Tom Stienstra) are trees and bushes sticking up out of the water, around old dock pilings, deep coves where trees and brush provide shade, and big rockpiles. Bass tend not to be found on the surface, except perhaps early in the morning or late in the day. Then, of course, as the time of year changes, the bass move around and they become even more difficult to catch, veritable Richard Kimballs of the water.

To catch bass or any fish, you must develop the instincts of a good detective. All it takes is a willingness to learn. The clues are all there, you just have to look for them.

Resolved: I keep on the lookout for clues that will lead me to fish.

September 22

"Suddenly the line went dead. Far off, the marlin broke into the sunshine—a sea-enamelled beauty, going away fast."

—Phillip Wylie

Quit thinking small when it comes to fishing. Think big. Think in terms of a fishing expedition to someplace like Bali or Fiji or who knows where.

Weekend trips are cool. There's nothing wrong with going on Friday and coming back on Sunday. At least you went. A lot of people don't even do that. At least you had a full day of fishing on Saturday. A lot of people can't claim that.

But it's time to think bigger than that. Fall is the traditional time for planning major excursions for the coming year. Now it's time to think about doing something . . . *huge.*

What's that? It's nice to dream, but you really can't afford it. You've got to get your act together before you do something like that.

Aw, forget that noise. You may never get your act together, you know? That's just an excuse for doing nothing. Your life will always be in a certain disorderly state. That will never change; it's in the nature of things. In the meantime, go to Bali. When you come back your life will be in the same disorderly state, but it will seem better somehow. Or you just won't care as much.

Start checking out the fishing magazines and the travel brochures. Something big is beckoning to you. It could be Bali or Fiji, or you name it.

Resolved: I start planning a big fishing expedition for next spring.

September 23

"Patience—and the mulberry leaf becomes a silk gown."

—Chinese proverb

Do one thing. Then move on to the next thing.

Check out the water. Walk up and down the shore. Take your time. See what's going on. Perhaps even take a moment to yourself. Sit still and close your eyes.

Open your eyes, and move on to the next thing.

Do the thing you're doing as well as you can. Tie a nail knot. Tie it as well as you're able. Then move on from there.

Find a spot and fish it. Really fish it. Then move on to the next spot when you feel it's time.

Focus on what you're doing, whatever it is, and do it as well as you can. What's next will come in its good time. Stay tuned to the thing you're doing at that moment and do it as well as you can.

You'll never be a patient fisherman if you are constantly looking ahead. In all likelihood when you get to the thing you've been so ardently desiring, your mind will jump ahead to the next thing after that. And do you ever get to the place you want to be? Good question.

To be patient is to do one thing, then to move on to the next thing.

Resolved: I practice patience. I finish one thing before moving steadily on to the next.

September 24

"Awake up my glory; awake, lute and harp; I myself will awake right early!"

—Prayer

Rev it up.

Can't get started this morning? Can't seem to get off the dime? Rev it up.

Get up out of bed; get off your sorry butt. There are fish to be caught. Need some coffee? Tea? Here, have a cup, or three. Just rev it up.

All right, you made it. You're out there. You're out of bed and on the stream. But the same principle applies: rev it up.

It's late in the morning, you're starting to fade. You're getting hungry and thinking about a salami and cheese lunch. *Now* rev it up. Give yourself another 20 or 30 minutes of hard fishing, then take your break.

Draw your energy from the sun or the fish or whatever is available at that moment, and rev it up.

It's after lunch. You've had your snooze. You want to take another crack at it but you can't seem to move. Well, move it. Rev it up. There's plenty of good fishing left.

It's nearly sundown. It's that peaceful, lovely time of day when everything gets still and even the birds quiet down and the light softens and the shadows lengthen across the water. Before you call it a day, rev it up one more time.

Resolved: I rev it up and hit the stream early today.

September 25

"If I fished only to capture fish, my fishing trips would have ended long ago."

—Zane Grey

How do you know when to quit at the end of the day? When you feel good about yourself and your fishing.

Catching a fish is the perfect capper for every day. It leaves you on a high note. It gives you something fresh to brag about and motivates you to get out fishing again as soon as you can.

Still, a lot of fishermen don't like to pack it in right after they've done something special. They're too jazzed. They want to keep the feeling going and land another.

But it's foolish to think that every day is going to end with a rock 'em–sock 'em performance that bags you a fighting ten-pound sockeye. That's the way Hollywood makes movies, but it's not fishing. So you're going to have to find your positives elsewhere.

Some fishermen find their positives in the simple fact that they are fishing. Any day spent fishing is a day well spent.

Other fishermen recall a hard battle or two they fought earlier in the day and carry that memory with them. Still other fishermen draw strength from the beauty of their surroundings. Others relish the time they've spent with their son or daughter or someone else who's important in their life.

There are plenty of positives in fishing that have nothing to do with catching fish. Those positives are on call to fishermen throughout the day, from beginning to end.

Resolved: I walk away from a day of fishing feeling good about myself.

September 26

"One may explain water, but the mouth will not become wet."

—Takuan

If he doesn't get it, drop it. You explained it to him, didn't you? You did your job. Now drop it.

It's like the old saw about leading a horse to water. You can tell your son how to fish, but that doesn't mean he's going to do it. You can explain and explain and explain and explain and explain. But it's just wasted breath if his mind is as closed as the door to his room.

Clearly, he's not listening to you. Live with it. He's a teenager and he's not going to. That's *his* job.

Sure, it's frustrating. Sure, you know how to fish and you could save him a lot of problems if he'd just do what you say. But ragging on him will only make it worse.

He'll get it. Or he won't. If he doesn't, it's not because you didn't do your part. You did everything you could.

Ultimately it's his deal. He's either going to catch on or not. It's hard to divorce your ego from caring because you're his father and you want him to learn and excel. Fishing is a thing that you value and you want to him to value it, too.

But he can never experience fishing the way you experience it. That's impossible. So back off and let it happen on its own. He'll find his way and when he does, it will lead back to you.

Resolved: I explain less and fish more with my son.

September 27

"Truth is the most valuable thing we have. Let us economize it."
—Mark Twain

When you're sitting at a trout pool and another fisherman walks up and asks how you're doing, tell him "terrible," and forget to mention the half-dozen rainbow trout you caught that morning.

When you tell the fellas at the tackle shop how you caught a half-dozen rainbows yesterday and they ask where, tell them, "You know, down at the bridge," even though it wasn't within forty miles of the bridge. The next morning when you drive by the bridge, be sure to wave hi to everybody.

When a fisherman you've never seen before asks if you know any hot places to fish, shake your head slowly and say, "Nope. Sorry, I'd be there right now if I did." Watch him drive away, then head off to your pool where the fish are packed in like spectators at an Ohio State–Michigan football game.

Truth is a very fine and noble concept, but it should not be applied too liberally else people may come to take it for granted. Finding a good place to fish is like striking gold. As soon as you tell one person, the whole damn town knows. Pretty soon it's the Gold Rush of '49. Better to apply a little misdirection to anyone who might come sniffing around your strike.

Resolved: Like every good fisherman, I economize with the truth if it's to my advantage.

September 28

"The lasting pleasures of contact with the natural world are not reserved for scientists but are available to anyone who will place himself under the influence of earth, sea, and sky, and their amazing life."

—Rachel Carson

What do you need to know as a man and fisherman? What do you need to learn? Nature will tell you.

Want to find fish? They're there all right, if you know where to look. How do you know where to look? Ask nature.

And how do you know when the fish are running? The paper won't have that information. Look in nature.

How do you rate as a fisherman? How do you handle a rod and reel? Nature will put you to the test.

Want to read a book that is limitless? Read nature's book. Want to engage in a lifetime of learning? Enroll in nature's school, where you never graduate.

Want to explore? Explore nature. Want to challenge yourself in ways you've never been done before? Face nature's challenges.

What are the answers? Nature has them. What are the questions? Ask nature.

The world outside you is a mirror of what is inside you. Feel at home with nature and you will feel at home with yourself. Those who feel fully themselves, feel in harmony with nature. Today, take your fishing rod and go into nature.

Resolved: I put myself in frequent contact with the world of fish and nature.

September 29

Know this: if it's meant to be, it will happen. If it's not, it won't.

The Muslims have a saying: If Allah wants you on the bus, he'll put you on the bus. If Allah says no, even if you're the Keanu Reeves character in *Speed*, you won't get on that bus.

Virgil expresses a similar thought in *The Aeneid*, writing about one of the challenges faced by his epic hero Aeneas. "It will come willingly, easily if you are called by fate," Virgil writes. "If not, with all your strength you cannot conquer it."

All this has relevance for fishermen. You're either going to catch fish, or you're not. Every fisherman has had those days where he tries everything, but nothing works. It almost doesn't matter what he does. It's as if it's been taken out of his hands.

For whatever reason, Allah didn't want to put him on the fish-catching bus that day.

This is not an argument against individual initiative or the value of persistence. By all means, keep after those rascally critters. Do everything you can. Fight the good fight.

But some days, if all your efforts come to naught, you may do well to accept the wisdom of fate, rather than railing against it. And try to get on that darned bus tomorrow.

Resolved: If Allah wants me to catch fish, I catch fish. (But I keep trying.)

September 30

"Nostalgia seems to infuse every aspect of fishing."

—Bill Barich

Always come back with something when you fish. Whether it is a memory or a photograph or a new piece of water lore, always come back with something.

In older, simpler times, fishermen came back with fish. They judged their day by the number of fish in their creel. But creels have largely gone out of fashion because fish are no longer as plentiful as they once were and it's wiser to return them to the waters where they live.

Nevertheless, come back with something when you fish. Even if it's nothing more than a whopping good yarn. A fish out of water has a finite life. It must be consumed else it will begin to smell. But a good story will last forever, even the smelly ones.

An abalone fisherman named Bob Kaehms had a favorite phrase. "Let's go make new memories," he'd say, dressed in a full wet suit with his mask and snorkel, just prior to plunging into the cold waters of the Pacific Ocean in search of abalone or rockfish.

That's a lot of what fishing is about: making new memories. Living in the present, to have stories to tell in the future. It's not always possible to bring back fish from your fishing expeditions. But always bring back something, whether it's a great memory, a photograph, or a new piece of water lore.

Resolved: I fish and make new memories.

October 1

"There are as good fish in the sea today as ever came out of it."
—English proverb

It's the first of October. A better day has arrived.

What's so special about today? Nothing. Or rather: *everything*. It's getting colder. But it's not the dead of winter yet. There's a nip in the air. The leaves are turning gold and red and orange. It's truly a special day.

Special? Heck, as Tony the Tiger might say, it's *grrrrrr-eat*!

Today's the day. This is it. It's unlike any other in your life, maybe even in the whole history of the human race.

What's so special about this day? Well, the salmon are running this time of year. That's pretty special all right. But that's not it, not all of it anyway. No, what makes this a better day than all the rest is . . . *you*.

You've decided to quit living for tomorrow. You've decided to stop thinking that things are going to get better in the future. A better day is here. In fact, it's perfect. There's no sense waiting around anymore because it's perfect today.

The fish in the sea now are as good as they ever were. The future has arrived. It's time to start living it.

Resolved: Whatever I want to do in fishing or anything else, I do it. Starting today.

October 2

"And God said, Let the waters bring forth abundantly the moving creature that hath life, and fowl that may fly above the earth in the open firmament of heaven."

—Genesis 1:20

You read in the newspapers and magazines about how this is "an era of limits." You think that's probably right in some ways, but then you go out and spend some time in the woods fishing and it doesn't seem all that limited.

Matter of fact, it seems abundant. The sky is huge. Is there a shortage of sky in the world? Not when you're fishing. Unless you're down in a canyon or tucked away deep in some pine forest, the sky mostly opens up and extends from horizon to horizon, the way it was designed to.

The sun is equally present. It's large and in charge. Forget your sunglasses on a bright, cloudless day with the light reflecting off the water, and you'll be in trouble.

When you're fishing, you hear nothing but the sound of rushing water. You get used to the cold (well, sort of) and closely watch a cloud of insects hovering above the water. There's definitely no era of limits when it comes to bugs. Trees and greenery surround you, more shades of green than in Ireland's County Kerry. The sun is high in a vast cloudless sky. Small birds buzz along the water's surface.

Despite the disappearing forests, despite the lack of wild, undammed rivers and wild, untamed fish, despite the array of environmental problems that need attending, the world of fishing is still a world of plenty. Lose yourself in it.

Resolved: When I'm fishing, I revel in the abundance of life.

October 3

"A bobber just barely visible in the dark water is one of the most beautiful sights known to man. It's not doing anything, but there's always the feeling that at any instant it might."

—Jean Shepherd

Fish till the sun sets. Fish into the night and beyond.

Be in a boat as the sun sinks below the horizon, turning the sky on fire. Watch as the clouds turn pink and red. Then keep fishing. Fish till the stars come out.

Race out of work, jump in the car, hit the road, and drive. Skip dinner (or eat it on the fly) and roar up to the river. Get your gear and get down to the lake. Daylight savings hasn't ended yet. You've still got time.

There's nothing like fishing in the late evening. All the other fishermen have given up and gone home. (Okay, maybe not. But there's always a chance.) Anyhow, it's a peaceful, easy time of day that spawns contentment no matter what the fish are doing.

Maybe you fish in the evening all the time, so it's no big deal to you. But if you do it all the time, you know it's nice and mellow. That's why you do it.

No matter how you began the day, you ended it right. No matter what happened during the day, you finished it perfectly. The sun is setting. Night is coming on. While the rest of the world retreats indoors, stay right where you are and fish.

Resolved: I usher in the night with fishing rod in hand.

October 4

"What in the world are you doing here? Because touching this wildness is the best way I know to undermine sadness."

—Pam Houston, on why she fishes

Maintain your resolve.

There will be good days in fishing and bad days. Maintain your resolve throughout the good and the bad.

Some days you will catch fish and some days you will not. Maintain your resolve whether you catch fish or not.

There will be times when you are about to pull in a fish, and your line will inexplicably break. Maintain your resolve even when it seems the fishing gods have got it in for you.

Some days will be sunny and mild. Other days the rain will pour and thunder will shake the heavens. Maintain your resolve whatever the weather brings.

Sometimes conditions will be perfect. Other times gale-force winds will blow in your face. Maintain your resolve whatever the conditions are.

There will be times when you feel like the world's greatest fisherman. There will be other times when you feel like a complete schmuck. Maintain your resolve whatever you happen to think of yourself or your abilities at any given moment.

Your fortunes in fishing will go up and down like a roller coaster. There will be sad days as well as happy ones. Maintain your resolve amid all the ups and downs of fishing.

Resolved: I hang tough in fishing, no matter what.

October 5

"When you are able to cast a dainty dry fly over a glassy trout pool of a mountain stream and make the trout come up and take it, there is a sensation that will long be remembered."

—Ray Ovington

Put it on hold. Whatever it is, put it on hold and fish.

You've got a book deadline staring you in the face. Ah, your editor will understand. Put it on hold and fish.

The backyard looks like hell. Nobody's mowed the front lawn in years. The weeds have taken over your flower garden. Runaway ivy is pulling down the fence.

Oh well, it's survived this long without you, another week or so won't hurt. Put it on hold and fish.

Your wife wants you to go with her to visit her mother. You haven't seen your mother-in-law in five or six years. Ah, what's the hurry anyway? She'll understand. Put it on hold and fish.

The car is leaking oil and needs to go to the shop. A headlight is broken. The glove compartment door came off its hinges and had to be removed. The driver's-side doorlatch has fallen off. So has the rearview mirror.

Yes, but it *drives*. There's no need to rush into anything, especially if what you're rushing into is a large repair bill. Put it on hold and fish. And take the car. It's got at least one more fishing trip left in it before it collapses.

Think cosmically. Is what you're doing—or about to do— really that important? The trivialities of life—they shall pass. But a fishing trip is something you will remember for a lifetime.

Resolved: I put it on hold and fish.

October 6

"Give me, kind heaven, a private station,
A mind serene for contemplation."

—John Gay

You're not sure what bait or fly to use. What do you do? Chew a reed and think about it.

You arrive at the river. You jump out of the car and head down to the water to check things out. While you're there, chew a reed and think about it.

A big ol' hairy Snake River cutthroat is camped in a pool beyond the rocks. There it is, ripe for the plucking, but you're not sure how to approach it for fear you might scare it. Before you move a muscle, chew a reed and think about it.

You've fished all day. You're beat but also curious about what it looks like upstream. Pack it in or go some more? That's the question.

Here's the answer: chew a reed and think about it.

Some fishermen smoke cigarettes. Some even smoke pipes. Some do their best thinking between slugs from a bottle. Sitting down and chewing a reed is another option.

It's a contemplative act. Maybe it's the chewing, but something about it helps you relax and get things straight in your mind. You gather it all in. You stop rushing. It's impossible to rush with a reed in your mouth.

Chewing a reed puts you in the right frame of mind to contemplate the vicissitudes of fishing. Whether you land a big fish, or (many condolences) lose one, you know what to do.

Resolved: I chew a reed and think about it.

October 7

*"The art of losing isn't hard to master; so many things seem
filled with the intent to be lost that their loss is no disaster."*

—Elizabeth Bishop

It is not a disaster to lose things, although it can seem that
way at first.

Maybe you lost a piece of tackle or even that precious new
Swiss army knife you just bought. Maybe you mislaid your
watch or a pair of expensive sunglasses or that beat-up old
pair of Converse waders that you've been fishing in for years.

You lose one of these things and it hurts. Plus it's irritating as hell. You used those waders so many times it was like
losing an old friend. A whole slew of fishing memories was
tied up in them.

But now they're gone. Like an idiot you left them on a log
by the car and drove off without them.

The first impulse is to immediately replace the loss. Go
down to the fishing shop and buy a new pair, as if the loss
never occurred at all. Certainly if you want to keep fishing,
you're going to need some waders.

But sometimes when you lose something, you realize you
didn't need it after all. There's a lesson here. It's not the disaster you thought. You can get along fine without it. In certain cases you don't even replace the thing you lost; it's not
vital.

A loss of this kind can simplify your fishing. In some mysterious way you realize that you're better off without the thing
that you once could not live without.

Resolved: When I lose a piece of gear, I question whether
I need to replace it.

October 8

"Sakyamuni once cried out in pity for a yogi by the river who had wasted 20 years of his human existence in learning how to walk on water, when the ferryman might have taken him across for a small coin."

—Richard Kehl

Go ahead. Ask him. He won't bite. He may even be able to help.

Okay, so it is your dad. So what? He's been around the block once or twice, in a fishing sense, and he knows what he's talking about.

Come on, don't be like that yogi. Do you want to take twenty years to learn to walk on water when someone will motor you across for pocket change? Fishing isn't walking on water.

It's the height of youthful hubris—ah, now there's a term for you—to think you can do it alone. You can do a lot of things by yourself, and you will, but every now and then it makes sense to seek out the counsel of your tribal elders.

But that's not the end, that's only the beginning. As a fisherman, you need to draw from all sources. Start with dad. But keep your eyes open for more fishing mentors. Learn from anybody and everybody.

And don't be afraid to ask dumb questions, which are probably not as dumb as you think. Every fisherman has likely troubled over the same problems at one time or another.

Asking a dumb question is the smartest thing you can do. Most fishermen will respond sympathetically and go out of their way to help you.

Resolved: I draw from all sources when I'm learning to fish.

October 9

"It was interesting and good to know about, and it always made me happy that there were men fishing in the city itself, having sound, serious fishing and taking a few fritures home to their family."

—Ernest Hemingway

Sound, serious fishing in the city. What a concept.

Hemingway was talking about fishing the River Seine in Paris in the 1930s. But those times are long gone, at least in the United States. Nowadays most urban creeks and rivers are polluted or lined with concrete or messed up in some way.

This is very sad. David Van Over is a Berkeley, California, fly-fisherman who grew up with two trout streams running through his family's Pennsylvania farm. He loves to fish in places like Russia, New Zealand, and Chile, but as he points out, "it's ultimately more satisfying to visit these distant destinations after becoming intimate with our local waters." But when your local waters aren't fishable, what do you do?

Somehow, some way, you get involved. Many fishing clubs are active in creek restoration projects in their area. So are schools and public service agencies. Some of these groups are making real progress too, though it's a long, tough battle to change generations of wrong-headed policies and public lethargy.

Think of it. Instead of driving three hours to find a trout stream—or flying halfway round the world—you grab your rod and fish the creek that cuts through your city.

Is it naive to think that this can actually happen?

Resolved: I find out about creek restoration projects in my area.

October 10

"It is permitted me to take good fortune where I find it."

—Moliere

Salute your good fortune. It's permitted. Some people never get a chance to do what you do. You're fishing. How tough can life be?

Salute your good sense. Some people work and work and work and that's all they know. You, however, have chosen to take a break and get a new perspective on things.

Salute your wisdom. Some people constantly bang their heads against a wall and wonder why they're not happy. You, however, have said good-bye to what was depressing you to engage in an activity that gives you pleasure.

Salute your outdoor nature. You have chosen to go outside and breathe fresh air and feel the sun against your face and listen to the birds chirp and walk in cold mountain streams and see the moonrise and do a thousand other things that indoor people will never see or do.

Salute your patience. Some people need immediate results. You, however, are willing to wait . . . and wait . . . and wait for a good thing in the form of a fish.

Salute your fighting spirit. Some people get depressed when they lose. You, however, know that losing is part of the game and that it is ultimately what makes winning (i.e., catching fish) so worthwhile.

Salute your genius. Yes, genius. Hey, you're a fisherman, right? You're doing what you truly love and what makes you happy. What's a better definition of genius than that?

Resolved: I salute my good fortune today.

October 11

"I feel that I am reserved for some end or other."

—Lord Clive

Get there. Just get there.

Where's there? It's not necessarily the end, sometimes it's only the beginning.

You may want to be a great fisherman. You may want to fish big water. You may want to fish in exotic locales. You may want to devote more time to fishing. You may want all of the above and more.

Wherever you want to go as a fisherman—whatever place you seek—it's within your reach. Keep going and you'll get there.

You won't get there if you quit. Nobody gets anywhere when they quit. The only way you'll get there is to keep going.

You haven't gotten there yet. But you will. Keep your eyes on the prize, and you'll get there.

You may need to try harder. You may need to try less. But you'll get there. Never doubt it for an instant.

Sometimes people get to where they're going without even realizing it. Sometimes people overlook what they have in the moment in their quest for what's just beyond. And sometimes a person must let go of his desires to find out what he really wants.

But not you. You know your destiny. You just haven't gotten there yet. But you will. You will.

Resolved: I keep working for what I want in fishing.

October 12

"The attraction of angling for all the ages of man, from the cradle to the grave, lies in its uncertainty. 'Tis an affair of luck."

—Henry Van Dyke

Some fishermen possess a strategic planning mentality. They plan their trips down to the minutest detail, as if preparing to invade an enemy land populated by a strange race of underwater swimming creatures. They look ahead and seek to anticipate every eventuality.

This is impossible, of course. A fishing trip never works out exactly the way it is intended. More frequently than not, all their finely wrought preparations are blown away in a moment by the weather or the fish or some hidden factor.

What's that old saying? Life is what happens when you're making other plans. It's the same with fishing. Fishing is what happens while you're making other plans.

Here's a thought: enjoy the uncertainty of it, for that's what makes fishing what it is. If everything went according to design, how much fun would that be? Fishing is a roll of the dice. You can't control what happens. That's why men and women keep coming back to it and why it can never be mastered.

Go ahead. Make your plans and preparations. That's okay. It helps to have a sense of what you want to do and where you want to go beforehand.

Just remember this: when things do not go according to plan, on some level that is when they start to go *right*.

Resolved: I enjoy the uncertainties of fishing and the absence of control.

October 13

Get past it. Whatever blocks or impedes your progress, get past it. Get past it, and go.

It is time. It is well past time, in fact. You've spent long enough in this place. Now is the time to get over the hump, and move on.

Take a good look at what you're doing. Have you been here before? Are you unconsciously following a pattern of behavior that is holding you back? Awareness comes first.

Get away from it for a while. Time is the best teacher. When you return to the problem, the answer that you were missing may be in the palm of your hand.

Seek advice. Watch other fishermen. You can learn from other people. They see things you may overlook.

Look at it from another point of view. Perhaps that is all that's needed. Approach your situation differently than you've done in the past. Look at it from a third point of view if necessary.

Simplify. If you're having trouble in fishing, you're probably making it more complicated than it is. Like swimming across the English Channel, the rules are pretty plain. Keep that in mind whenever you find yourself blocked for any reason.

Resolved: I simplify, and move on.

October 14

"O sir, doubt not angling is an art. Is it not art to deceive a trout with an artificial fly?"

—Izaak Walton

Think sharp, fish well. That's an axiom to live by. Fuzzy thinking leads to fuzzy-headed fishing.

When you have a clear thought in fishing, follow it. If the thought is to stray, by all means, stray. If the thought is to stay put, then stay put. The only way you'll know whether the thought was a good one is to follow it. Don't live a life of fishing regret. Do what you think to do.

Follow your thoughts upstream and down. Follow your thoughts to Montana or Maine or the Caribbean. Follow your thoughts out of the office and into the nearest trout stream. Follow your thoughts wherever they lead.

The brain is a fertile spawning ground. The more you think, the more thinking you will do, and the more precise your thoughts will become. Generally, in fishing and in life, this is a good thing, although there are exceptions.

Your fly rod is at its best when harnessed to your thoughts. Angling is the art of converting thoughts into action. Ignore your thoughts and you will come to distrust and doubt yourself. Follow your thoughts—first thought is best—and you will grow in streamside confidence daily.

Resolved: I think sharp and fish well.

October 15

"The little things? The little moments? They aren't little."

—Jon Kabat-Zinn

Pack up the food. Get the gear. It's time to hitch up the boat.

No kidding around now. This is serious. Back up the truck. Come on back, a little farther. There. Put the hood over the ball and hitch it up. Got it? Let's go.

There's no turning back when you hitch up the boat. What are you going to do, drive around town dragging a boat? No, there's only one thing to do when you hitch up a boat, and that's fish.

Before you leave town you stop at the tackle shop. You run in, get what you need. You park in the lot at an angle because you can't park in a normal space with a boat. Other people have to adjust to you, and you like that.

"Hey, that guy's going fishing," you imagine people are thinking when they see your boat. You like that, too.

Next stop: the gas station. The truck and the boat take up about three gas pumps. Any car that wants to fill up will have to wait until you're done.

You practically drain Saudi Arabia to fill your tank. While that's happening, you go into the mini mart and buy ice and stock up on munchies. You never go too fast when you're pulling a boat, so you might as well eat.

The lake is five hours away, four with a tailwind. At first you're real aware of this thing you're hauling behind you, checking to make sure it's still there. After a while you get used to it and relax. It's a nice feeling. You'll be there in no time.

Resolved: I hitch up the boat and go fishing.

October 16

"I scarcely recognized myself; the fanatical fisherman in me had died. I was someone I barely knew, lying on my side, watching a star."

—David James Duncan

Easy day, hard day. That's a good rule for fishing trips, now or at any other time of the year.

Take it easy on Sunday if you go all out on Saturday. Two hard days in a row is one too many.

The same holds true if you stay for a longer period of time. Push yourself a little on Monday, then maybe take Tuesday off. After your off day, jump back to it on Wednesday.

Some athletes train in this manner. They put in a hard day, followed by an easy day, followed by hard, and so forth. This gives them both a mental and physical break from their regime. No one, fishermen included, can push hard all the time and still get results.

Granted, this is not always easy to do. You come into an area and you've got X amount of time for fishing. You've paid good money for the privilege. You want to see everything you can, *now*. And you want to catch big fish.

Relax. In fishing, certainly, hard effort does not necessarily equate with results. It's like quicksand. The more you struggle, the deeper the hole you find yourself in. Better to lighten up a little and open up sides of your personality that normally do not get adequate air or light. In this relaxed state—surprise, surprise!—your fishing may experience a boon as well.

Resolved: I fish hard one day, then easy the next, and see what happens.

October 17

"We may our ends by our beginnings know."

—Sir John Denham

Be easy on yourself in the beginning.

Getting started may be the hardest part of any new venture, so be easy on yourself. You can only get to the end if you get past the beginning.

When you're learning to fish, be easy on yourself. There's a lot to learn. All this line you've got to take care of; these sharp, pointy little hooks; this big, long rod that you've got to make sure you don't stick into someone's eye; these squirmy worms—it's a lot to take in. So be kind to yourself, particularly at the start.

That's not bad advice even if you're an experienced fisherman who knows all the ropes. As everyone knows, those ropes can tangle your feet like vines and trip you up. Maybe you're coming back to fishing after a long layoff. Or maybe it's a simple case of too many beers the night before and a rocky start the following morning. In any case, be kind to yourself when you're just getting going. You'll be up to full speed in no time.

A good beginning frequently means a good ending. A good beginning can carry you a long time. No matter what happens later on, you'll always have that good beginning to look back on and draw strength from as you move along.

It's hard to get started on the right track with an unforgiving attitude. Be generous with yourself in the early going. Give yourself plenty of room to make mistakes and grow, and what follows after will go much more smoothly.

Resolved: I take it easy on myself in the beginning.

October 18

"The face of the sea is always changing. Crossed by colors, lights, and moving shadows, sparkling in the sun, mysterious in the twilight, its aspects and mood vary hour by hour."

—Rachel Carson

Coming back after a day of fishing, it just stops you. You're walking along, thinking about dinner or the drive home or whatever's next, and it just stops you.

The light.

It's late in the day, nearing twilight. The sun is low in the western sky. Deep shadows cut into the hills. The water is calm, not a trace of wind. The sky is a dusty blue. It's low tide. The shore is muddy and rocks that aren't normally visible rise out of the shallow blue-gray water.

You've seen this scene (or scenes like it) plenty of times, except for the light. It's a light show on the water, impossible to describe. Points of light radiating off the water, glowing and sparkling, in a mysterious diamond shape. The longer you stare at it, the more you see. Colors emerge. Blue, red, green blinking like ethereal Christmas tree lights.

You look around to see if anyone else is nearby, if anyone else sees it. You want to share this moment with someone. Do you see it? Do you see what I see?

But there's no one else. It's just you and the lights. Just you and the sky. Just you and the hills. You shake your head at the profound beauty of it all.

Reluctantly you start walking again, turning your back on the still-twinkling lights. Finally you reach your car, and head home.

Resolved: I stay tuned in to nature's amazing beauty.

October 19

"Some say trout fishing is a contemplative sport, but it never is when you stick a tiny fly into a big unsuspecting trout."

—Vincent Marinaro

Feel the power of fishing.

Feel what it's like to stretch your limbs in the sun. Feel the warmth against your face. Feel the sweat around your hat band. Dip your face and hands in a cold running creek, and feel revived.

Feel what it's like to be out in the woods with the birds and the squirrels and the deer as your only company. You'll meet no finer group of friends anywhere.

Feel what it's like to drop down into a creek channel and jump a bear feeding in the stream. It's a black bear, not a grizzly. Even more frightened than you, it runs off through the bushes with remarkable speed and grace.

Feel the power of water. Even shallow moving water can knock you off your feet if you're not careful. Fail to show the proper respect for water, and sooner or later it will bring you to your knees.

Feel the power of a strike. That is the most amazing feeling: when you realize suddenly that you're onto something big. It's like you've hooked into an elemental force. The fish puts everything on the line, holding nothing back, while energy surges into you on the other end of the line.

Then the fish leaps, incredibly, out of the water, and you almost jump out of your skin with it. There's nothing like it. Nothing else can match that sensation. For that moment at least, you feel wholly . . . *alive*.

Resolved: I feel the power of fishing.

October 20

"Rich in the simple worship of a day."

—John Keats

A warm, sunny day is good almost any time. But it's especially good when it occurs at this time of year.

In the summer, warm days are a dime a dozen. People take them for granted. It's hot again today? Oh no, not another day of sticking like Scotch tape to your car seat. A succession of warm, sunny days wears on you after a while and makes you long for the cooler days of fall.

Fall is more "variable," as the TV weathercasters say. You still get warm days, but the nights are cooler. Then winter comes around and both nights and days get cold, with snow and freezing rain thrown in for good measure. After a little of this you begin to pine for those long, hot days of summer. And so it goes.

But around this time of year (and even later), you may receive an unexpected bonus when you're fishing and it suddenly turns warm. It's like the seasons have gotten confused and it's July again, only you appreciate it more now because you know it won't last and the cold, hard days of winter loom around the corner. It's a gift of sorts, like finding an envelope of cash (with no owner in sight) on the sidewalk.

And what do you do when you receive such a gift? You say, "Thank you very much," and go out and enjoy it.

Resolved: I relish a day of unexpected warmth.

October 21

"Look not thou down, but up!"

—Robert Browning

See a far sight today. Look to distant vistas.

That's one of the (many) great things about fishing. There are no buildings to block your view. You're not seated in front of a computer screen or TV. You're outside where your eyeballs can see faraway things.

You stand on shore and look down the straits to the bridge. You have a clear, wide view of it. The bridge connects hills on either side. The hills are brown with green pockets of trees here and there. A line of electrical towers climbs out of sight up and over the hills.

Between you and the bridge there is only water. Today is calm and the water is flat and smooth. Beyond the bridge are more flat, smooth expanses that open into the waters of the Pacific.

It's good fishing weather. It's that time of year. The salmon are out in numbers. The other day, while walking on the beach with your dog, he stuck his nose around a two-foot salmon that had washed onto shore. You'd like to land one of those yourself.

In the meantime, you wait. And look. You pay attention to your fishing, but you like the fact that there's nothing stopping your view. You look above and see sky. You look west and see the brown hills and bridge. You look in front of you and all you see is water.

Resolved: I lift my sights to distant vistas. I fish.

October 22

"It is good food and not fine words that keeps me alive."

—Molière

Follow pleasure with pleasure. After a day of fishing, eat a good meal.

You're tired and hungry and cold. You deserve it any time, but you especially deserve it after a long, hard day of traipsing around a high-country trout stream. You've tortured your body long enough. Now it's time to pamper it.

You may feel like you could eat a horse, but a horse will not taste nearly as delicious as fowl or fish or a nice bloody sirloin. Have a baked potato with butter and sour cream on the side.

With the steak, order a red. With the fish, white is preferable. With the chicken, you're on your own. In any case, a good bottle of wine is mandatory.

A good meal and a bottle of wine after a day of fishing will provide more inspiration than any words on a page. They are the very stuff of inspiration.

A good meal will take a good day and make it better. A good meal and a bottle of vino—especially the vino!—will make a bad day much easier to swallow. You may even forget it by dinner's end.

Bring as much pleasure as you can into fishing, however you can do it. Associate good things with fishing and you will want to fish more. A good meal is one way to do this, and you don't have to catch a thing.

Resolved: I end every day of fishing with a good meal.

October 23

"Perched on the loftiest throne in the world, we are still sitting on our behind."

—Montaigne

You're back at it. Sitting on your butt, fishing. And you feel good about it.

You meant to fish more over the summer. Hell, you mean to fish more *all the time.* But one thing led to the next like it always does, and you could never find the time.

But finally you did. It's not for as long as you'd like. It never is. But at least it's something. You're sitting by a stream playing Spider to the fish's Fly and that feels pretty good.

My my my, said the Spider to the Fly. Jump right in to my web.

Conditions aren't ideal, but are they ever? There's always gonna be some bee in your bonnet in fishing. The great thing is, you're back at it. Think of all the things that come between you and a simple day of fishing. Nah, it's too depressing. Just be glad that you came out from under those things for a day or two, and got back at it.

The workaday world seems to get along okay without you. There's no real difference between you and those kingpins of commerce and industry anyway. Like the man says, they're all sitting on their butts, too.

When you come back to fishing after being away for a while, you wonder why it took so long to get back to it. Maybe next time it won't take so long.

Hello, is that you Mr. Fly?

Resolved: I feel good about sitting on my butt and fishing.

October 24

"In every species of fish I've angled for, it is the ones that have got away that thrill me the most, the ones that keep fresh in my memory. So I say it is good to lose fish."

—Ray Bergman

What are you so bummed out about? Okay, so you lost a fish. Snap out of it, man. You're lucky to lose fish.

What's that? It was a big one, you're sure of it? You're even luckier then. It's always better to lose a big one than a small one. You'll have the memory of that fight and that fish a lot longer than if you'd led him docilely into your net.

A picture gets filed in a box somewhere, to be forgotten or lost. A memory gets filed in your head and you never let go of it.

Another thing: you learn more when a fish beats you. It's like learning at the feet of a Zen master. He'll show you whether or not you've reached enlightenment.

Sometimes a fish gets away because of those proverbial factors beyond your control. Another name for it: pure dumb rotten luck. But that's part of fishing. That's what you have to learn about, too.

Look at it this way: you lost a fish. Okay, that's a drag. But at least you're out there, doing what you want to do. You're in the mix. You're not sitting around moping about all the great opportunities that have passed you by in this life.

If every now and then a piscine pugilist earns a decision over you on points, well, that's the way it goes. Make yourself stronger by the loss. Get back into the ring as soon as you can, and come out fighting.

Resolved: Every fish I lose makes me a better fisherman.

October 25

" 'You've missed the point, Nick,' he said, taking my hand in his bony fingers. 'Until next year.' "

—The angler Hawkes, to Nick Lyons

What's the point of fishing?

The pretty farmgirl that you pass on the road and who waves at you with a shy smile.

The fruit-and-vegetable stand alongside the road, where you buy a big bunch of sweet and juicy purple grapes.

Turning up into the mountains, and saying good-bye to the city.

Opening up the sunroof when night falls, gazing up at the stars as you go eighty-five on the interstate.

The charge you get when you see the river for the first time in way too long.

The beers you drink while sitting on a rock, checking out the water.

The beers you drink when you're hungry and tired and content after a day of fishing.

Being in the woods, being in nature. Stalking around like a madman in the trees and brush. Getting dirty and wet. Sticking your toe in freezing cold water, then the rest of you up to your calves.

Waking up to the sun, not an alarm clock. Ordering your day according to the earth's movement in the sky.

Getting to know yourself a little better. Letting go of what seems so urgent but isn't and rediscovering some other neglected aspects of your life.

Resolved: I never miss the point of fishing.

October 26

*"A fish story backed by visual evidence is something you don't
run into every day."*

—Red Smith

It's true. You don't come across all that many fish stories
backed up by hard evidence.

But you're the exception. You did it, and you've got the
goods to prove it.

There you are, grinning like some goofy cartoon character, framed by the gorgeous blue water of the Florida Keys,
holding up an even more gorgeous tarpon.

Nobody would believe you without the photo. You caught
that? No way. The fish is simply too big. But there can be no
doubt (thanks to the real hero, your wife the photographer).

Now, this is what you do: get the negative, take it to a film
shop, and make an eight-by-ten print.

That's right: eight by ten. Blow it up. You need a suitable
representation for an achievement of this magnitude. Poster
size might be pushing it. An eight by ten is just right.

Then buy a nice frame and stick it on the wall. In your
office or fly-tying room or wherever. But get it up there so
people—and you—can see it.

You deserve it. You catch a fish like that, it ought to be recognized. What's more, looking at a picture like that, you will
want to go out again ASAP. Every day you're not fishing will
seem like a wasted day.

Resolved: I frame a great fishing photo and put it on the
wall.

October 27

"I wondered if as a child I longed to go fishing. In an old family album there is a picture of me wearing a buckskin jacket, casting on a lawn covered with snow."

—Ailm Travler

Every fisherman remembers the first place he or she went fishing. For Ailm Travler, it was a lake in the Adirondacks.

"I spent a few weeks of many childhood summers on a small island," she writes, "a three-acre slab of grown-over granite in the middle of an Adirondack lake, forested with tall white pines and strewn with blueberry and wintergreen bushes." She fished with clam innards on a hook and caught bluegills off the dock.

Everything on the island was old, or seemed that way, to her. The boathouse and the cabins where she and her family stayed were more than a century old. There was no electricity. But there were canoes and guide boats, the same ones her grandparents and great-grandparents used when they caught brook trout on the river the lake fed into. But that was a long time ago, and Travler says, "You don't hear much about trout anymore."

So it goes, sadly. The places you fished when you were a kid are no longer fishable. Sometimes they don't even exist any more, except in your memory.

Take a moment to think back on the first place you fished, what it looked like, the things you did, the people who were there. It can't hurt, can it? The place has changed and many of the people are surely gone. But it's still a nice place to visit now and then, if only in your mind.

Resolved: I remember the first place I fished and the people I fished with.

October 28

*"I am satisfied that nothing can take the place of a real
knowledge of the trout we fish for—how they live, how they
see, what makes them do what they do when they do it."*

—Eugene V. Connett

Here's your mission, should you choose to accept it: go out
and buy a how-to fishing book. Or pick up *Field & Stream* or
any of the other fishing magazines that are always chockful
of how-to articles.

Now pick out something from it. Whatever subject you like,
it doesn't matter. How to double haul, how to handle your rod
when a big fish jumps, how to make nymph presentations,
how to dig an ice hole—you name it.

Follow the instructions exactly, and see how you fare.

A ridiculous concept, right? Nobody follows those articles
word for word. Most fishermen are just looking for a tip or
two, some kernel of wisdom they hadn't thought of that will
help them catch fish.

You may indeed pick up a trick or two from these articles.
But the only stuff that will sink in for real is the stuff you learn
yourself. On your own, on the stream, with a fishing rod in
the palm of your hand.

There are no shortcuts. Nothing will take the place of a real
knowledge of trout other than a real knowledge of trout. As
much as possible, get your information about fishing firsthand. Go to the source. It's far more reliable and lasting.

Resolved: I get a real knowledge of fishing by fishing.

October 29

"Fly fishermen spend hours tying little clumps of fur and feathers on hooks, trying to make a trout fly look like a real fly. But nobody has ever seen a natural insect mate with a Fanning Ginger Quill."

—Ed Zern

Fly-fishermen who tie their own flies like to make a big deal out of tying flies—the art and science of it. Ed Zern is not impressed.

"Every once in a while a fly fisherman catches a trout on a trout fly, and he thinks this proves something," says Zern. "It doesn't. Trout eat mayflies, burned matches, small pieces of inner tube, each other, caddis worms, buttons, crickets, lima beans, Colorado spinners, and almost anything else they can get in their fool mouths." In other words, they're not exactly picky.

Trout do not have an aesthetic appreciation of a well-tied fly. They may not confuse it with a hatching insect. They may not be confused at all. As Ed Zern says, "It is probable they think the trout fly is some feathers tied to a hook. Hell, they're not blind. They just want to see how it tastes."

It's good to keep this in mind if ever you get too wrapped up in the art of tying flies. It's a very worthwhile practice. You learn a lot about insects when you tie your own. You even learn about yourself. As long as you're going to do something, it always makes sense to do it as well as you can.

But the trout? Ah well, they may not care at all.

Resolved: I tie flies the best I can and leave it at that.

October 30

When you fish, let this be standard operating procedure: check it out. Always, check it out.

You like where you are but you're still curious about what's happening upstream? Well then, check it out.

You want to go to this new spot upstate where you've never been? Quit stalling around. Check it out.

You're tired. You want to pack it in. But your buddy wants to try over by the dam. He thinks something is happening there and he'd like to see.

Sorry, your buddy wins. When in doubt, check it out.

Fishing's over. You're fifteen minutes from the nearest town. There's this great Mexican place that serves heaping platefuls of cheap food and it's got a bar where supposedly a lot of girls like to hang out after hours.

You gotta check *that* out.

You will learn more with a check-it-out attitude. You will lead a fuller, richer, and more enjoyable life. You will have more fun. You will become a better fisherman. You will stay out of ruts and know more about the world, both natural and human.

Always, check it out. Never be afraid to check it out.

Resolved: I check out that Mexican food place with all the girls. That sounds like fun.

October 31

"Fishing lets the child in me come out."

<blockquote>
—Mel Krieger
</blockquote>

It's Halloween. What are you wearing for fishing today?

What do you mean you don't understand the question? Aren't you dressing up?

There once was a dedicated—perhaps *fanatical* is a better word—fisherman who used to dress up as a tree in order to fool the fish. His name, believe it or not, was Dr. Thomas Birch. He was an Englishman (naturally), and every time he went a-fishin' he slipped into costume.

He covered himself with leaves and branches before approaching the stream. He thought if the fish mistook him for a tree, he stood a better chance of catching them off guard.

How he did is not known. Probably not all that great. If he had achieved great success in this gambit, other fishermen would have followed suit and there would have been trees stalking trout all over England.

However ridiculous he may have been, old Doc Birch made an inadvertent point about fishing: it is a little goofy. It is something that you do as a kid. Even as you get older and more experienced, the idea is to retain that youthful enthusiasm, the enthusiasm you had when you were first starting out.

Who knows? Maybe this means occasionally dressing up as a tree.

Not.

Resolved: I keep the fun in my fishing, but I never dress up as a tree.

November 1

"What is truth? I don't know, and I'm sorry I brought it up."

—Edward Abbey

Relax. You don't have to feel inspired today.

Not every day needs to be a day that reveals eternal truths. Some days are just what they are. Nothing more, nothing less. They're average, ordinary, run-of-the-mill days in which nothing even remotely inspiring occurs. You neither feel inspired, nor act inspired.

You may even feel downright cranky. The sun is a bother. The birds sound like noise. The weather is a terrible nuisance. Not even the fish do anything for you.

You know it's bad when even the fish don't inspire you. Still, it happens and there's nothing wrong with that.

You're getting by, right? It's not a great day of fishing, but it's also not a terrible one. You're doing what needs to be done and you're doing it pretty well, considering.

So take the day off from inspiration. Forget anyone even mentioned the word.

How does it feel? Pretty good, huh? Like a great burden has been lifted off your back. Suddenly you feel free. You feel transported.

You feel, uh, inspired.

That's the way it goes sometimes. Don't push for a thing and it will come to you. Whether it's inspiration or love or fish. Don't push for it, and it will come to you.

Resolved: I let inspiration come to me naturally.

November 2

"Glorious was life when standing at my fishing hole on the ice."

—Eskimo song

The cold weather is coming. The official start of winter is more than a month away, but the cold weather is coming. You can feel it.

Maybe the cold weather has already arrived in your neck of the woods. If it's not here yet it will be soon, like the aliens in *Independence Day*. It's relentless, unstoppable, and not even a drunken Randy Quaid can save us.

There are a lot of things to be said about cold-weather fishing. One, it's cold. Two, sometimes it's very cold. Add in a north wind blowing across the lake, and you've got conditions better suited for penguins than fishermen.

Cold-weather fishing is as much about attitude as anything else. You've got to have the right mind-set, as the TV football announcers say.

You're going fishing. It's going to be cold for a while. It won't kill you, and at some point, you will come back indoors and get warm again. In the meantime, get into it.

A lot of fishermen swear by cold-weather fishing. They think it's the best time to go. The weekenders have all gone home and they've got the place pretty much to themselves. Cold-weather fishing boils fishing down to its basic elements: fishermen, fish, and freezing buns. Dress warmly, and enjoy.

Resolved: I get in some cold-weather fishing days.

November 3

*"I fell in love with a fly fisherman. Come Opening Day, I lose
him to dawn hatches and evening rises."*

—Allison Moir

One of the nice things about having children is being able to take them fishing.

You take them with you when they're kids, and you take them with you when they're teenagers and young adults.

You watch them learn. You watch them make mistakes. You watch the delight in their eyes when they catch fish. When you were a kid you could never understand how your parents could derive such apparent enjoyment from watching you play sports and do things. Now you know.

But inevitably, it happens. They grow up and fly the coop. Those little fireplugs running around in diapers are now adults in their own right, with families, jobs, and commitments of their own.

So the question begs: with the children raised and gone, who do you fish with?

Look around the house. Recognize anybody familiar? Yes, *her*. Well, why not?

She's been there all the time. Probably by now, she's as good a fisherman as anybody in the family. She's a trooper. Hell, she stuck with you all these years.

Maybe the two of you will rediscover each other on a fishing trip. Maybe you'll rekindle a romance. Maybe you'll find a new fishing partner. Or maybe you'll get so pissed off that you'll never speak to each other again. Anyway, it's worth a try.

Resolved: I take my wife on a fishing trip.

November 4

"Only connect! That was the whole of her sermon. Only connect the prose and the passion, and both will be exalted."

—E. M. Forster

Step off the merry-go-round and fish.

What merry-go-round? You know, the one you're on. The one that won't give you enough time to do the things you love. The one that drains all your energy. The one that makes you feel like you're wasting your time and possibly even your life.

Step off the merry-go-round for an afternoon, a day, a weekend. Step off it and fish.

How do you do it? You just do it. How do you find the time? You just find it.

You don't need permission from anybody. Not your boss, not your spouse, not your children, not your friends, not your parents. You're following a higher authority: your heart.

If what you love to do is fish, why is your life filled with other things you don't love? That makes sense only to the millions of others who are also stuck on the merry-go-round.

Stop making sense. What they think has to be, doesn't have to be. There are other paths to follow.

Step off the merry-go-round for an afternoon or a day or a weekend, and explore those paths. Connect the prose of your life with the passion. When you do, those explorations will last a lifetime.

Resolved: I step off the merry-go-round for an afternoon and fish.

November 5

Make the vow, swear it in blood, raise it to the heavens: I'll
do anything and go anywhere for big fish.

I'll freeze my tail off in sub-zero Arctic weather to catch
big fish.

I'll go into debt to fly to Idaho or Alaska or New Zealand
or wherever it takes to catch big fish.

I'll brave teeth-rattling, appendage-numbing, snow-melt
streams and lakes to catch big fish. I'll go to the remotest locations, in the worst weather imaginable. I'll go in the dead of
winter and be half-dead when I return.

I'll trudge upstream and down and back again to catch big
fish. I'll crawl on my hands and knees if necessary. Hell, I'll
dress up like a tree to catch big fish, if that's what it takes.

I'll pull myself out of bed before sunrise to catch big fish,
and I won't come back till after dark even though staggering
with exhaustion and down a quart of blood from mosquito
bites.

I'll endure long periods of not catching anything. I'll tear
my hair out and curse and stomp around like a maniacal
child, but I will never cease moving toward my inevitable goal.

I'll endure the extremes of misery and heartache and
depression and frustration and agony, to experience the ultimate joy.

Resolved: I'll do anything and go anywhere to catch big fish.

November 6

"The past is a foreign country; they do things differently there."

—L. P. Hartley

Okay, you did it. Great going. You caught a big fish yesterday, a real beaut. Now what?

First, give yourself credit. You did what every fisherman dreams of doing. Truly relish that fact.

Now, put it behind you. Yesterday's yesterday. Today's today. In fishing, they can be a million years apart.

One thing *not* to do: play "Top This!" with yourself and others. You know how it goes: "See what I did yesterday? I can do better than that. What? What do you mean you don't believe me. Listen pal, let's see if you can do any better!"

Anyway, you get the idea.

Playing the "Top This!" game creates unreasonable (and unreal) expectations. You put unneeded pressure on yourself. You set up conditions for disappointment by attempting to match or exceed what you did in the past. Times have changed. You need to change with them, and that includes changing your expectations of yourself and your fishing.

You can never top the fish. In the long (and short) of it they're always going to top you. Boast about your prowess and accomplishments, and they will rapidly cut you down to size.

That you did better in the past does not necessarily mean you are doing poorly now. You may be doing very well, given current conditions. But trying to top your past achievements, and feeling frustrated when you do not, will only make things worse.

Resolved: I never try to top myself in fishing.

November 7

"Readiness is all."

—William Shakespeare

It's not too early to start thinking about your fishing goals for next year.

You may want to fish more. You may want to take a big trip somewhere. You may want to hit some of the local hot spots that you've never fished before. You may want to fish more with your family. You may want to learn to fly-fish or do the Ernest Hemingway thing and go saltwater fishing for trophy fish.

Thinking things out will not only help you plan your fishing for the year, but also for your life.

You make fishing a priority in your life through your thoughts and plans. If you never think about it, clearly it is not a priority. By making room for it in your mind—or more room for it—you make room for it in your life.

There is an additional benefit. When you make fishing a priority, it has a domino effect on the rest of your affairs. You are saying, in effect, that there's more to your life than your job or merely making money. You are going to take time for yourself and do the things you love. You will have to create the time to fish. Some things in your life will obviously have to give.

Thinking about the year to come in fishing is a worthwhile process. It will give you a sense of where you're going and help you get there. And it will create more opportunities to fish.

Resolved: I start thinking about my fishing goals for next year.

November 8

"The fish I love more than any other is the brook trout. I love the brook trout not because he is the biggest and strongest of all gamefish (he is nowhere near it). But because he belongs to the Yankee forest that I live near or am often in."

—Ted Williams

Congratulations. You found your spot. You're a lucky man.

Not everyone is lucky enough to have a spot. A lot of people live their whole lives without ever finding their spot. But you found yours.

It's not the world's greatest spot, not even close. You like it because it's a little bit away from everything, but not totally. It's a rock and sand outcropping along a small bay. It's exposed to the wind, which sometimes blows your hat off. Other days the water is flat as a board. A stand of tule reeds ranges along the shore.

You've caught stripers there, some big ones, too. That's mainly what you fish for: stripers. There's another spot down at the end of the road where most of the other fishermen go. But you don't go there very often. You like your spot better.

You can't exactly explain why you like this spot so much and why you keep coming back to it. It's peaceful and calm and you can get away and let the knots in your mind untangle. That's part of it, but not all of it.

Maybe it's because it's yours. Not yours, really. But yours in the sense that you've developed a relationship with it and a loyalty to it. It's brought you good times. You feel close to it.

Let other fishermen chase their dreams where they will. You've found your spot. You're staying put.

Resolved: I find a good spot and stick to it.

November 9

*"There must be a beginning of any great matter, but the
continuing unto the end until it be thoroughly finished yields the
true glory."*

—Sir Frances Drake

There was a famous racehorse named Silky Sullivan. He was
known for his all-out dashes to the finish line. Inevitably, he
would get off to a slow start and stay well back in the pack
or even lag behind it as the race progressed.

But when he hit the clubhouse turn, something got into
Silky. He turned it on, putting on a thundering charge that
nearly always overtook the other horses in the field and won
him the race by a nose. His name became synonymous with
a late-charging winner.

Be a Silky Sullivan when it comes to fishing. Turn it on the
later it gets.

For most people, their time in fishing is short. They get a
weekend here and there and maybe take a week or two in
summer. They feel the need to get the most out of their fishing because they're not sure when they're going to be able to
do it again.

Maximize your fishing time the way Silky Sullivan maxi-
mized his horse races. When it gets late in the day, turn it
on. Concentrate for that last hour or two as if they were your
last moments on earth.

Maybe you'll catch fish, maybe you won't. But when you
quit for the day, you leave with a very satisfied feeling no matter what the fish do. You gave it everything you had. You put
it all out there. Silky Sullivan would be proud.

Resolved: I finish my fishing day strong.

November 10

"If you find yourself camping by an unknown brook, and are deputed to catch necessary trout for breakfast, it is wiser to choose the surest bait."

—Bliss Perry

Go with the sure thing. Why not?

It's sitting there, right in front of you. If it was a snake, it'd bite you, and all that. It's got a proved track record. Go with it.

It's too obvious, you say? What's wrong with obvious if it helps you catch fish?

Fishing is hard enough as it is. Plenty of hard knocks await you even if you have the supposed sure thing. Go with the sure thing and see what happens. Who knows? You could get lucky.

Some people distrust a sure thing, and for good reason. Every fisherman knows there is no sure thing in fishing.

Everybody else could be using minnows and pulling out lunkers, but that doesn't mean you will. You hear there are great things happening down at the levee, but by the time you show up it's dry as a bone. So much for sure things.

Sure things never pay off. Well, that's not quite right. Every fisherman knows you can never say never in fishing.

So at least start with a sure thing. That's a good rule of thumb. Then move on from there when it doesn't work.

Resolved: I go with the sure thing and see what happens after that.

November 11

"All men are equal before trout."

—Herbert Hoover

It's Veteran's Day, a holiday for most people. What do you do on a holiday? Fish.

Veteran's Day is a day to honor the men and women who fought and died in our nation's wars. How can you honor them? Fish.

Fishing is no small thing. It is a part of our national heritage. Presidents fish. Senators, representatives, and governors fish. Pioneers of industry fish. Teachers, coaches, union leaders, newspaper reporters, poets, plumbers, doctors, nurses, roofers, carpenters, software engineers, garbage collectors—they all fish.

Wars were fought so the people of this country could have life, liberty, and the pursuit of happiness. Fishing is part of that.

Two of the defining characteristics of America—what we think of when we think of America—are wide open spaces and great natural resources. Fishing is wrapped up in both. Fishermen enjoy both and know firsthand the continuing threat they're under.

Think of the young men who lost their lives in war. They lived in small towns and big cities in every state in the nation. They were all races, virtually all religions. If they were alive today, many of them would go out and fish.

What better way to honor them than to do what they would if they had the chance?

Resolved: It's a holiday. I fish.

November 12

"Mankind always sets itself only such problems as it can solve."

—Karl Marx

Okay, you've gotten off track. It happens. What do you do? Get back on track.

Sounds simple, right? Sometimes it's not so easy. After all, you totally screwed up. Well, not totally. But enough to really piss you off. You know better than to do what you did. But you did it anyway and now look at you.

You fished too long and got way too tired. You stayed too long at a spot that wasn't working. But you stubbornly refused to give in and you created problems for yourself.

If you had just stepped away for a moment, you would have been all right. You would have figured it out. But that would have been a failure of sorts, and you couldn't admit that to yourself.

You got into trouble because you had certain expectations in your mind about how things should go and you felt you weren't fulfilling them. You pushed too hard, and that's never a good approach in fishing or anything else.

The problems you face in fishing are solvable, every one of them. Next time, step away for a moment and clear your head. The answer will come. Fishing is an exercise in catching fish and solving problems. You need a clear head to do both.

Resolved: I step away and clear my head when I get off track in my fishing.

November 13

"Fishermen are born honest, but they get over it."

—Ed Zern

A well-crafted lie, like a thing of beauty, is a joy forever. What's the harm in a small fib? And if there's no harm in a small one, can a really big whopper hurt?

A fisherman who tells a lie is a person who cares about people. Everybody wants to hear a good story. It's in the nature of human beings. We've been sitting around the fire telling stories to one another since the days of the cavemen.

A caring fisherman does not want to disappoint. He tells the story that everybody wants to hear. Some may call that lying. It's not. It's creative storytelling.

Some people think that to get away with a good bald-faced lie, all you have to do is make up a story and tell it without blushing. This is hardly the case. Jerome Mermone explains, "Mere bald fabrication is useless; the veriest tyro can manage that. It is in the circumstantial detail, the embellishing touches of probability, the general air of scrupulous—almost pedantic—veracity" that separates the ordinary lie-telling fishermen from the true masters of the art.

The truth of a good lie is in the details. A big story alone with big flourishes will not do the trick. What is needed are the small touches that fill in the larger picture. These details create an air of probability that is certain to ensnare the listener. Of course, the more details there are, the more the possibility for contradiction. So watch out.

Resolved: When I tell a lie in fishing, I pay careful attention to the details.

November 14

"Besides the past, it is well to look to the future. We, too, shall grow out of date. Fishers of a hundred years hence will cast an easy smile on ourselves and on our methods, which we think so delicate and so final."

—John Waller Hills

It's fun to look back on turn-of-the-century fishing photographs. The fishermen have such crude-looking implements, and appear so stiff and awkward in their antiquated dress as they pose for the camera. You just have to smile.

How could they have even fished in such getups? Compared to what fishermen use today, it all seems so backward and primitive.

Of course, you must realize that a hundred years from now (or sooner), people will say the same things about us.

How crude they look! How quaint! How could they have even fished in such weird getups?

What unites the fishermen of the past with the fishermen of today and tomorrow is fishing itself, the journey we are all engaged in, the common pursuit.

Each of us embodies, at this moment, the fisherman we once were and the fisherman we will become. The boy is there, as is the old man and all the stages in between. Each of us is progressing toward—what? Well, no one can be sure of that.

One thing we can be sure about: we will someday be—in the words of John Waller Hills—"just as antique, as obsolete and as far away" as those old fishermen in the photographs.

Resolved: I look to the past, and to the future, and reflect on my place in it.

November 15

"Civilization is a stream with banks. The stream is sometimes filled with blood from people killing and doing the things historians usually record—while on the banks, unnoticed, people build homes, make love and raise children. The story of civilization is the story of what happened on the banks."

—Will Durant

One of the great joys of fishing is sharing it with children and young people, introducing them to the great outdoors and all the wonders therein.

Aye, but there's a catch. You like kids but you don't have any of your own.

Matter of fact, you're kind of happy about that. You prefer the role of uncle or godfather or grandparent—someone who comes in, spreads presents and joy, then leaves the parents to clean up the mess. You don't really want to be a full-time parent; you're more of a part-timer in that regard.

Perfect solution: get involved in a "fishing buddies" program.

Your fishing club may sponsor a program of this nature. You can try your local parks and recreation office or even Boy Scouts and Girl Scouts or Big Brothers/Big Sisters. Basically, through the program, fishermen take kids out to a lake or reservoir and show them a fishing good time. These youngsters may be hard-luck urban kids who've never handled a rod and reel before.

It's a privilege and honor, really, to be some kid's first fishing teacher. It gives you a real charge and renews your own enthusiasm for catching fish.

Resolved: I find out about a fishing buddies program in my area.

November 16

"During the winter I dream about fishing."

—Ailm Travler

It's cold outside, raining in fact. It's not quite winter but it sure feels like it. It's a good day to stay indoors and dream about fishing.

Dreaming about fishing is a pretty good way to kill some time. You never get wet, bugs never bite, and you always pull out record-size trophy fish.

After you log some heavy time in dreamland, however, you may feel in the mood for something more substantial. Why not go to a lecture about fishing?

Listening to someone talk about fishing is nearly as good as dreaming about it, and just as dry. Usually there are pictures, too. More often than not an expert will bring along slides to accompany the presentation, and if you get bored you can look at pictures of fish, which is always entertaining.

You can learn all kinds of stuff at these talks. You can hear travelogues on new places to go. Just consider it part of your continuing education as a fisherman.

Of course, sometimes you may want to hear what nonfishermen have to say. Fish-and-game biologists are good. They talk about fish and birds and wildlife and how they all fit together in the ecosystem.

Your local fishing shop or club probably holds lectures all the time. They're great for getting out and rubbing shoulders with other guys who have been cooped up dreaming about fishing, too.

Resolved: I go to a lecture about fishing.

November 17

"Let me, less cruel, cast the feathered hook."

—John Gay

Some people criticize fishermen for inflicting pain on fish in the name of sport. These critics are mostly off the wall because, as Nick Lyons writes, "The trout is not a human being and the repeated Disneylike, anthropomorphic assertions that a fish feels pain the way human beings feel pain are worse than simply misleading and spurious. They're downright dangerous."

If you're like most fishermen, you're careful about fish. You don't want them to suffer unnecessarily, if at all. You use barbless hooks and other methods to quickly catch and release fish.

Lyons adds, "Get the fish in quickly and whack it abruptly on the head if you're going to eat it, or off the hook if you're not. This requires balance and judgment, which everything worthwhile requires. Your equipment should not be too heavy to raise your quarry or your leader so light."

A fish is not the enemy, a creature to be conquered. But it's not a human being either. There's got to be a middle ground in there somewhere, though the antifishing zealots will probably never be satisfied.

Nick Lyons personally fishes with a fly because he finds it more demanding and challenging, and less cruel. But every fisherman in every type of setting needs to show balance and judgment when it comes to hooking and landing fish.

Resolved: I use balance and judgment—and barbless hooks—when I fish.

November 18

"Live as on a mountain."

—Marcus Aurelius

Live as on a mountain, but come down and fish from time to time. And when you fish, carry these words of the great Roman emperor with you.

Detach yourself from the act of fishing, even as you are engaged in it.

This is not so easy to do—to maintain an Olympian detachment when you're fishing. You care about it. You want to catch fish. It's important to you.

That's a problem.

Attach yourself too strongly to fishing (especially the desired end result of catching fish), and you are sure to be gravely disappointed. But it's not fishing's fault; it's yours. You're too ego-involved, and you need to step back and get perspective.

Know that inevitably you will lose a fish or fall in the lake or not draw scratch for hours and hours. Some days everybody else on the boat will land lunkers while you can't draw scratch. As hard as it may be, you must disengage yourself from these disappointments to some degree, anticipate them as an inevitable part of fishing, and look beyond them. In this way, you will reduce their sting when they occur.

Resolved: I detach myself from the disappointments of fishing.

November 19

"I'm prepared to swear that a fisherman is only at his relaxed best when he knows that nothing is watching him except the scampering chipmunks and God."

—Robert Traver

This morning greet the sunrise with a fishing rod in hand.

It's not that cold yet. It's not even winter. Get going, get out of bed, and send an early morning hello to the fish.

Shout it the way Robin Williams did in *Good Morning, Vietnam*: "Goooooood morning, fish!"

Oh well, maybe that wasn't such a good idea. You've now alerted every fish within a square mile of you. But heck, it's early and there's plenty of time to recover.

That's the great thing about rising and shining: the whole day stretches out in front of you like a magic carpet. You've made the big effort and rousted your aging and tired body out of the sack. Now you're reaping the benefits: plenty of fishing time.

No one ever regrets getting up at the break of day. You grumble while you're doing it, but once you're up and out and you meet the day and see how beautiful it is, you forget it. You're *there*.

No other fishermen are out but you. They're all still in bed, poor fools. The lake is smooth as polished glass. The birds are fraternizing in the trees. A squirrel runs away, thinking you're going to steal the nut he's gathered. It's quiet as a library or a church. Finally the sun climbs up over the western hills and beams its smile across the lake toward you. You pull in your line, and cast again.

Resolved: I greet the sunrise with a fishing rod in hand.

November 20

"Wash what is dirty, water what is dry, heal what is wounded."
—Archbishop Stephen Langton

It's time for a fresh start. Get out the tackle box and clean it.

Everybody's tackle box could stand a good cleaning. Yours is no different. Get it out and spiff it up.

You're going to find things in there you don't need. Get rid of them. You may find outright junk. Round-file it.

There's something strange about a fisherman who keeps a clean tackle box all the time. It's like owning a pickup truck with a clean bed. A pickup with a clean bed is a pickup that isn't working. A pickup has got to have a locking toolbox, empty beer cans, dirt and pine needles, a broken shovel, a wood splitter, one crummy workboot without a mate, and a barking dog in the back.

It's the same with a tackle box (absent the dog). A tackle box has got to look like they carried it on the Bataan Death March. Otherwise, it's just not right.

Still, every tackle box needs to be cleaned out now and then. Heck, every tackle box needs to be taken out in the yard and hosed down, the way they do prisoners in county lockup.

A tackle box is a reflection of its owner. People can look in a tackle box and know what kind of fisherman you are. Clean out the tackle box, and you'll be able to fool them for a while.

Resolved: I clean out my tackle box.

November 21

"It's a magical time in these parts, where species have converged for a few weeks of world class fishing. Guides who are willing to put in a long day, can get their clients into salmon, steelhead and lots of trout."

—*San Francisco Chronicle* fishing report
on the Sacramento River

In fishing or business, this cliche applies: strike while the iron is hot.

It's a magical time on the upper Sacramento? They're pulling out world-class salmon, steelhead, and trout? By all means, go for it. Strike while the iron is hot.

You—and your guide—better be willing to put in a long day when this happens. If your guide is lukewarm about it, get a new guide.

It's like that old saw about opportunity knocking (sorry, another cliche). If you don't answer the door, it's not going to wait around forever. It's going to get fed up and knock on someone else's door.

Good fishermen are like surfers. There are times when nothing is happening. The waves aren't breaking. Then somebody yells, "Surf's up!" and men with boards rush to the ocean.

Be ready to answer the call when the call comes. Be willing to put in a long day. You will reap world-class rewards if you do.

Resolved: In fishing (and business), I strike while the iron is hot.

November 22

"Every day, in every way, I am getting better and better."

—Emile Coue

Give yourself credit today. Like the good French doctor, you're getting better and better, too.

You're a better fisherman than you were six months or a year ago. You know more. You've experienced more. You're more aware.

You've thought more about it. You've read more about it. You've fished more. You keep growing as a person and a fisherman. It's there for all to see, plain as day.

You may not be as good a fisherman as you want to be. Who is? You're good now, and you'll get even better.

You're more attuned to nature. You're less wrapped up in results. You've stopped kicking yourself for your alleged shortcomings. Everybody has faults. You're no different. But you see the broader picture now, one that keeps those alleged faults in perspective, balanced against your many other virtues.

You're a better fisherman when you feel better about yourself. You're better at *anything* when you feel better about yourself.

You're not just dreaming about making progress. You really are. It's happening. You're moving forward. You're growing as a fisherman. Ain't it grand?

Resolved: I keep getting better and better at fishing.

November 23

"If there is magic on this planet, it is contained in water."

—Loren Eisley

Sometimes fish appear in abundance, sometimes they can hardly be found. Accept the magic of it.

Sometimes the lake seems like a limitless treasure chest, while at other times it feels empty as a donut hole. Accept the magic of it.

Sometimes the sky is serene and beautiful, and sometimes it pours out rain and thunder and lightning. Accept the magic of it.

Sometimes you feel lucky to be alive, a blessed heavenly being, while sometimes you feel cursed and unwanted, a forgotten child. Accept the magic of it.

Sometimes your well-considered fishing stratagems work like a Swiss watch, other times they crash miserably. Accept the magic of it.

Sometimes the wind blows and blows, other times it is meek as a whisper. Accept the magic of it.

Sometimes it seems as if you can peer into the vibrant wild heart of the universe, redolent with meaning, while other times all you see is a dark void. Accept the magic of it.

Sometimes you sing a happy tune in fishing, while at other times you sing low-down, dirty blues. The important thing is to keep singing and to accept the magic of it all.

Resolved: I accept the magic of nature and my fishing life.

November 24

*"The fish you release is your gift to another angler and
remember, it may have been someone's similar gift to you."*

—Lee Wulff

Give the gift that keeps on giving. Release a fish back into the
water after you catch it.

You know the expression "Bread upon the waters"? In this
case, throw the fish upon the waters and see what comes back
to you.

Who knows, maybe it will produce good karma for you.
Maybe something good will happen to you because you have
wisely and selflessly returned a fish to its home.

Catch and release is good policy. The more fish there are,
the better it is for everybody, particularly fishermen.

It can't be emphasized enough that in order to throw a fish
back, you must first catch it. So you have achieved success
and probably had a memorable day regardless of whether you
actually consume the product of your effort.

As Lee Wulff says, the fish you catch may be a gift from
an anonymous fishing donor. Today, be an anonymous donor.
Catch a fish, then release it back into its home.

Resolved: First I catch a fish. Then I release it.

November 25

"The thirsty earth soaks up the rain
 And drinks, and gapes for drink again."

—Abraham Cowley

Go out to fish after a fresh rain. The earth seems to have taken a bath. The trees, the grasses, the plants, everything alive appears more alive somehow. The trail is soft and moist, no longer dry and beaten down as it was.

Fishermen, above all, know the healing powers of water, and after a fresh rain, such healing abounds. Water is in plentiful Eden-like supply. You step over pools of water as you walk, pushing away the still-wet branches. The creek is swollen. Beads of water drip from the leaves of the trees ranged along the shore.

Even the sky is fresh scrubbed. Yesterday's dark clouds have given way to a clear blue surface, as if the canopy of the sky was taken down, given a good washing, then strung back up.

Now, it's true the fish may or may not be in a receptive mood after a fresh rain. But that is often the case, whatever the weather. If you only go out when you are sure the fish are in a receptive mood, you will never go out.

By all means, though, go out. Catching fish seems almost a secondary consideration after a fresh rain. It's so great to be outside—and alive!—that you may temporarily suspend your desire to outwit and outthink fish. Let them do as they wish, you think. They deserve to enjoy the day, too.

Resolved: I go out to fish after a fresh rain.

November 26

"The harder you work, the luckier you get. As far as I'm concerned, I'm the luckiest guy in the world."

—Joe Torre, Yankees manager, after his ballclub won the 1996 World Series

Feel lucky today.

Why not? What have you got to lose?

Okay, so millions of New Yorkers haven't sung your praises and showered you with confetti during a crosstown parade to celebrate your team's comeback victory in the World Series. But you're a lucky guy anyway.

Look around you. Luck abounds.

Start with the fundamentals. You're alive, right? That's lucky right there.

You've got your health. There are people who love you. You've got food on the table. You've got a job. All that's lucky.

You're fishing (or about to), right? That's a piece of great luck.

Your luck goes up and down. There's no way to control it. But starting a new project with an attitude of "uh-oh, this is going to be trouble" becomes a self-fulfilling prophecy. When you expect trouble, trouble usually obliges.

Why not expect good things to come to you? You've worked hard, you deserve it. Why not feel lucky today? Because if you truly look at your life and all the good things in it, you are.

Resolved: I feel a lucky streak coming on, in fishing and in life.

November 27

"Most men forget to pay their praises to Him that made that sun and us, and still protects us, and give us flowers and showers, and stomachs and meat, and content and leisure to go a-fishing in."

—Izaak Walton

'Tis the season to give thanks.

Give thanks for all the fishes that swim in all the waters of the world. Where would we be without them? We'd have to take up golf or some fool thing like that.

Give thanks for all the fishing manufacturers who make such wonderful and amazing things that drain any and all surplus funds from the household budget.

Give thanks for the sun, which warms us and makes plants grow, and give thanks to sunglasses, which keep it out of our eyes.

Give thanks for the earth, without which we would have no place to stand in space.

Give thanks for the clouds and the rain, though it'd be nice if they both stayed away until after we were done fishing.

Give thanks for water, which makes all life possible, although Phil Harris refused to drink it. Harris, the late entertainer and legendary imbiber of alcohol, said he'd never drink anything fish swam in.

Give thanks for Jack Daniels and Jim Beam and Johnny Walker and other traveling companions favored by fishermen.

Give thanks that there are no polygraph tests in fishing.

Give thanks for a sense of humor. Fishermen need that as surely as they need bait and tackle.

Resolved: I give thanks for all the blessings of my life.

November 28

"In so doing, use him as though you loved him."

—Izaak Walton, on baiting a hook with a live frog

Do you have tension? Are you under stress?

Does this stress manifest itself in the form of an achy lower back? What about your neck? When you turn your neck does it sound like you're cracking a walnut?

How about headaches? Does an occasional migraine make you climb the walls? What about heartburn, indigestion, chronic fatigue, or other signs of stress in our over-amped modern lifestyle?

Here's the solution for it all: give your tension to the fish.

Go ahead. Go to the doctor and load up on drugs. Exercise. Even try gutting it out. But giving your tension and stress to the fish is a far more effective method of treatment than any of these.

Fishing. An alternative healing therapy.

The way it works is simple. When you hook a fish, release the tension from your body. Send it out through your hands to the fishing rod, up the rod onto the line, then out along the line into the fish.

There. Don't you feel better already?

The fish hardly mind. They don't notice a little extra stress being downloaded into their bodies. They're too worried at the moment about saving their skin. Then when you release them, you can watch them swim away carrying your tension with them.

Resolved: I unload my tension onto the fish.

November 29

"The suspense created by the slow, deliberate and visible rise of a big trout to your fly is agonizing."

—Vincent Marinaro

Go for the hit. That's why you fish anyway: the hit. Go for it.

The pride of the catch is good. It's always nice to come back to camp with a real nice eating fish (if you're eating it) or a real nice picture of it (if you're not).

But the thing that really moves you, the reason you go out in the first place, is the hit.

It almost doesn't matter what size the fish is. You can get a thrill from a big or a small fish. The hit's the thing, and it jolts you like an electric shock.

You wait and wait and wait. You watch that big trout move like a submarine toward your fly. It's agonizing, that wait. Then boom! It hits, and you're off in another world, like a junkie who's just gotten a dose.

The hit is a rush. It's like caffeine. It's like a roller-coaster ride. It's like bungee-jumping. It's like Springsteen in his rock-and-roll days. It's like powder-skiing. It's like good sex.

Someone is complaining about being bored with fishing? Let him have a hit. If that doesn't do it for him, he needs to go to a doctor and have his vital signs checked.

The pride of the catch is nice. The hit is where it's at.

Resolved: I go for the hit.

November 30

"I refuse to rise to the tempting fly. . . . I am too wise a fish to gobble that angler's bait."

—Njal

You're not looking to reinvent the wheel. You don't want to be the second coming of Charles Cotton. All you want to do is fish.

You want to get away from the rat race for a while and spend a little quality time on a stream or lake near you. You don't want to go to the Caribbean and catch these strange exotics. An ordinary bass or maybe a salmon or trout will do just fine.

You don't want to catch huge numbers of fish. That's not the plan. All you want is to catch two or three. Or even one will do.

You're not looking to land some amazing specimen that breaks the scales at the weigh-in place. What you seek is a fish that is modest, but respectable.

You want to get a fish to rise to your fly. You don't care if it's a smart fish or a stupid one. All you want is to hook it and net it. Is that too much to ask?

Not at all. Modest goals, like modest fish, are quite fine, all a person needs really. For you know your time and resources are limited right now. You know you cannot go in search of Moby Dick. In fact, you don't even want to. All you want to do is spend a little quality time fishing on a stream or lake before winter sets in for good.

Resolved: I set a modest goal and catch a modest fish (or two).

December 1

"If you play cornerback and haven't been beat, you haven't been on the field."

—Albert Lewis, pro football cornerback

Fishermen are like football cornerbacks. If you haven't been beaten, you haven't been in the game.

Furthermore, if you haven't been made to look downright silly by a fish, you haven't been in the game.

If you haven't tangled your line in a buckeye tree, you haven't been in the game.

If you haven't gotten a hook imbedded into several different parts of your body, often at the same time, you haven't been in the game.

If you haven't tipped over your canoe and gone for a sudden swim, you haven't been in the game.

If you haven't stood around for hours on a dock, checking your watch and waiting for a bite that never comes, you haven't been in the game.

If you haven't sat on a boat, watching someone else haul in fish after fish while you can't draw scratch, you haven't been in the game.

If you haven't been utterly and totally frustrated and fed up with fishing and ready to hang it up once and for all, you haven't been in the game.

To be a fisherman is to be beaten. But at least you are playing—fishing. The important thing isn't winning: it's being in the game. But the only way you can win is to play.

Resolved: I fish. I get beat. I come back.

December 2

*"A moderator of passions, a procurer of contentedness. . . .
[Fishing] begat habits of peace and patience in those that
professed and practised it."*

—Izaak Walton

How long do you fish a spot? This is one of the grand philosophical questions of fishing.

Your favorite spot by the bridge isn't happening. It's been good to you in the past, but you've been there an hour or two and your line hasn't drawn so much as a quiver. How long do you stay before moving on?

Here's a suggestion: stay a while longer.

Then stay a while longer after that.

Then, when you are absolutely sure that nothing is happening and nothing is going to ever happen, stay a while longer.

Stay and stay and stay and stay and stay.

Stay night and day. Stay through summer and fall, winter and spring. Stay through rain and thunder, stay through Sahara-like heat.

Be like a tree. Throw down roots in that spot and grow. Let kids on a hot day find shade under your branches. Let an old man who needs rest lean against your trunk.

This you must know: the world will come spinning toward you if only you stay where you are. Sooner or later your patience will prevail. If you stick with a spot long enough, you will catch fish.

Resolved: I stay where I am and fish on.

December 3

"Frequently for the fisherman, the circumstances in which the prey is caught is of more delight than the size of the fish."

—Charles Traub

Where are you going to fish today? Why not the bridge?

The bridge is a cool spot. It's not exactly the heart of wilderness, but so what? You don't have to be Davy Crockett to catch fish.

You could move upstream. You hear that people are catching fish near the campground a mile upstream. Instead, you stay put. You like it at the bridge.

Fishing on the bridge is a John Mellencamp rock song. It's Sunday afternoon at the ball game. It's an ice cream on a hot day. It's the Macy's Thanksgiving Day Parade. It's America.

Cars drive slowly by, watching you lean against the railing. Kids stare out the windows at you. A dad in a minivan asks, "Any luck?" "Not yet," you say, and grin.

Later on, some teenage girls come by. They're just goofing off, having fun. There are some other guys on the bridge, too. Everybody's joking around with the girls and it's a lot of laughs.

Finally, one of the guys on the bridge—a big, fat, tattooed guy in a Stanley Kowalski T-shirt who's using salmon eggs as bait—pulls out a fish. It's wriggling on the line as he pulls it up toward him. Someone yells, "Hey girls, come on over and look!" And they run over, express their amazement, and giggle, as the fishing goes on.

Resolved: I fish the bridge.

December 4

When you fish, fish all the way. Whatever type of fishing you do, wherever you go, fish all the way.

Fishing all the way does not mean taking unnecessary risks. It just means milking it for all it's worth, squeezing every last precious drop out of it, before you pack it in and call it a day.

Go to the end of the point if you're fishing along a point. Know what's at the end of the point before you turn back home.

The view from the end of the point—and the fishing as well—may be different than anywhere else, perhaps radically so. Sometimes what you will find there is so awesome it will change your life. You may never forget it.

But you will never know what it is like unless you go to the end of the point.

The fishermen who do not go will never know. They stop halfway, and as a result, they never know what you know, and as hard as you try, you are never be able to tell them what they have missed.

Finish the job. Go to the end of whatever it is you are doing. See it (and seek it) all the way through. You will gain all the satisfaction there is to gain in this life when you do.

Resolved: I go to the end of the point.

December 5

A bright day of promise (and fishing!) begins. It ends.

A miserable day at work (and no fishing) begins. It ends.

The daylight begins. It ends.

The darkness begins. It ends.

Warm, luscious, lovely weather begins. It ends.

Cold, sloppy, wet weather begins. It ends.

A run of salmon (or striped bass or bluefish or whatever) begins. It ends.

A good run of fishing luck begins. It ends.

A bad run of fishing luck begins. It ends.

That long-awaited tarpon-hunting trip to Florida begins. It ends.

Your time away from the job and the house and the kids and the wife and all your conventional responsibilities begins. It ends.

A three-day weekend (to be filled with fishing) begins. It ends.

The year begins. It ends.

Your life begins. It ends.

Everything that begins, ends. Every beginning contains the seeds of its end. Relish and cherish the beginning of things and you will be that much closer to accepting their inevitable end.

Resolved: I relish my beginnings and make peace with my endings.

December 6

"I have a simple definition of character: it's doing right when nobody's looking."

—J. C. Watts

Be a fisherman you can respect.

Be a fisherman who does right when nobody's looking.

Be a fisherman who throws the really big ones back.

Be a fisherman who eats what he catches, if he doesn't throw them back.

Be a fisherman who doesn't leave pieces of trash lying around, and maybe even picks trash up if he sees any on the ground.

Be a fisherman who's quiet around the water, in deference to the rights and wishes of other fishermen.

Be a fisherman who grants plenty of space to other fishermen and who does not barge in on someone else's area.

Be a fisherman who gives advice to others if they seek it but otherwise keeps his thoughts to himself.

Be a fisherman who does not patronize young fishermen but who lends a generous and sympathetic hand.

Be a fisherman who is patient with himself and others.

Be a fisherman who respects nature and the outdoors and actively works to preserve it.

Be a fisherman who knows and respects fish.

Be a fisherman who plays by the rules.

Resolved: I do right when nobody's looking.

December 7

"Their strength is to sit still."

—Isaiah 30:7

Get a comfortable chair when you fish.

Every fisherman, like every writer, needs a comfortable chair. You cannot do good work without one. A well-equipped fisherman carries a rod and reel, tackle, some salmon eggs and other bait, and a comfortable chair.

Most fishermen use folding lawn chairs, although some go in for more deluxe models. A good chair needs to be light because you have to carry it from the car to wherever you're fishing. It supports the back and it's even comfortable enough to let you nod off now and then.

Some fishermen stand when they fish. Others grimly pace, smoking unfiltered Camels, one after the other. Others lean against a railing or tree. At some point, everyone sits. You need a comfortable chair for those times.

You can sit on the ground if you wish. But the ground is uneven and frequently muddy or rocky and it may not make for good sitting. A chair is preferable at those times.

You set up your rod and you sit. You sit and you sit. You have your ice chest within easy reach. You kick back and drink it all in. When you get a hit, you jump to your feet and haul that baby in. That's fishing as practiced by millions of people all around the globe, and one of the ingredients for success is a comfortable chair.

Resolved: I bring a comfortable chair when I fish.

December 8

Adopt a policy of nonintervention when it comes to fishing. If it ain't broke, don't fix it. If it is broke, don't fix it.

Let things work out. Things *will* work out, you know. One way or the other, they will work out.

Let's be real. Fishing is not a life or death issue. It's not going to kill you (unless you get drunk and stupid and fall out of a boat). Within this context, every problem you encounter in fishing must be considered minor.

So how do you handle minor problems? Well, you get around to them sooner or later. And if it takes longer than you thought, you work around it. You cope. No biggie.

Switch it around. Suppose fishing is a matter of life or death importance. You look at it the way a starving man looks at a bag of Doritos. You gotta have it.

An attitude of *mañana* might be healthy for you, too. In your piscine zeal do you make molehills into mountains? Leave those molehills alone for a while and see what happens. It's like the children's story about the ugly duckling. A creature that was once ridiculed for its strange looks grew into a beautiful swan. What you perceive now to be a handicap in fishing may, with a little time, shade, and perspective, turn into something positive.

Resolved: I say *mañana* to whatever is bugging me in fishing.

December 9

The days are shorter and colder now. Still, a day is a day. Use it for all it is worth.

How many fishing days do you have in a year? Twenty, fifty, one hundred? Every one of them is precious, even in the cold. Use it for all it is worth.

In the summer, the days stretch out languidly forever. Not so in the cold. The days start cold and end cold. In between, even when the sun comes out, there's an edge to the air. You can see your breath, and the air is so sharp it almost hurts to take it in.

When you get a fishing day in cold weather, it's a rare day. Use it for all it is worth.

There is less idleness in a cold climate. Every fisherman becomes more matter-of-fact, more businesslike. He has a job to do and a certain amount of time to do it. Tying knots in the cold, doing *anything* in the cold, becomes that much harder but all the more satisfying when you do it right and well.

It is inevitable that you will seek the comfort of the indoors as the cold weather sets in for good. There will be less fishing, and less good fishing. But every now and then you will find yourself out in the cold, with the late afternoon shadows falling across the water, not a person in sight, not a sound anywhere except your footfalls on the hard dirt, the lake rimmed by mountains, and you will know why you are there. You will know.

Resolved: I use every fishing day for all it is worth.

December 10

"There are three characteristics of a really fine walk: 1) You have to get lost; 2) You have to get muddy; 3) You have to arrive home after dark."

—Jon Carroll

What's true for walking is true for fishing. For a really satisfying day of fishing, you must get lost, get muddy, and come home after dark.

Getting lost means going off the trail. It means going up or down the river where other fishermen do not ordinarily roam. It means wandering well past that.

The point of your meanderings is to find fish. So there is always a grand design in your getting lost.

When you hike along a river or creek or stream or lake or wetland, you inevitably get wet and muddy. This is the second part of the equation. You will be plenty wet and muddy before you even start fishing, which of course will make you wetter and muddier still.

Because you are lost and far away from all that is civilized and good, it is going to take a while to get back home. It is going to take a while to get back to your car, actually. You stumble and climb and fall as the sun drops low and daylight fades. When you ranged along the stream in search of fish, you did not realize how far you were going. Now, staggering back, you realize how far it really was and how tired you are.

But what a feeling, what a grand feeling, when you open the door at home, tired and muddy and holding a trout for dinner!

Resolved: I get lost, I get muddy, and I come home after dark the next time I fish.

December 11

"Trust God, see all, nor be afraid."

—Robert Browning

Every now and then, take your shades off when you fish. See the world without tinted glasses.

You take your shades off on some bright days and the glare will turn your eyeballs to toast. So you have to be reasonable about this. Maybe on the walk back from fishing, or when the glare is not so strong on the water, or in the early morning or late afternoon when the sun has tapered off—pick your spot, but take your shades off.

You get a different view of things when you do. Some fishermen act like they're Tom Cruise or somebody. They wear shades all the time.

Think of sunglasses as a metaphor. When you have them on, there's a filter between you and the world. When you take them off, you remove the filter. You see the world as it really is. You know, it's really not such a bad place. It's really kind of beautiful.

Okay, so you squint a while. Nothing wrong with that. A little squinting is good for a person.

You can get along fine in fishing without a lot of the things that conventional wisdom regards as absolutely essential. One of those things is sunglasses. Free your mind and your eyes. Check out the view with your naked eyeballs, and see what there is to see.

Resolved: I take my shades off from time to time.

December 12

Think how much bigger your world is because of fishing.

Because of fishing, you know fish. You know about salmon and trout and bluefish and bass and catfish and tarpon and a lot more. Maybe you don't know all there is to know about every species of fish, but you know *something*, and how many people can say that?

Because of fishing, you know about water. Every body of water has its own identity, is its own world, and you know the worlds of lakes and rivers and bays and oceans because you've spent time, a lot of time, in and around them.

Because of fishing, you know nature. You live an outdoor life. You're more tuned into the weather's moods than any meteorologist you've ever seen on TV. You know insects (you've killed a few in your time). You know birds and trees and mountains and flowers and the color of the sky at dawn. Maybe you don't know the names of every bird and every plant, but you know a lot of them, and you know them in important ways that have nothing to do with remembering their names.

Because of fishing, you're plugged into what is deep and lasting in this life. You're not exactly sure what *that* is, and if someone asked you might be embarrassed to talk about it, but you know it's there all the same and when you go fishing, that's where you find it.

Resolved: I think about how much bigger my world is because of fishing.

December 13

"Fishing was part of the mysterious and unattainable Adult world. I wanted in . . . I wanted to go fishing more than anything else in the world."

—Jean Shepherd

Let your son in. Let him become part of the mysterious and seemingly unattainable World of Men. Give him a fishing rod.

You don't have to spend a fortune. Give him a little starter set from Wal-Mart or somewhere. For what he's going to do with it, it'll work just fine.

Your dad gave you your first rod. Now you're giving your son his first. It's a passing of the torch, a generational rite.

Maybe your son already has one. What about an upgrade, then? While you're at it, what about an upgrade for you, too? You both deserve it.

A fishing rod is not a toy, but toys are important. Toys say a lot about a person, whatever his age. Toys are a peek into a person's true personality.

Does work define you? If you're like most people, probably not. Probably you work at something you don't really like, but you hang onto it as a way to pay the bills and keep the wolf from the door. Work enables you to play, which is really what sends your spirit soaring.

What gift can equal a boy's first fishing rod? A boy is no longer a boy when he owns a fishing rod. Is he a *fisherboy*? No, he becomes a *fisherman*! No prouder title than that.

Give your son a fishing rod. It will make all the difference in the world to him, and to you.

Resolved: I give my son a fishing rod.

December 14

"The finest fishing often takes place not on water but in print."
—Sparse Grey Hackle

Here's another thing to give your son: a good book about fishing.

He has a good sturdy rod and reel. Now give him a good sturdy book. You don't need to look far. The one you hold in your hands will do very well.

A rod and reel and *The Angler's Book of Daily Inspiration.* What more could a young fisherman want? Indeed, what more could any fisherman, young or old, ask for?

A good fishing book contains adventure, history, nature, tall tales, tips on the craft, philosophical reflection. It also contains ample heaps of inspiration, for what good is a book about fishing if it doesn't make you want to go out and do it?

Ultimately, the lessons you learn from fishing will be direct and firsthand. No book can replace that. Wisdom in fishing derives from experience; it's earned.

But when you fish, you naturally want to know more about the different species of fish and their habits and the lives they lead and the insects they eat and the amazing miracle of spawning and a whole raft of other subjects. The only way you're going to get this information (unless you bend the ear of some old-timer) is inside the pages of a book.

A young fisherman's mind is a terrible thing to waste. Give your kid a good book about fishing.

Resolved: I give *The Angler's Book of Daily Inspiration* to my son (or a friend).

December 15

You're ready. You're always ready to go fishing, even at this time of year.

Your son's ready. He's got a new rod (or will have, come Christmas) and he's been boning up on fishing books with a dedication he never shows his schoolwork.

Now, call Granddad. That's your dad, in case you've forgotten. The one who taught you how to fish.

Maybe he won't want to go out in the cold weather. Maybe he'll want to wait until it warms up. But you never know. He may surprise you. Those old guys can be pretty hardy at times.

Sure, he can be cantankerous and a pain in the rear. But all things considered, he's your dad, and you love him, man. So invite him.

Granddad, dad, son. What a fishing trip! Better not wait forever, though. Granddad is as robust as the Eveready bunny, but that won't always be the case. And your son, if he hasn't already, will soon enter that dark tunnel known as the teenage years in which he will want nothing to do with you and your kind and the "phony" (favorite teenage word) values you represent.

Fishing is a nexus, a means of connection between you and the wilderness, you and fish, you and the deepest parts of yourself. Another of fishing's fundamental connections is between you and your family, and you and your father. Explore that connection while you have the chance.

Resolved: I bring my dad and my son on a fishing trip.

December 16

There are certain things you need to be a fisherman. One of
them is a fishing cap.

How can anyone fish without a fishing cap? It's simply not
done. To be a fisherman you need a rod and reel, bait and
tackle, a comfortable chair, sunglasses, and a cap.

Most fishing caps are converted baseball caps. You also see
wide-brimmed jobs and caps with rear flaps that keep the sun
off your neck. But baseball caps are the most popular.

Once you use a cap for fishing, it becomes strictly a fishing cap and it's good for no other use. It gets soiled and
sweaty and possibly odoriferous. Your wife may not let you
bring your longtime fishing cap into the house, like a dog with
muddy paws.

A fisherman gets attached to his cap. It becomes a part of
him, like his nose. He can't bear to fish without his hat on. If
he leaves it hanging from the hook in the garage, it ruins his
entire day. The fish sense the fisherman's disappointment, and
shy away from him like he's got the plague.

A fishing cap, like a fisherman, develops character over
time. A fisherman who sports a brand new cap is most likely
a part-timer and not to be trusted.

You can trust a man in an old, soiled fishing cap. A man
like that radiates integrity. The older and dirtier his cap, the
better it is. If yours looks shockingly bad and makes children
and babies cry, you know you've got a keeper.

Resolved: I wear my fishing cap with pride.

December 17

Have a clear concept when you fish. Know what you want to do before you do it. Vague thinking leads to aimless fishing.

When you arrive at your spot, check it out before you get out your gear. Have a plan in mind before you put a line in the water. Fishing is like anything else. A little forethought will pay big dividends later on.

You may go to the same spot on the river every time because it's worked for you in the past. Still, the same rules apply: think about what you're doing. Be open to what the river tells you. It changes from day to day, though it may appear the same on the surface.

Every good fisherman has a plan. The plan almost never works out exactly as he envisions it, but at least he starts with a clear idea of what he wants to do. Every good plan allows room for spontaneity and surprises.

Fishing is a process of outwitting fish. The fish are not witless; they're very clear on what they want: food. You need to be clear on how you can match their desires with yours, and ensnare them.

It'd be nice if you could just walk down to the lake or river and start pulling out fish. While some lucky days are like that, fishing wouldn't hold much of a challenge if that were the case every time. Follow your heart down to the water. Then use your brain to catch fish.

Resolved: I have a clear concept of what I want to do before I start fishing.

December 18

"A trout is a fish known mainly by hearsay. It lives on anything not included in a fisherman's equipment."

—H. I. Phillips

Have fun with fishing. Winter, spring, summer, or fall, have fun with it.

It don't mean a thing if it ain't got that swing, as Duke Ellington used to say. Have a clear concept of fun. This is the first and last rule of fishing. The pleasure principle overrides all other angling principles, within the bounds of reason and good sense.

There is the story of the fisherman who wanted to examine what fish see under the water. So he filled his bathtub with water and got in. Using a diving mask, he took a fish-eye view and studied several dry flies floating on the surface.

Then there is the story of the fisherman who, seeking to get close to the fish without scaring them, dressed as a tree whenever he approached his fishing spot.

These fishermen weren't having fun, strictly defined. They earnestly believed what they were doing would help them catch fish.

Even so, they brought a spirit of creativity and invention to the enterprise. Look at the way a child approaches a new toy. He does not view it in the boring and conventional way of adults; he immediately turns it around, flips it over, bounces it, tips it, looks under it, jumps on it, even tastes it, all in the spirit of play.

Approach fishing as a child would, even though you have been doing it for years. Do it with creativity, invention, and flair.

Resolved: I fish. I have fun.

December 19

"A fishing line is a piece of string with a worm on one end and a darn fool on the other."

—Saying

Be a darn fool. Go out and fish.

It's cold enough to make a penguin think twice about going outside. Snow is piled up above your chimney. The roads are impassable. The weather forecasters are warning of apocalypse. A new Ice Age has set in.

Be a darn fool. Go chop a hole in the ice and fish.

Who's being foolish, really? The people with cholesterol-hardened hearts who sit inside all day watching "Geraldo" and living in fear of what will happen if they venture out? Or people like yourself—hardy, hard-living, hard-drinking, hard-charging fishermen who get off their duff and go adventuring in the great (if very, very cold) outdoors?

Be foolish. Go out and fish.

What's more, be proud of your foolishness. It's better to be a fishing fool than any other kind of fool. Fishing fools are the best kind of fools, a truly rare breed of men and women. A fishing fool is like a mail carrier. Not rain nor sleet nor hail will stop him from making his appointed rounds.

To be foolish (as defined by some) is to live with passion. A fishing fool truly loves what he does. What's crazy about that?

Resolved: I act like a darn fool. I go out and fish.

December 20

"Let us, then, be up and doing, with a heart for any fate."
—Henry Wadsworth Longfellow

When you are fishing from an ocean pier, stand on the railing.

Some pier fishermen are sitters. Others are leaners. The ones who really want to catch fish—well, they stand on the railing.

A pier railing consists of two or more supporting boards. Some fishermen will put one foot on the lower rail and one on the pier. More energetic types will place both feet on the lower rail or even up on the second rail. It takes balance and coordination to make a cast while standing on the railing.

You get a better view of things from the railing. You can clearly see the water and your line disappearing into the water. You can look out across the bay and along the long, curving shoreline.

Posture means all in this case. Your position on the railing says to the world (and any fishermen or tourists who may pass by), "I am ready and eager to catch fish. I am so ready and eager that I will climb the railing for them. In fact, I would even jump in after them if it brought me closer to my goal."

Critics may say that standing on a pier railing suggests impatience. This is balderdash. A fisherman who stands on the railing is into it; he's engaged, he's involved. Fishing is no mere spectator sport for him; he's a player, a participant. He will not meekly accept what life (or the ocean) hands him. He will do whatever it takes to catch fish, and he will succeed.

Be ready and eager to catch fish. Be a player in life. Be a person who relishes what he does. Get up on that rail!

Resolved: I stand on the rail when I fish from a pier.

December 21

To be great at anything, you've got to do it on a regular basis.
You've got to make a habit of it.

To be a great chef, you've got to cook. To be a great writer,
you've got to sit your butt down and write. To be a great photographer, you've got to shoot film.

Of course, to be a great (or good) fisherman, you've got to
fish.

The problem is (actually it's no problem, but it does make
it very uncomfortable at times), fishing is a year-round activity. To do it on a regular basis, you must do it in winter. That
means coping with numbingly cold weather and wind that
peels the porcelain off the crowns in your teeth and sleet and
snow and sudden lightning storms moving down the canyon
toward you and whatever else Ma Nature cooks up.

Obviously, it's easier to develop and maintain excellent
fishing habits in warm weather. It easier to do *anything* in
warm weather, except perhaps ice-fish.

But with effort and determination, you can be regular about
your fishing in winter, too. Go out once or twice a month. Pick
your spots. Make sure you're prepared. Fishing in winter is a
habit of mind as much as anything else. Overcome the mental obstacles and the physical ones will follow.

Resolved: I keep fishing a regular habit, even in winter.

December 22

"It shall be a rule for me to make as little noise as I can when I fish."

—Izaak Walton

Keep your own inner counsel when you fish.

You may scare the fish away if you raise your voice. You may also annoy other fishermen in the area.

Be quiet out of respect for others. Be quiet because it may help you catch fish. But more important, be quiet out of respect for yourself.

When you are quiet, you can think. You can think about fishing and you can think about other things. You can observe and listen. None of this is possible if there's a constant chatter around you (either yours or another person's).

Give yourself some internal space. Quit being busy for a while. Allow yourself to open up and let go.

Fishing is a meditative act. Surely this is why after you return from a day of fishing you are more composed, more at peace with yourself. Your head is clear. Your thoughts are sharp.

Even as you are searching outside for fish, look inside yourself. You'll be amazed at what you find.

Resolved: I keep my own inner counsel when I fish.

December 23

"If there is a cold, whistling wind and it be a dark, lowering day, then the fish will usually bite all day. For a dark day is much better than any other clear weather."

—Dame Juliana Berners

Any tourist can fish on a bright and sunny day. Go out on a dark and gloomy day.

Who needs the sun anyway? Not the fish. They don't have any misgivings about a dark day. They may even prefer it. Easier to catch their food.

That's a good rule of thumb in fishing: if the fish prefer it, you do it. It may be pitch-black outside, but if the fish are biting, be there. Wear a miner's lamp on your head if you need to, but be there.

Over the course of a year, there will be more dark and gloomy days than the other kind. If you only fish when the sun's out, you won't fish (or catch) much. It goes without saying that a cold, whistling wind goes along with a dark day like an evil twin.

You can't change the weather, so you might as well accept it for what it is.

Dark days have more mood and character. Fish on a dark and gloomy day, and you can almost imagine the Loch Ness monster rising out of the pond. Now that would be something to tell the guys at the tackle shop!

Every day has its virtues, even the darkest and gloomiest ones. The simple fact that you are alive and have an opportunity to fish—there's nothing gloomy about that. On the contrary, it's a bright and rich bounty.

Resolved: I go out to fish on a dark and gloomy day.

December 24

"A faithful friend is the medicine of life."

—Ecclesiasticus

There is no better partner than a fishing partner.

A fishing partner can be a man or woman, a wife or husband. It can be a son or daughter, a father or mother. It can be someone you've known since the two of you were kids, an old college buddy, or a person you met on the river last year with whom you felt an instant kinship.

Some fishing partnerships, like some marriages, last a lifetime. You're a pretty lucky person if you have one of those.

A good fishing partner stays quiet when it's time to stay quiet and cracks jokes when it's time for a joke. A good fishing partner will share a beer or whiskey with you. A good fishing partner will offer advice when asked, but knows when it's time to step back and let you handle it yourself. A good fishing partner has been through good times and bad with you. He's someone you can count on in a pinch.

If you ask a good fishing partner to go fishing, he doesn't think of reasons why not. He figures out ways to do it. Then a week or two later, or at most a month, he returns the favor and asks you to go on a trip.

Your fishing partner ranks right up there with the most important people in your life. Give him a call in the spirit of the season and wish him Merry Christmas or Happy Hanukkah. Then ask him when he wants to go fishing again.

Resolved: I plan a fishing trip with my partner.

December 25

"To put it rather bluntly, I am not the type who wants to go back to the land; I am the type who wants to go back to the hotel."

—Fran Lebowitz

Today, take a day off from fishing.

Forget about trout and salmon and char and bonefish and grayling and other swimming creatures.

Forget about leaders and lures and tippets.

Forget about poppers and streamers and nymphs.

Forget about reading water.

Forget about blood knots and clinch knots and nail knots.

Forget about Izaak Walton and anything he ever said or did.

Forget about caddis flies and mayflies and every mosquito bite you've ever had.

Forget about making plans for your next fishing trip.

Forget about spring fishing.

Forget about Alaska and Costa Rica and New Zealand and all the places you want to go.

Forget about the big one that got away and still tortures you.

Forget about going back to the land. Just go back to your house, gather your family around you, and count all the blessings in your life.

Then tomorrow, go fishing.

Resolved: Today I rest. Tomorrow I fish.

December 26

"The best all-around bait is a worm. Hardly a fish swims that will not take a worm."

—Tom McNally

There is something reassuring in the fact that the best all-around bait is still a worm. Worms were the best all-around bait a hundred years ago, and they will likely be the best all-around bait next century as well.

Fishing is simple. Worms are simple. Fishing and worms go together like pie and ice cream.

You can find worms in your own backyard. There's something reassuring about that, too. You get an old coffee can and a spade and you dig them up. There's dirt in the can and you put the worms in. You take the can down to the stream. When you need a worm, you reach into the can and get one.

Any boy or girl can find worms. That's reassuring, too. Worms are free. A kid doesn't need any special skills to get them. All the bait a kid could ever need is right there in his backyard. All he has to do is dig.

You learn a lot about worms when you stick them onto a hook. They're slippery little devils. They move around like crazy. Sometimes you lose pieces of the worm while you're trying to get it onto the hook. You keep working at it until you get enough of the worm on the hook that a fish might be interested.

Fly-fishermen may turn up their noses at worms, but what do they know? A trout looks just as pretty when it's caught with a worm as it does with a pale morning dun. Worms are what fishing is all about—worms and kids, that is.

Resolved: I dig up some worms and go fishing with a kid.

December 27

"Nothing great was ever achieved without enthusiasm."

—Ralph Waldo Emerson

Go for the extraordinary, in fishing and in life. Whatever you want to do, whatever wild plan you hatch, pursue it with everything you have.

Chase a crazy dream. Follow your imagination wherever it leads. Other people will tell you no; your response must be "Yes!"

Seek a higher destiny. Lead a life of attempt. The only way to determine what a person wants to do in life is by what he or she does. Do much, want little.

It is possible. Whatever you see for yourself in your heart's core, can exist in fact. Dreams come true all the time, and not just in the movies. Why not for you, too?

You can reorder your priorities to give yourself more time to fish. You can take faraway trips. You can become a fishing vagabond if you like. It doesn't take a miracle; you just have to do it.

Worry less about luck. Let luck take care of itself. Luck is fickle; you remain steadfast. Luck ultimately bends to the fisherman who keeps his purpose fixed in his mind.

Nobody can stop you, unless it's you. Nobody can distract you, unless it's you. Nobody can make you waver and quit, unless it's you.

Why settle for less when you fish? Why go only halfway? Do it always with energy and enthusiasm, and you can—you can!—achieve great things.

Resolved: I go for the extraordinary, in fishing and in life.

December 28

Learn your craft. Learn it from the ground up and build a ladder to the stars. Give it a good base and a sturdy foundation, and work at it. When you are tired of working and feel you can work no more, take a break. Then work some more.

Work is today's lesson, tomorrow's lesson, next year's lesson. It's all you need to know. The way you get better at fishing, the way you get skilled at catching fish, is to work at it.

No man is born an angler. No woman, either. The great anglers all got to be great the same old boring way: they worked at it.

Fishing is a lifetime endeavour. It will exhaust you before you even come close to exhausting all its possibilities. So keep pushing. You've got a lot of work to do.

Forget about art. Let art take care of itself. Work is how you attain what you want in this life. It's an old message, a message repeated in this book, a message that you've heard a hundred times since you were a kid. But its familiarity does not lessen its power, or its truth. Its familiarity *is* its power.

Fishing is play. But to be good at the playing, you've got to work. It's a contradiction to be sure. While you're figuring out the contradictions, keep working.

You've got a goal: catch fish. Work toward your goal and you'll get it. Learn your craft. Learn it from the ground up and build a ladder to the stars.

Resolved: I work at fishing and I keep working at it.

December 29

"My desire to catch as many trout as possible didn't change in one season. It was when I started tying my own flies that I began to notice a transformation."

—Ailm Travler

When you fish, a transformation occurs. Let it happen.

It doesn't happen overnight. You may not even be aware of it. It may sneak up on you over time and only then do you realize that something is different. Your attitude about fishing has changed somehow. You have changed.

For Ailm Travler, the transformation occurred when she started tying her own flies. But it can occur whether you tie your flies or not, whether you're a fly-fisherman or not.

The transformation is this: she saw herself as connected to fish. Their destiny was not separate from hers but linked to it. They were not her enemy; she did not want to conquer them. She no longer saw fishing solely in terms of the number of fish caught.

She saw fishing was more than that. It was about establishing connections—with fish, with the natural world, with herself.

Hooking a fish is a symbol of these mystical connections. For a brief time, fish and fisherman are joined together by an umbilical-like strand. The fish represents the strange, fertile, scary, miraculous world from which the fisherman came.

Fishing is the process of seeing and making these connections. This is how the transformation begins. It's not a divine transformation, nothing of the sort. But it is a transformation that can change your life.

Resolved: I see the connections between fish and myself.

December 30

"Gamefish are too valuable to be caught once."

—Lee Wulff

Become a guardian of fish.

When you catch a great fish, return it to where it came from. And if you keep it, eat it. Then carry its power within you like an internal flame.

Protect and respect fish. Fight for their rights. When you fight for the rights of fish, you fight for your own rights as a fisherman.

People who don't know any better may ask, "How can a fisherman be a guardian of fish?" Every fisherman is keenly interested in the welfare of fish. He knows and loves fish far more than people whose only experience with them is in a restaurant.

To become a guardian of fish, you must learn about them. The search for knowledge is a quest for understanding. The more you understand fish, the more you will love fishing.

You will be a better fisherman when you become a guardian of fish. You will see how interwined the lives of fish are with wild water and open spaces and fresh air, and you will fight for these ideals even as you are fighting for fish.

See fishing as a higher calling. See yourself as a savior of fish even as you seek to capture them.

Resolved: I become a guardian of fish.

December 31

"We shall not cease from exploration. And the end of all our exploring will be to arrive where we started and know the place for the first time."

—T. S. Eliot

So how'd you do?

At the start of the year you pledged to make this the best fishing year of your life. Now the year is over. How'd it go?

You did it, you say? This was, beyond doubt, the greatest fishing year of your life? All right. Way to go, dude!

Huh? What's that? You in the back row, please speak up. The others can't hear you.

You say you had a pretty good year but not the best ever. You fished more than you have in a long time, but you didn't get away to as many different places as you would have liked. And that dream trip to New Zealand is still that, a dream.

Oh well. What you need to do next is the same as the guy who's had his best year ever.

First, it's New Year's Eve. Go out, have a few beers, and celebrate a job well done. Ring in the new year with a bang. Then get up in the morning (or afternoon, if it was a really long night) and rededicate yourself to making next year the best fishing year of your life.

Resolved: I make next year the best fishing year of my life.

About the Author

This is Kevin Nelson's eleventh book. His previous book, *The Golfer's Book of Daily Inspiration*, was published by Contemporary Books. He lives in the San Francisco Bay area.

Index